Culture

A Reformer's Science

Tony Bennett

SAGE Publications
London • Thousand Oaks • New Delhi

First published in Australia in 1998 by
Allen & Unwin Pty Ltd

SAGE Publications Ltd
6 Bonhill Street
London EC2A 4PU

SAGE Publications Inc
2455 Teller Road
Thousand Oaks, California 91320

SAGE Publications India Pvt Ltd
32, M-Block Market
Greater Kailash – I
New Delhi 110 048

British Library Cataloguing in Publication Data

A catalogue record of this book is available from the British Library.

ISBN 0 7619 5922 X (hbk)
ISBN 0 7619 5923 8 (pbk)

Library of Congress catalog record available

Set in 10/12pt Goudy Old Style by DOCUPRO, Sydney
Printed by South Wind Productions, Singapore

Series introduction

The relations of government and culture are currently undergoing significant change. The rationales for government involvement in the management of culture that accompanied the social welfarist conceptions of the post-war period have been called increasingly into question since the 1980s. At the same time, debates about diasporic communities, multiculturalism and the rights of indigenous peoples have placed the recognition and maintenance of cultural diversity at the centre of current policy debates. Paralleling these developments, new media and communications technologies have presented governments with distinctive regulatory and policy challenges, while also offering new ways of responding to earlier demands of cultural access and entitlement.

The *Cultural and Media Policy Series* will develop and promote work that responds critically and creatively to these new realities. Its approach to these concerns will be characterised by five signatures.

- *A broad policy range* Titles will explore the relations between government and culture across a broad range of cultural and media policies, including broadcasting and communications policies; film, video and the new media; arts policies and funding structures; museums, art galleries, libraries and the new information economies; heritage policies; cultural statistics; cultural policy and planning; cultural diversity; intellectual property; cultural tourism; and the culture industries.

- *Policy and practice* The series will explore the relations between policy and practice, looking at how policies formulated at the level of governments influence, and are influenced by, the policies and practices of cultural and media institutions and industries, NGOs, the institutions of civil society, and cultural actors and consumers.

- *Interdisciplinary and pluralist* Titles in the series will draw on the full range of humanities and social science disciplines—history, sociology, cultural and media studies, women's studies, economics, and anthropology—rather than being limited to policy studies in a narrow sense. Similarly, the series will be wide-ranging in the theoretical traditions it will draw on, aiming to promote a many-sided debate rather than a single orthodoxy.
- *International and comparative* The series will promote an engagement with cultural and media policy debates and issues as they are posed across national boundaries, as well as with comparative studies examining related policy practices and structures in different national settings.
- *Historically informed and theoretically challenging* The series will publish titles which help to place our understanding of contemporary relations of government and culture in an historical perspective, and will contribute to recent debates and developments which have brought policy studies into the centre of contemporary cultural theory and practice.

Contents

Acknowledgements

Many hands, and many voices, have contributed to this book, which owes a good deal to the generous conventions and habits of scholarly exchange which allow work presented under a single name to be the beneficiary of so many different inputs.

The first debts to record are those that I owe to the individuals who have commented—always constructively—on the different chapters at various stages in their development. I am especially grateful to Ian Hunter for his helpful comments on an early draft of Chapter 1, as I am to David Saunders and Peter Williams for their insightful criticisms of an early version of Chapter 2. I am similarly grateful to John Frow, Larry Grossberg and Stuart Hall for their helpful comments on the first draft of Chapter 9.

I am grateful to Kuan-Hsin Chen for the opportunity to present the arguments that are published here as Chapter 3 at the *Trajectories: Toward the Internationalisation of Cultural Studies* symposium he convened in Taipei in 1992. I also thank the symposium participants for their comments, which have proved helpful to me in revising the paper for publication.

Chapter 4 has had the benefit of many dress-rehearsals in a number of different contexts. I learned a great deal from the discussion generated by presenting an earlier version of this chapter at the *Cultural Policy: State of the Art* conference organised by the Institute for Cultural Policy Studies in 1995. I especially valued the contributions of Stuart Cunningham and Liz Jacka. An extended and revised version was presented as the inaugural lecture in the University of North Carolina Program in Cultural Studies: I am particularly grateful to Robert Allen, Larry Grossberg and Della Pollock for this opportunity. Close-to-final versions of the paper were presented at the

Development and Communication conference organised by the Human Sciences Research Council and the Department of Communication at the University of South Africa in Pretoria; as guest lectures in the Institute for Communications Research, Seoul National University, and the Cultural Studies Program at the Chinese University of Hong Kong; and as a workshop presentation for the Australian Academy of the Social Sciences. I am grateful to Charles Malan, Pieter Fourie, Christo von Standen, Myung-Koo Kang, Stephen Chan and Stewart Clegg for inviting me to present my work in these contexts and to the participants for the wealth and diversity of their comments. Thanks also to Graham Martin for a helpful reminder of some aspects of Raymond Williams' work I had overlooked.

I am grateful to the many individuals who commented on earlier versions of Chapter 5 in the context of presentations at the Department of English, Cultural and Media Studies, de Montfort University; the Centre for the Study of Popular Culture, Manchester Metropolitan University; the Pavis Centre for Sociological and Anthropological Research, The Open University; the Unit for Criticism and Interpretation, University of Illinois; the Chicago Humanities Institute, University of Chicago; the Tisch School of Art and Film, New York University; the Department of English, University of Melbourne; and the Faculty of Humanities, Griffith University. I am especially grateful to the following for making these presentations possible: Stephen Knight, Steve Readhead, Ken Thompson, Paul du Gay, Larry Grossberg, Arjun Appadurai, Toby Miller, Simon During and Ken Ruthven. Special thanks are also due to Larry Grossberg and Toby Miller for their insightful and detailed criticisms of the paper, and to Bronwen Hammond for her invaluable research assistance. I am also indebted to Mari Schindele of *Critical Inquiry* whose detailed editorial suggestions helped to improve the clarity of my argument in this chapter immeasurably.

Chapter 6 had its origins in a paper first presented at the *History of the Human Sciences* conference that was organised by Deborah Tyler and David McCallum in Melbourne in 1994. I am grateful to both for this opportunity and to Deborah Tyler for her subsequent helpful editorial comments on the chapter. The chapter has also benefited from the discussions generated by related presentations to the Cultural Studies Association of Australia conference *Intellectuals and Communities* held at the University of Technology Sydney in 1994 and to the *Race, Identity, and Public Culture* conference held at the Institute for Liberal Arts of Emory University in Atlanta in 1995. I am especially grateful to Ivan Karp for inviting me to contribute to the Atlanta conference, as I am also for the helpfulness of both his and Annie

Coombes' engagements with my arguments. John Frow has also helped me think through the issues this chapter addresses in his insightful comments on my earlier work in the same area. Most of all, though, I am indebted to Robin Trotter for the inestimable value of the research assistance she contributed to this chapter. I am similarly indebted to Robin for her research contributions to Chapter 8.

A number of the chapters draw on a project examining the relationships between museums, the historical sciences and liberal government in a variety of late-nineteenth century colonial and metropolitan contexts. I am grateful to the Australian Research Council for its award of a Large Grant in support of this project.

To John Frow and Meaghan Morris, I owe thanks for their initial comments on the shape of the book as a whole, and for their support in judging the project worthwhile when it was still at the drawing-board stage. I owe a further debt to Meaghan Morris for her careful, encouraging and productively critical comments on the final typescript. Her scrupulous commitment to intellectual rigour and political clarity helped me immeasurably in the final stages of preparing the book. My debt to James Clifford is of a similar kind: generous in his assessments of my arguments, his reading of my work was unfailingly accurate in its identification of its shortcomings and diplomatically to the point in suggesting how I might overcome them. My thanks also to Elizabeth Weiss of Allen & Unwin for her patience in waiting for the book to arrive, and for her confidence that it was worth supporting.

The book wouldn't exist in material form at all but for Bev Jeppesen's text-entry and formatting skills: my thanks to Bev, then, both for those skills as well as for her helpful assistance in many other matters without which I should never have found the time to write the book. Thanks, too, to my sons Oliver and James for their help in proofing the final stages of the typescript.

Some of the chapters published here have been published in other contexts. Chapter 1 was first published in J. McGuigan (ed.), *Making a Difference—Theory and Research in Cultural Studies*, Sage, 1997; Chapter 2 in *Southern Review*, vol. 26, no. 2, 1993; Chapter 5 in *Critical Inquiry*, vol. 21, no. 4, 1995; Chapter 6 in *Economy and Society*, vol. 26, no. 2, 1997; and Chapter 9 in *Cultural Studies*, vol. 10, no. 1, 1996. I am grateful, where relevant, to the journals and publishers concerned for their permission to republish these articles. They are all published here without significant changes except for the final chapter, which omits a section from the original published version. However, I have made minor adjustments to avoid needless repetitions and, where relevant, to help strengthen the connections between different chapters.

Introduction: For cultural studies

To write for something is also, and at the same time, to write against something else. Louis Althusser encapsulated this dual orientation succinctly in the title he used for the collection of essays he published as *For Marx* in signalling, as Robert Resch describes it, a concern to subject Marxism to a constructive critique—a critique, that is, that would be *for* a critically renewed Marxism in being *against* the existing Hegelianised versions of Marxism which, as Althusser saw them, deformed Marxism's true scientific spirit (see Resch, 1992: 33). To write for something, then, is to argue a case for its reformation. It is to engage in a transformative project which, in seeking to bring about a change in its object, entails a commitment of support that is conditional on the transformations it aims to bring about. It is in this sense that I see myself, in what follows, as writing for cultural studies: not, to be sure, in an uncritical and complacent advocacy of cultural studies in all of its existing forms, but rather in advocacy of a critically revised understanding of what cultural studies is and can most usefully aspire to be.

My project, in short, is a revisionist one, although not in the sense of seeking to rescue some earlier moment of cultural studies from the history of its subsequent deformations. It is here that I part company with Althusser. For the tendencies within cultural studies that I shall take issue with are ones that have been there from the outset. They are not incidental exterior accretions that have been added through subsequent debates and which have now only to be scraped away to reveal some more useable and resilient set of theoretical and political positions. This is not, then, a work of restoration. My purpose, rather, is to probe some of the key concepts, theoretical procedures and political stances that have characterised the central traditions of argument within cultural studies and to do so with a view to suggesting that it is precisely these—the central and defining aspects of cultural studies—that need to be, in some cases, qualified and, in others, jettisoned if work in the area is to proceed on a surer theoretical, institutional and political footing. By the same token, however, I shall also be concerned to identify those other defining features of cultural studies which have had, and still have, a continuing value and validity. Indeed, it is only because I believe that, in the final analysis, these positive and enabling aspects of cultural studies outweigh the problems that inhere in the intellectual legacies the field has bequeathed us that writing from within and for cultural studies remains both a valid and worthwhile enterprise.

My purpose, then, is to sketch out a program for cultural studies that will be responsive to the now-changed realities that intellectual work must take account of if it is to be connected effectively to, and into, the present. Yet, inevitably, an undertaking of this kind can only be conducted from a particular point of view. From what perspective, then, do my assessments of what are the sound and useful tendencies within cultural studies, and what are its more questionable aspects, derive? Three main issues stand to the fore here. First, I have sought to think consistently and realistically about the implications for cultural studies of the fact that the primary institutional conditions of its existence as an area of critical intellectual work have been supplied by the tertiary education sectors of advanced capitalist societies. In many canonical accounts of cultural studies, these institutional contexts have been regarded either as largely incidental—a convenient setting for an intellectual practice which has defined its true political vocation in terms of its extra-academic affiliations and connections—or as a danger embodying a threat of institutional entrapment that will deprive cultural studies of its radical cutting edge. My purpose, by contrast, is to suggest that the dynamics of higher education have played a key role in shaping the intellectual agendas of cultural studies, and that they have done so—supposing that such moments can be isolated—from the very beginning. Pierre Bourdieu has warned that 'agents engaged in the university field' are often blind to the role that their own activities, when looked at from the perspective of the institutional contexts in which they are located, play in connecting 'the hierarchies organising academic space' to 'the hierarchies inscribed in the objectivity of social structure'. In doing so, he makes a special point of saying that this includes 'those who, in writing about power . . . spontaneously think of themselves as exceptions to their own analyses' (Bourdieu, 1996: 4). The embarrassing tendency within cultural studies for those whose objective position is that of salaried government employees (that is, academics) working within large organisations (universities) governed by elaborate committee procedures and engaging in all the usual aspects of professional academic activity (attending conferences, publishing, grading and assessing) to write of cultural studies as if it were somehow outside of or marginal to institutions, and to speak of 'institutionalisation' as if it were a looming external threat, shows just how vulnerable it is to Bourdieu's characteristically acerbic critique. By way of a corrective to this tendency, then, I have sought to ground cultural studies more concretely and more specifically in the practices of the educational contexts which provide its most typical institutional settings and to argue the need for its future programs to take account of these conditions in a more thoroughly self-conscious and strategic fashion.

This is not to suggest that the significance of work within cultural studies should remain limited or confined to the educational sphere. To the contrary, one of the most valuable insistences of cultural studies has been its contention that academic work should not remain merely academic; that intellectual work conducted within universities or other educational contexts should seek to relate itself to other spheres of activity and involvement in the wider society. That said, the insistence is not one that cultural studies can claim as uniquely its own. It is just as strongly present in Marxist, feminist and postcolonial writings, for example. Just as important, though, it is also a claim that could be made with equal validity by pretty well every academic discipline or intellectual tradition you might care to mention. Indeed, Foucault's perspectives on the relations between knowledge and power have shown that all knowledges are in some way imbricated in the exercise, or contestation, of particular kinds of power in ways which entail constitutive connections between the intellectual dispositions of those knowledges and the organisation of particular fields of social relations or forms of social administration.

A stress on the relations between knowledge and practice, then, is not in itself a distinguishing characteristic of cultural studies. Rather, it is in the kinds of connections between the two that it has sought to organise that its arguments have been more distinctive: in connecting its concerns with the relations between culture and power to the politics of social movements, for example, or in its contributions to the personal politics of sexual relations. Although they have not been at the centre of my own interests, I have no quarrel with these concerns (which is not to say that I always agree with how they are formulated—I don't). What I do quarrel with, however, is the view that these should be regarded as the primary or only forms of practical connection with other spheres of activity and involvement that those working in cultural studies should seek to cultivate.

This brings me to the second perspective shaping my arguments in this book: the need to accord questions of cultural policy a more central place within the concerns of cultural studies. Of course, this is not to suggest that the two should be equated: there are many topics of valid concern within cultural studies which do not require—at least not in any direct or immediate way—the input of a policy perspective. Equally, cultural policy studies, as it presently exists, is a somewhat heterogeneous field that is by no means reducible to the contributions that have been made to it from within cultural studies: there are quite independent traditions of work in arts management and cultural economics, for example. The arguments of this book, however, are predicated on a triple wager. The first is that perspectives derived from cultural studies have a significant contribution to make to our understanding of the role which cultural policies play as parts of a distinctive configuration of the relations between government and culture which characterise modern societies. The role played by specific discourses of culture in organising particular fields of policy; the ways in which these are related to broader objectives of social management; their implications for the kinds of social and political tasks that cultural resources are conscripted to perform; the ways in which critical discourses get translated into the policy process and its bureaucratic mechanisms; the grounds on, and means by, which policy outcomes are taken issue with by political constituencies of various kinds: these are questions that need the critical input of cultural studies if their analysis is not to be merely anodyne and descriptive or complacently apologetic. By reverse, the second aspect of the wager is that a cultural studies that does not take account of the varying and complex forms in which culture is managed and administered in modern societies will be considerably impoverished in terms of both its historical understanding and its theoretical capacities. The third aspect of the wager, finally, is the contention that an engagement with policy issues needs to be seen as a central component of the practical concerns of cultural studies, and one that entails the development of effective and productive relationships with intellectual workers in policy bureaux and agencies and cultural institutions—but *as well as*, rather than at *the expense of*, other connections and, indeed, often as a means of pursuing issues arising from those other connections.

Reactions to arguments of this kind as aired in the context of the 'cultural policy debate' of the late 1980s and early 1990s—conducted mainly in Australia but with some spill-overs into British and American debates—have been varied. Some have suggested that the proponents of a policy perspective within cultural studies have overestimated the novelty of their case. Meaghan Morris points to the traditionally strong ties which have characterised the relations between universities and policy bureaux in all areas of Australian intellectual life (see Morris, 1992), while many commentators have called attention to Raymond Williams' strong practical and intellectual engagement with arts and cultural policies. These are useful correctives. However, they do not gainsay the fact that questions of cultural policy had previously been largely absent from both theoretical discussions about cultural studies and programmatic statements made on its behalf. Why this should have been so was made clear in the other genre of reactions to the policy debate—those which construed a concern with policy as, variously, a sellout to bureaucracy, a sacrifice of critical edge for a complacent managerialism, a Faustian pact with the state, or as the manifestation of a wish to sit down with (and perhaps even *in?*) 'the suits'.[1] For the terms in which these objections were couched testified clearly to a number of operative assumptions within cultural studies which functioned and, although I think the tide has now turned considerably, still function as serious theoretical blockages to an adequate engagement, both theoretical and practical, with the horizons of policy.

The sources of these theoretical impediments are various: in some cases, they arise from libertarian formulations that have been the worm in the bud of American cultural studies ever since it made its trans-Atlantic passage; in others, they have reflected the influence of essentialist theorisations of the state as an apparatus unified, in its entirety, by its role in the service of the ruling class; and, in others again, they have reflected the antinomies of critical theory which, for all its commitment to the prospect of a universal communicative rationality, splits the world of reason into two—critical reason and practical reason—in a manner which forecloses on the possibility of there being mutually productive relationships between them except, of course, for ones in which the former lords it over the latter.[2] Whichever the case, I believe that objections of this kind are fundamentally misconceived. This brings me to the third of the general perspectives which animate my concerns in this book. For my views on these matters derive from a set of perspectives on the relations between culture and government arising out of a particular approach to, and adaptation of, Foucault's writings. The tradition of work I have in mind here is that associated with the loosely interacting 'history of the present' groups in Brisbane, Melbourne and London which have sought to cull from Foucault's work a set of theoretical resources for examining the composition and operation of modern forms of government across a diverse range of contemporary fields of social management and administration: economic management, citizenship, ethics, the psy-complex, education (see, respectively, Rose and Miller, 1992; Meredyth and Tyler, 1993; Minson, 1993; Rose, 1990; and Hunter, 1994).

The merit of this body of work, from the point of view of my concerns here, has consisted in the manner in which it has undercut and disabled those ways of thinking about intellectual work which situate the intellectual in some self-subsistent and transcendent site of critique located in a position of exteriority in relation to the object of that critique: in this case, the state or the management of culture. This misconstrues the matter entirely. When we speak about the relations between cultural studies and policy, I shall argue, we are not discussing the relations between two separate realms (critique and the state) but, rather, the articulations between two branches of government, each of which is deeply involved in the management of culture. It is here that my earlier remarks, derived from Bourdieu, regarding the extent to which theorists of power always imagine themselves to be immune to the effects of their own analyses apply most tellingly. What else could account for the resolute failure of so many university teachers working within cultural studies to recognise that their position within a university objectively situates them within the realm of government? What else could account for their failure to see that 'working with government' is, in this sense, what they do every day and that the problems, experience and often the theoretical and practical concerns of those intellectuals who work in cultural policy agencies and bureaux are remarkably similar to their own? They are not identical, of course—the conditions of work in universities are different in the degree of freedom and autonomy they afford, and these are conditions that should be valued, respected and put to good use in generating and sustaining work that can connect productively with other branches of government. This is simply not possible where those conditions are misrecognised as an autonomous, uncontaminated realm of critique: to claim this status is to play, unwittingly, the role of state-funded court jester.

None of this, of course, is to suggest that one should be any more starry-eyed about a practical engagement with cultural policy than about working in the modern university. The scope for useful work is, in both cases, clearly influenced by broader political considerations. It is thus no accident that policy issues should have entered actively into the concerns of cultural studies perhaps more insistently and enduringly in Australia than anywhere else in view of the more auspicious circumstances created by a continuous period of Labor government from 1983 to 1996 at a time when the United States was undergoing the Reaganite 'revolution' and Britain was suffering from the worst ravages of Thatcherism. These are obviously important considerations, as are the longer-term political and administrative traditions which make for relatively direct and interventionist forms of cultural policy in Australia compared with the more *laissez-faire* approaches which, with the exception of the New Deal period (see Harris, 1995), have prevailed in countries like the United States. It is also true, as Hugh Collins (1985) has argued, that Australian traditions of government have historically tended to be more strongly directive and utilitarian—more Benthamite, even—than those associated with British forms of liberal government.

All of these things matter in determining the specific nature of the political, intellectual and administrative ground that has to be negotiated to produce useful points of connection between work in cultural studies and actual cultural policy processes and outcomes. Difficult though this work may be and, no doubt, often in conditions not of our own choosing, it cannot be sidestepped in view of the significance which attaches to such processes and their outcomes. Equally, though, the influence of different national traditions and conditions needs to be recognised if we are to speak with, rather than past, one another. This has been clear from the ways in which echoes of the cultural policy debate have been picked up and replayed in the context of North American debates. While there have been few impediments to effective dialogue between Canadian and Australian debates in these areas, it is clear that the language of policy has as much difficulty in being translated across the Pacific as it does across the 49th Parallel. Yet it is equally clear that similar issues concerning the need for intellectual work to more clearly articulate the kinds of connectedness it can and should aspire to have been very much to the fore in work—like that of Bruce Robbins (1990) and Andrew Ross (1989)—concerned with the public role of intellectuals, or that of Michael Bérubé (1996), addressing the question of a publicly relevant cultural criticism or, finally, that of Tom Streeter (1996) who, while noting the relevance of Australian cultural policy studies to his concerns, is equally clear about why, in the United States context, it makes more sense to talk about law than about policy in view of the particular kinds of technocratic association the latter term has acquired. I have therefore, where relevant, sought to develop my concerns in ways which emphasise their connections with these debates in the interest of a more productive international dialogue on these questions.

These, then, are the general arguments running through and connecting the essays collected here. As such, they reflect my experience of working in cultural studies in a number of contexts. Most obviously, they reflect some of the things I have learned in moving from Britain to Australia and, in the process, encountering traditions of intellectual work, of politics and of culture which have required more than minor adjustments to the terms of reference I brought with me. They also reflect the equally significant process of learning and unlearning that has formed a part of my practical involvement in policy—not as a 'policy player' or a policy-maker, but as the director of research centres with a policy focus. My arguments, finally, in both their substance and their form, owe a good deal to my ongoing work on the history and present practices of museums and art galleries, which I draw on in a number of places in order to develop my points through an engagement with particular issues and materials.

The chapters are grouped into three parts, each of which has a distinctive thematic coherence, although there are also links and continuities between these different parts. My concerns in the first part are with two different aspects of the theory of cultural studies: first, its view of itself and of its relations to adjacent intellectual enterprises; and second, the relative merits of contrasting theoretical paradigms within cultural studies. My interests in the first two chapters focus on what I can perhaps best characterise as the bashfulness of cultural studies regarding its own status as an intellectual discipline. This has been manifest in the degree to which it has fought shy of defining itself in terms of definite theories and methods, preferring instead forms of self-characterisation which allow it to be thought of as a permanently mobile and adaptive practice unencumbered by the kinds of intellectual restrictions that disciplinary status brings in its wake. In the first chapter, 'Towards a pragmatics for cultural studies', which sets the tone for the book, my purpose is to identify, in the midst of this disciplinary bashfulness, the kinds of minimally shared ground—the general arguments and positions—to which most people working in the field would subscribe. I then proceed to argue for a particular interpretation of these general arguments—one that would, in my view, allow cultural studies to connect more successfully than it has so far with the diverse fields of practical engagement which have characterised its work to date. It should be recognised, however, that suggesting cultural studies needs a pragmatics is, in some respects, a provocation to the degree that many tendencies within cultural studies have defined themselves in opposition to the kinds of reconciliation with the field of the practicable that the concept of a pragmatics implies.

Chapter 2, 'Being "in the true" of cultural studies', approaches the disciplinary bashfulness of cultural studies from a different perspective, suggesting that this constitutes a particular mode of being 'in the true', the consequences of which, in displacing debate from theoretical and methodological issues on to the moral qualities which intellectuals supposedly derive from their social characteristics, have been regrettable. The argument is carried via a critique of the role that is accorded the status of social marginality, whether construed in terms of relations of region, gender, race or class, within the epistemic gambits of cultural studies. This is accompanied by a critical assessment of the role that the status of marginality plays in conventional accounts of the history of cultural studies and a sketch of a counter-genealogy which instead traces its origins to the requirements of postwar secondary education. In bringing these two arguments together, this chapter suggests that 'disciplining cultural studies' in the sense of defining its intellectual attributes more clearly and thinking about its practical articulations in terms which, like any other discipline, include the role it plays in the education system, offers the prospect of developing a clearer and more acceptable politics of knowledge than the sometimes heroic accounts of a knowledge-forged-in-opposition which have tended to govern the terms of debate on such questions.

The final chapter in the first part of the book, 'Cultural studies: The Foucault effect', returns to a question I have addressed before: the nature of the relationship between Foucault and Gramsci within the concerns of cultural studies (see Bennett, 1990), but, this time, from the perspective of their respective theorisations of the nature and organisation of the forms of cultural power that are peculiar to modern societies. With thinkers as complex and many-sided as Gramsci and Foucault, there is, of course, little point to be served in siding with the one in an unqualified way against the other and no point at all in discounting the contributions of either. The argument of this essay, however, runs in favour of Foucault in regard to two central concerns of cultural studies: how to account for the distinctive place that culture occupies within the forms of power which characterise modern societies and, perhaps more important, how to account for the distinctive *productivity* of culture. The Foucault in question here, however, is a very particular one: it is the Foucault whose writings on liberal government permit, so I contend, a revised understanding of the relations between civil society, culture and the state which allows culture its autonomous spheres and forms of action in a manner that Gramsci was never quite able to accommodate. This was due to the degree to which the work of culture always finally remained, for Gramsci—in however indirect and mediated a manner—a question of the effect of the economic structure on itself. It is fair to add, though, that I may well be putting words in Foucault's mouth here, as the subject of culture was not one Foucault himself wrote about directly. My account, then, is an extrapolation of how culture might be theorised given a particular set of theoretical axioms, rather than a summary of what Foucault said—or might have said, had he got round to it.

The theoretical perspectives outlined in this concluding chapter in Part I provide me with my bearings for Part II. My concerns here are historical in the sense of seeking both to describe and account for an historically specific set of relations between culture and government through which, since the Enlightenment, the realm of culture has been regarded as a set of resources which are to be strategically managed with a view to bringing about specific changes in the conduct of populations. It is as a consequence of its inscription in such practices of government, I suggest, that culture has come to be tangled up in the exercise of power in historically specific ways which have resulted in its acquisition of distinctive kinds of productivity and effect.

This argument is carried at a general level in the first chapter of this part of the book—'Culture: A reformer's science'—by means of a critical review of the concept of culture as a way of life. Although—indeed, perhaps because—it now enjoys a more or less canonical status as the founding concept of cultural studies, there has been little critical discussion of this concept in the literature. When looked at more closely, I suggest, the yield of this concept proves to be far more complex and ambiguous than conventional assessments suggest. Surveying its use in nineteenth century anthropology, in the work of Raymond Williams and in the discourses of contemporary cultural policy, I suggest that the concept in fact remains deeply normative in ways which have allowed it to function as an adjunct to—or, better, as an indispensable component of—the reforming practices of government. This, however, is not a reason for abandoning the concept. To the contrary, my purpose in offering this reading of the concept is to offer, so to speak, a scandalously moderate genealogy for the concept that will rescue it from an unqualified radicalism and for a reformist cultural politics.

The theoretical concerns which provide the backdrop to my arguments in this chapter are derived from Foucault's account of the mechanisms of liberal government. This has had significant implications for our understanding of 'the social' or 'society' as a realm that is independent of government and yet one with which, inevitably, government must concern itself. It is now common for the emergence of the social sciences to be accounted for in terms of the gap between government and society which liberal problematics of government open up. For Andrew Barry, Thomas Osborne and Nikolas Rose, for example, the social sciences 'provide a way of representing the autonomous dynamics of society and assessing whether they should or should not be an object of regulation' (Barry, Osborne and Rose, 1996: 9). There is also a much broader tradition of analysis, nicely summarised by Bruno Latour in his reference to the role that sociology, in its administrative application, has played in fashioning the social as an effect of its own actions (see Latour, 1987: 257). Somewhat less attention has been given to identifying the implications of such conceptions for the ways in which the realm of culture might be theorised in terms of its relations to both government and society.[3] This chapter contributes to such an endeavour in showing how culture is increasingly envisaged, within liberal systems of rule, as a *means of acting* on the social. Indeed, the fashioning of culture into an historically specific set of resources for managing conduct is essential to the mechanisms of liberal rule in providing a varied set of means through which the freedom which arises from the autonomy of society can be subjected to direction and regulation. In its approach to these questions, then, this chapter offers a different way of thinking about the relations between culture and society from those we have become accustomed to: one in which culture emerges as a set of relations and practices that is involved in managing the social by acting *on* it rather than as a mediated reflection or expression of relationships that are rooted *in* the social.

The remaining two essays in Part II illustrate this conception of culture as a means of acting on the social in the context of two particular historical deployments of cultural resources for reforming purposes. In Chapter 5, 'The multiplication of culture's utility', I try to recover the discursive conditions which made it intelligible to nineteenth century cultural reformers to suppose that the provision of public libraries, museums and the like might be of service in making the workingman sober and sexually prudent. One aspect of my concerns in this chapter is to offer a case study of the relations between culture and liberal government in showing the detailed planning that went into designing the programs and regimes of museums to make them places where people would learn to become self-governing and self-civilising. Another, however, is to trace one of the more surprising consequences of this endeavour in the anti-auratic and bureaucratic orientation to art that it entailed. My interests here focus on the respects in which the utilitarian calculus that informed these endeavours might provide a useful counterfoil to the romantic construction of the art museum that is inherent in the legacy bequeathed to us by Theodor Adorno and Walter Benjamin. Chapter 6 seeks to be similarly revisionist in relation to the role that is accorded evolutionary narratives in the functioning of late nineteenth century ethnology and natural history displays—usually, that of functioning, in social Darwinist terms, as a conservative antidote to socialism. The difficulty with such accounts is that they posit an essentially negative mechanism for culture: they see it as functioning oppressively by stopping something happening—in this case, the working classes from becoming revolutionary. As a counter-argument, then, I look closely at the ways in which Darwin's work was originally received, interpreted and translated into programs of social and cultural management by the liberal scientific intelligentsia who were Darwin's contemporaries. In doing so, I suggest that the light in which Darwin's work was originally interpreted allowed it to be used as a way of managing the insertion of individuals into new orders of historical time in ways that would promote in them a 'regulated restlessness' that would enlist them in the task of progress by making them self-developing subjects. Here again, the stress is placed on the productivity of culture in organising new forms of self-activity into being.

Studies of this kind have their obvious limitations. It particularly needs to be stressed that analysing the discursive properties which inform the programs of cultural institutions is one thing and that studying the ways in which audiences or visitors then use, interpret or make sense of these institutions is another. Ideally, of course, the two should be studied together; in practice, this is often not possible, either because of constraints on the researcher's time or the lack of any relevant forms of historical evidence. For both of these reasons, I have, in Chapters 5 and 6, restricted my attention to the first set of issues. This reflects a decision, made for a combination of theoretical and practical reasons, to focus on a particular delimited object of study, rather than an erroneous belief that the ways in which users and audiences relate to the discursive properties of cultural institutions can simply be read off from those properties themselves. These are questions that I engaged with, although indirectly, in an earlier phase of my work when, in the context of debates within literary theory, I proposed the concept of 'reading formations' as a means for conducting an empirically grounded analysis of the socially variable ways in which texts were used, viewed and interpreted (see Bennett and Woollacott, 1987). Although I have not invoked that concept in my subsequent work on museums and art galleries, I have seen nothing in later developments in reader-response or audience theory that would make me want to walk away from it either. I mention this in case readers interested in visitor and audience studies might find this concept helpful in pursuing their own concerns in this area.

The final part of the book addresses three different sites of practice for cultural studies: politics, policy and pedagogy. In Chapter 7, 'Culture, power, resistance', I take my bearings in relation to the first of these from the role that the concept of resistance has played in the concerns of cultural studies. My primary purpose in doing so is to prise apart the often very different and even incompatible accounts of the relations between subordinate groups and dominant forms of cultural power that take cover beneath the common shelter of this concept. This involves comparing and contrasting two canonical cultural studies texts—the Birmingham Centre's *Resistance through Rituals* (Hall and Jefferson, 1976) and Michel de Certeau's *The Practice of Everyday Life* (1984)—as a means of circumscribing the concept of resistance and limiting the weight that is placed on it if we are to account for the diversity of the political relations to dominant cultures that can be developed by those whom they subordinate. This, in turn, prepares the ground for a more detailed discussion of de Certeau's analysis of the practices of everyday life, particularly from the point of view of their applicability to the forms of cultural resistance developed by indigenous Australians.

Chapter 8 returns to the 'cultural policy debate' of the late 1980s. My purpose in doing so is to try to understand the discursive antinomies which, for most participants, organised the terms of that debate and, in tracing the history of those antinomies, to plot a route beyond them that would put culture and policy on the same, rather than the opposite, sides of an equation. This involves a consideration of Adorno's (1967) account of the relations between culture and administration, and of the inadequacy of his attempt to resolve what he sees as an inherent opposition between the two. My final concern in this chapter is to illustrate how contemporary radical cultural politics can themselves be seen as attempts to governmentalise—and so also to bureaucratise—culture in specific ways. My examples here are taken from contemporary debates regarding the relationships between museums and communities, especially James Clifford's perspective of museums as contact zones.

My concerns in Chapter 9, 'Out in the open: Critical reflections on the history and practice of cultural studies', have a dual focus. First, in focusing on a particular episode in the history of British cultural studies comprised by the making of the Open University *Popular Culture* course, I return again to the role which 'myths of the margins' have played in histories of cultural studies. My more substantial concerns, however, are with questions of pedagogy. In defending the *Popular Culture* course from the charge that it failed to 'teach resistance', I take issue with the notion that this either can or should be a coherent goal for a cultural studies pedagogy and show how the supposition that it might be is the reflex action of a libertarian strain within cultural studies that has paid insufficient attention to its relationships to the political paradigms of American liberalism.

A final word on what I hope the reader will take away from the book: ideally, a sense of being provoked, of looking at some issues in a different light—a feeling, in short, of productive irritation that might promote a similar inclination to work for cultural studies by thinking against the grain of its received formulations. And a word on what I hope the reader will not take away from the book: namely, a sense that its engagements, although often sharp, have been gratuitously polemical. Cultural studies is, at the end of the day, a practice whose theoretical coordinates are still mapped in terms of a number of key names. I am aware that I have approached a number of these key names—some of which are also the names of mentors and of friends—fairly robustly. To them, as indeed to all readers, I say that what is in a name is, in this case, a position and not a person. True, the distinction is often a difficult one to maintain. It is, however, vital that we continue to do so if debate is to remain open, frank and productive.

PART I

Theory

1 Towards a pragmatics for cultural studies

Perhaps my title begs a question or two. For, putting aside what a pragmatics for cultural studies might look like, it is not altogether clear that cultural studies either is, or will come to be, greatly troubled with or by the need for one. After all, from the perspective of a certain style of radicalism, the concept of a pragmatics might seem inherently compromised, conceding from the outset the oppositional stance which, in some accounts, has defined the cultural studies project. To be pragmatic means, according to my dictionary, to be concerned 'with practical consequences or values' or with matters 'pertaining to the affairs of a state or community'. Few of the traditions within cultural studies with which I am familiar have been notably pragmatic in the first of these senses. There has, it is true, always been a clear insistence on the practical, in the sense of political, relevance of the concerns of cultural studies. However, this theoretical interest in practice has seldom resulted in any developed interest in the conditions—institutional, discursive, political—which define the limits and forms of the practicable. As to the second definition—the affairs of a state or community—these, in their actually existing forms, are often precisely what cultural studies has defined itself against.

To suggest that cultural studies might aspire to, and stand in need of, a pragmatics, then, is to propose a revisionary program for cultural studies. This is partly a matter of arguing the need for cultural studies to be developed in a closer association with the policy concerns of government and industry as a means of developing a more prosaic concept of practice, one that will sustain actual and productive connections with the field of the practicable. This is not a new argument; indeed, it is one which—although often using a different vocabulary—has been made a number of times in earlier phases in the development of cultural studies in critique of the reluctance to tether questions of culture and policy too closely together that stems, in part, from the history of the concept of culture itself. It will therefore be useful to bring an historical perspective to bear on this question in order to rediscover an earlier pragmatic strain within cultural studies that now needs to be retrieved 'against the grain' of, and as a corrective to, what have since proved to be more influential libertarian and oppositional formulations of the practical stances that should be adopted by cultural studies. In doing so, however, I shall also seek to locate questions concerning the relations between cultural studies and policy as part of a broader pragmatics rooted in a recognition of the real institutional conditions of cultural studies' existence within the education system.

It is from considerations of this kind that I want to take my initial bearings as a way of signalling the need to root debates about the theoretical and political agendas of cultural studies more closely in the circumstances affecting the forms in which it is, and is most likely to be, produced and disseminated. Two such factors might usefully be mentioned at this point. The first consists in the growing body of writing that is concerned to describe and assess the limitations of cultural studies from the perspective of rival critical paradigms. This is not to say that cultural studies has previously lacked critics. To the contrary, its claims to intellectual seriousness have had to be advanced in the face of those familiar kinds of elitist disdain which typically greet any intellectual project concerned with the power relations of the cultural field rather than simply training a new generation of cultic consumers. Then also, politically, there have been sharp disputes within cultural studies, as well as between it and closely related intellectual traditions, regarding its understandings of the relations between culture, race, gender and class. On the whole, however, throughout most of the 1980s, cultural studies registered what seemed to be a more or less irresistible advance. Its currency as a term became widespread internationally as its spiralling ascent—registered in terms of publications, conferences and the growth of cultural studies curricula—encountered little serious criticism or opposition.

The early 1990s, by contrast, witnessed the publication of a number of critical studies which—mostly from the disciplinary paradigm of sociology—sought to call cultural studies into question on both theoretical and political grounds. Jim McGuigan's (1992) criticism of the populist aspects of cultural studies is a case in point whilst David Harris, in his *From Class Struggle to the Politics of Pleasure* (1992), casts a broader critical net in chastising cultural studies for what he characterises as the narrowing and doctrinaire qualities of its most influential intellectual styles and paradigms. As it happens, I think both books fall short of their targets. This is not to deny that many of their criticisms of cultural studies are valid—far from it. But both tend to attack positions which had already been substantially criticised within cultural studies while failing to register the new positions that have been taken up in their place. Both also limit their attention more or less exclusively to Britain, and consequently take inadequate account of the extent to which much of the impetus for new initiatives and directions in cultural studies has come from 'other' places (see Blundell et al., 1993). For all that, the tendency which such studies represent is, I believe, to be welcomed, precisely because it places much-needed limits on the kind of intellectual project cultural studies might aspire to be. While a claim to embody new kinds of interdisciplinary understandings of cultural forms and practices by placing these in the context of relations of power has always been an important aspect of the self-definition of cultural studies, this view has also often been tangled up with the more polemical argument that cultural studies has the potential both to displace and to surpass those specialist disciplines which also have a stake in the analysis of culture.

While the first of these arguments is, in my view, valid and in need of further development, the second is not. Cultural studies may, of course, influence the concerns of sociology, history, art history, literary studies and so on. Indeed, there are ample signs that it already has. However, to expect that it might displace or transcend these disciplines, or that it is in some way inherently superior to them because of its interdisciplinary characteristics, is a fantasy that is neither to be wished nor desired. To the contrary, the value and specificity of distinctive intellectual skills and trainings within the social sciences and humanities need to be both defended and promoted instead of being 'white-anted' by misplaced and over-generalising assessments of the value of interdisciplinariness. In place, then, of imagining a future for cultural studies in which it provides for a kind of intellectual wholeness in overcoming disciplinary specialisms, the need now is to fashion a clearer sense of the specific and therefore limited frameworks of analysis and inquiry that cultural studies might claim as its own in relation to, and alongside, the concerns of more established humanities and social science disciplines. This will involve thinking clearly about its place in the education system. For the success of cultural studies, the rate at which it has become a regular feature of the curriculum landscape of higher education, is not unrelated to its value as a device for organising broadly based undergraduate degrees for an expanded student population, most of the members of which have little need for specialist disciplinary trainings so far as their likely career trajectories are concerned.

This brings me to my second point: if cultural studies now has its critics, it also has its textbooks and primers. If publishers' catalogues are anything to go by, this looks set to become a burgeoning industry. This development has, predictably, been vehemently opposed by many working within cultural studies as embodying a form of institutional co-option which represents the beginning of the end so far as its radical credentials are concerned. Where cultural studies is seen as an inherently oppositional and resistive intellectual practice, the very concept of a cultural studies textbook is something of an oxymoron since, in place of seeing cultural studies as a constantly mobile tactics of intellectual opposition, it reduces it to a body of knowledge which has been codified to allow for its transmission to be institutionalised. For Stuart Hall, for example, the prospect of institutionalisation represents 'a moment of profound danger' for cultural studies (Hall, 1992: 285). In contrast to such views, then, I want to argue that the cultural studies textbook is very much to be welcomed (the issue is not whether cultural studies should or can have its textbooks, but whether it gets good ones) and welcomed precisely because it calls attention to the fact that, among other things, cultural studies has always been, and is always likely to be, an institutionalised form of pedagogy.

Yet this is a contentious proposition. In many of the more influential versions of cultural studies that we have, its relations to educational institutions and practices have been portrayed as less important than its relations to social movements of various kinds. Indeed, in some versions, cultural studies itself figures as a kind of phantom social movement, a substitute for the working class or for the counter-hegemonic alliances of social forces which, in the days of 'rainbow coalitions', were to take the proletariat's place. This view of cultural studies as, in essence, 'politics by other means' has resulted in a regrettable neglect of the respects in which, to the degree that its primary institutional location is within tertiary educational institutions, cultural studies is inescapably shaped by the agendas of such institutions and so must consciously seek to shape its own future in ways which take account of those agendas.

The general direction of my arguments, then, will be in favour of more limited and circumscribed—but, by the same token, more specific and clearly formulated—understandings of the ambit, concerns and procedures of cultural studies. If its ambitions have often hitherto seemed vaunting and ill-defined, my purpose in proposing a pragmatics for cultural studies is to map out more definite and practicable paths for its future development. As this will involve a critical assessment of more conventional views of cultural studies, it will first be useful to distinguish the kinds of criticism to which cultural studies can validly and usefully be subjected from less helpful forms of critique and commentary.

CULTURAL STUDIES IN THE PLURAL

In a number of essays written in the late 1980s and early 1990s, Ian Hunter—who has been more astringent than most in his criticisms of cultural studies—has argued that, far from having transcended traditional aesthetic conceptions of culture, cultural studies has remained powerfully subject to the influence of such conceptions in ways which, although largely unacknowledged, have had a significant bearing on the direction and tenor of its intellectual projects and on the manner in which such projects have been conducted. Having argued that the 'cultural studies movement conceives of itself as a critique of aesthetics', here is how Hunter summarises its central ambitions in this regard:

> In short, the limits that cultural studies establishes for aesthetics are those of a knowledge or practice of cultivation segregated from the driving forces of human development—labor and politics—and retarding further development by diverting culture into the ideal realm of ethics and taste. Given this specification, the way to transcend these limits is clear. The narrowly ethical practice of culture associated with aesthetics must be subsumed within culture as the whole way of life. Then it will be possible to actualise the promise of self-realisation by harnessing aesthetics to the processes of economic and political development. (Hunter, 1992: 348)

It is precisely in this ambition to restore a lost form of wholeness, Hunter argues, that cultural studies most readily bears witness to the continuing influence of Romantic aesthetics as inflected, via the work of Raymond Williams, through the prism of Marxist thought. Romantic aesthetics, Hunter suggests, was essentially a practice of the self through which the aesthetic personality sought to overcome incompleteness and aspire to full humanity by using techniques of self-cultivation which aimed to harmonise and reconcile—to bring to interactive fullness—the different, and in themselves fractured and divisive, aspects of personhood. One part of the argument, then, is that the intellectual agendas of cultural studies translate this dialectical technique of person-formation into a dialectical-historical method through which the antinomies which have racked the sphere of culture are to be both traced and, through a political project aimed at the production of a common culture—of a shared way of life as a whole—overcome. Second, and as a corollary, cultural studies places its political bets on those social and cultural tendencies within the present which, in being interpreted as attempting to pierce through alienating cultural divisions, seem to prefigure new and emerging forms of cultural wholeness. This is the role accorded the concept of emergent culture within Williams' conception of the relations between dominant, residual and emergent forms of culture (see Williams, 1977). In a third aspect of the argument, however, Hunter relates the legacy of Romantic aesthetics more directly to the style and persona that cultural studies intellectuals seek to construct for themselves. Speaking of the tendency within cultural studies to eschew any determinate and definite knowledge claims in favour of grand and general claims to an interdisciplinarity that is beyond existing divisions of intellectual labour, Hunter relates this to that current of thought within cultural studies which expresses disdain for making use of available and existing instruments of political action in favour of practices of critique that will make the intellectual ready to act only once more auspicious political circumstances have been produced, and sees in both of these an adaptation of the styling of the self derived from Romantic aesthetics. 'Both ideas,' as he puts it, 'are symptomatic of a practice of the self that displaces the objectives of existing knowledge and politics with the objective of the permanent preparation of a self worthy to know and to act.' (Hunter 1992: 355)

These are powerful arguments which, in the main, hit their targets, although it can fairly be said that the bow Hunter draws is sometimes a long one, with the mechanisms of connection between historical discourses and present practices remaining somewhat obscure and conjectural. There are times also when the targets Hunter has in view seem too generalised and diffuse. For it is doubtful how far the positions he takes issue with can be attributed to cultural studies as a whole, as distinct from particular traditions and branches of inquiry within cultural studies. And if this is so, it is because it is also doubtful how true it is to say either that cultural studies can be defined as a critique of aesthetics or that, where this is so, its criticisms of aesthetics necessarily take the form Hunter attributes to them. It is true, of course, that work within cultural studies both depends on and contributes to criticisms of aesthetic conceptions of culture to the degree that it holds all forms of culture to be worthy of analysis irrespective of the places they occupy within the rankings of conventional aesthetic hierarchies. It is also true that, throughout the history of cultural studies, Williams' concept of culture as a whole way of life has been more or less routinely invoked to legitimate such a concern—but often as no more than a convenient shorthand which carries few of the specific and complex meanings associated with the concept in Williams' own work. When the authors of *Resistance through Rituals* wish to define what they understand by the term 'culture' in ways that will justify its extension to deal with the everyday cultural practices of young people, for example, they draw on Williams' notion of culture as a way of life. Here is the definition they offer:

> The 'culture' of a group or class is the peculiar and distinctive 'way of life' of the group or class, the meanings, values and ideas embodied in institutions, in social relations, in systems of beliefs, in mores and customs, in the uses of objects and material life. Culture is the distinctive shape in which this material and social organisation of life expresses itself. A culture includes the 'maps of meaning' which make things intelligible to its members. These 'maps of meaning' are not simply carried around in the head: they are objectivated in the patterns of social organisation and relationship through which the individual becomes a 'social individual'. Culture is the way the social relations of a group are structured and shaped: but it is also the way those shapes are experienced, understood and interpreted. (Hall and Jefferson, 1976: 10–11)

This definition is not without its difficulties, not the least of which are the respects in which culture doubles as both itself (a distinctive organisation of social life) and its own representation (maps of meaning). However, these difficulties have nothing to do with those aspects of Williams' usage of the concept in which culture as a whole way of life anticipates the restoration of a lost cultural wholeness in which hierarchising and divisive forms of cultural difference will have been overcome. To the contrary, the analytical agenda of *Resistance through Rituals* is one in which relations of cultural division and subordination—between different class cultures and, within the same class, between youth subcultures and their parental class cultures—proliferate with a view to understanding how particular ways of life (youth subcultures) are structured by relations of multiple social contradiction. Something similar is involved when John Frow and Meaghan Morris refer to Williams to define culture as 'the "whole way of life" of a social group as it is structured by representation and by power . . . a network of representations—texts, images, talk, codes of behaviour, and the narrative structures organising these—which shapes every aspect of social life' (Frow and Morris, 1993: x). In both cases, the reference to Williams is a more or less ritual incantation; and, in both cases, the object of analysis that is established is significantly detached from the semantic horizons in which the concept of culture as a whole way of life is embedded in Williams' own writing. The usage proposed by Frow and Morris, for example, is perhaps closer to Bourdieu's concept of *habitus* than it is to Williams' own usage while, in *Resistance through Rituals*, the interpretation of culture as a way of life draws far more on sociological subcultural theory than on Williams.

My point, then, is that Hunter offers too generalised a critique of cultural studies and does so mainly because he places too much stress on the originating context of some of its key terms in Williams' work and vocabulary and, consequently, is not always fully alert to the wider range of uses and meanings that have come to be associated with those terms when deployed in contexts which have little to do with the specific kind of critique of aesthetics offered by Williams. Such concerns are simply not visible in *Policing the Crisis* (Hall et al., 1978). Yet, in view of its ambitious orchestration of the relations between media practices, the shifting ground of class cultures and the changing field of political discourses in postwar Britain, this study is deservedly regarded by many as an exemplary text of and for cultural studies. Moreover, even where a concern with the critique of aesthetics has predominated, such work has not always been conducted under the aegis of Williams. Indeed, a good case could be made for seeing Bourdieu's work as having been more influential in this respect.

The more general issue to which these considerations point—and my reason for raising them here—is that cultural studies is now, and always has been, too diverse and polyglot for it to be susceptible to any general form of critique. It lacks, and always has lacked, the kind of unity—of a developed discipline, say, or of a movement—which might render it liable to successful prosecution on the grounds of the general effects of any single set of foundational concepts. Yet, for all that—although it is important to set some limits to the potential purchase of Hunter's criticisms—these remain of compelling relevance to contemporary concerns and debates within the field, in view of the light they throw on the question of the institutional location of cultural studies. Hunter's remarks thus most clearly hit home where they are directed against those tendencies within cultural studies which have been developed in a close association with the field of literary studies. For it has been here—where cultural studies has been thought of as both heir and successor to English while also furnishing a critique of its winnowing specialisms—that those formulations of Williams most clearly derived from Romanticism have been most influential. And it this aspect of cultural studies which, in Hunter's view, is likely to be responsible for its most significant long-term institutional legacy. For, to the degree that the critique of aesthetic culture derived from Williams' work is one that is still dependent on Romantic aesthetics, and to the degree, therefore, that such a critique signals a renewal rather than an end of aesthetic forms of social and cultural criticism, Hunter suggests, in a more recent assessment, that this 'helps to explain why the most lasting contribution of the cultural studies movement looks like being its refurbishment of literature departments in Australia and the USA' (Hunter, 1993: 172).

Of course, there are literature departments and literature departments and, within these, many approaches to the study of literature that remain unaffected by these developments. It is not the choice of literary texts as an object of study that is at issue here, but rather the question as to how such texts should be studied and with what purpose. The downside of Hunter's prognosis consists in the suggestion that cultural studies may well prove to be merely the catalyst through which aesthetic and moralising forms of critique and pedagogy regroup themselves and, in being applied to an extended array of objects (culture as a 'whole way of life'), extend their influence. Again, it is not critique that is at issue, but the form of critique and the purposes for which it is conducted. Where cultural forms are examined from the point of view of understanding the role which they play within specific fields of power relations, of criticising their political consequences in this regard and debating the forms of practical action through which their existing political articulations might be modified, this is all well and good. There are ample signs, however, that where cultural studies is being fashioned as an heir to English, the forms of critique it lays claim to are concerned more with cultivating a certain ethical style and demeanour than with the pursuit of any practicable courses of action with specific political or policy goals in view. One sign of this has been the enduring concern with 'speaking positions' which, in its focus on where the intellectual speaks from (as opposed to what he or she speaks to, and with what competence), has embodied precisely that interest in the endless preening of the intellectual's persona that is the hallmark of aesthetico-moral styles of criticism.

However, institutions connected to the literary field (which, let me stress again, I do not wish to falsely unify) have not supplied the only contexts from which cultural studies has emerged and in which it is presently practised. During its formative years in Britain, it was closely connected to developments in the fields of media and communication studies, sociology, history and art history, and often with important institutional bases in these different fields. It has also, but in plural and diverse ways, and from the beginning, been shaped by its connections with socialist, feminist and anti-racist political movements. When viewed in relation to this dispersed set of institutional and political contexts, it is not difficult to locate areas of cultural studies debate where the influence of the Romantic legacy traced by Hunter has been either, to say the least, marginal or, on some issues, actively opposed. Paul Gilroy, for example, was quick to identify the respects in which notions of the organic community lay behind Williams' argument that Britain's black migrants could be regarded as only legally, but not wholly—that is culturally—British. He was also quick to argue the importance of formal, legal definitions of citizenship, and of the role of the state in securing these, against Williams' Romantic fantasy that such matters are superficialities, reflecting 'the limited functional terms of the ruling class' (Williams, 1983: 195), compared with the deeper and more authentic cultural aspects of national identity (see Gilroy, 1987). Stuart Hall, in tactfully disentangling himself from this aspect of Williams' work—and doing so in a way which shows his clear awareness of the extent to which Williams' assessments on this matter derive from the elements of Romanticism that linger on in his commitment to the view of culture as a whole way of life and the criteria of cultural belonging that this generates—is emphatic in his insistence that, for black migrants, '"formal legal definitions of citizenship" matter profoundly' and 'cannot be made conditional on cultural assimilation' (Hall, 1993: 360). If, then, we are going to speak of the origins of cultural studies, we need to recognise that these have always been plural and diverse, as have been the traditions to which these 'origins' have given rise. This is even more so when we consider cultural studies in its international formation. This is, indeed, where the problematic of origins most evidently breaks down. However much the early developments in British cultural studies may have influenced the early formation of cultural studies in Australia or Canada, for example, it is equally clear that this influence was inflected via, and interpreted through, nationally specific intellectual traditions and concerns to which the agendas of aesthetic critique derived from Williams were of only passing interest. The relationship of cultural studies to the traditions of radical nationalism was of more pressing relevance in Australia whereas, in Canada, the concern with the role of communications technologies in organising socio-spatial relationships derived from the work of Harold Innes has proved of enduring relevance, accounting for what is often most distinctive in Canadian cultural studies.

Given such an understanding of cultural studies, two questions arise. First, what do these dispersed traditions of work have in common that merits their being called cultural studies and makes such a common designation useful? And second, which tendencies in this body of work are most worthy of support and further development, and which now need to be jettisoned or revised? Although each leads to a whole series of further questions, these are, in the main, the questions that have to be faced in developing an intellectual program for cultural studies. Let me, then, offer some brief indications as to how I should like to answer them.

CULTURAL STUDIES: ELEMENTS OF A DEFINITION

The first question is perhaps the most difficult to deal with. For the rate of growth of cultural studies has been such that some, including Michael Green, have doubted whether it is any longer possible—or desirable—to meet the 'urgently needed sense of what the whole area is about' (Green, 1993: 519). My own view is that the enterprise is both possible and worth undertaking, but only provided that not too much weight is invested in such definitions and that what is aimed for is relatively limited in scope and practical in orientation. Certainly, any attempt to impose a highly unified definition on the field—to describe it in terms of such and such a set of theoretical and political positions—will meet with failure. Instead, let me propose a number of propositions which might, if they are relatively loosely formulated, recruit broad assent.

1 Work in cultural studies is characterised by an interdisciplinary concern with the functioning of cultural practices and institutions in the contexts of relations of power of different kinds. Its interdisciplinariness, however, does not take the form of an alternative to or transcendence of those disciplines (history, sociology, literary studies, linguistics) which may lay a claim to similar interests. To be sure, it may challenge the effects of particular specialist foci within these disciplines, but it does not offer—or aspire to offer—a wholesale critique of them as disciplines any more than it dispenses with the need to draw on the specialist techniques, skills, knowledges and trainings associated with these disciplines where these are appropriate to the topic under investigation. Rather, cultural studies supplies an intellectual field in which perspectives from different disciplines might (selectively) be drawn on in examining particular relations of culture and power. In this respect, cultural studies performs a clearing-house function in coordinating the methods and findings of different disciplines insofar as they bear on the role played by cultural practices, institutions and forms of

cultural classification in the organisation and transmission, or contestation, of particular relations of power. It does not embody a putative intellectual synthesis in which existing disciplinary specialisms would be overcome or rendered redundant (although it will, and clearly has, promoted new forms of alliance within and between existing disciplines).

2 If relations of culture and power supply cultural studies with its object, the understanding of culture that animates its concerns is a broadly inclusive one. For reasons which have already been alluded to, and which will become clearer, the formulation that cultural studies is concerned with culture in the sense of whole ways of life as well as the officially valorised forms of high culture creates more problems than it solves. A more open-ended formulation might be to say that cultural studies is concerned with all those practices, institutions and systems of classification through which there are inculcated in a population particular values, beliefs, competencies, routines of life and habitual forms of conduct. To say this is not to assume that all the practices, institutions and systems of classification that are thus brought under the heading of 'culture' are constituted in the same way or function in a common manner. The likelihood is that they don't and that, therefore, the search for a common set of principles underlying the terrain of the cultural will prove abortive. Establishing such a set of principles, however, is not a necessary condition for securing cultural studies as a coherent enterprise.

3 The forms of power in relation to which culture (as defined above) is to be examined are diverse, including relations of gender, class and race as well as those relations of colonialism and imperialism which exist between the whole populations of different territories. The forms and manner in which these relations of culture and power might be interconnected is also a matter for concern within cultural studies. This concern with the nature, makeup and interactions between the different ways in which culture operates in the context of different power relations, however, is not scholastic in motivation. The ambition of cultural studies is to develop ways of theorising relations of culture and power that will prove capable of being utilised by relevant social agents to bring about changes within the operation of those relations of culture and power. This inescapably involves competing political estimations of who the relevant social agents are, how they/we are to be involved in the process of changing the functioning of such power relations, and who the beneficiaries of those changes will be.

4 The primary institutional site for cultural studies has been, and will continue to be, within tertiary educational institutions. It is, in this sense, like any other academic discipline; it is, like them, too, in that it faces the problem of how most effectively to arrange for the dissemination of its arguments, ideas and perspectives in ways calculated to maximise their influence with and upon those social agents capable of utilising its intellectual resources in specific regions of practical social action. In some formulations, this is posed as a problem regarding the relations between cultural studies and the various social movements (the women's movement, postcolonial struggles, black liberation movements) which, from time to time, cultural studies has claimed as its constituencies. In other formulations, the issue is posed as one of establishing appropriate relations with those who work in specific cultural institutions or fields of cultural management. In others, again, the polarity between these two options is viewed as a meaningless one, cultural studies needing to establish both kinds of relations depending on the point at issue. Whichever the case, the political agendas of cultural studies pose problems of mediation or connection that need to be resolved if cultural studies is not to be merely academic.

I am aware that already, in some of these formulations, I have introduced elements that some will find contentious. To suggest that some relations of culture and power might be regarded positively, for example, rather than regarding any twinning of culture and power as inherently repressive, is to introduce a perspective, derived from Foucault, that would not recruit the assent of everyone working in the field. For the most part, however, the positions sketched out above are susceptible to different interpretations that are capable of accommodating a broad spectrum of the opinion that defines current controversies within cultural studies. In answering my second question—which tendencies in this body of work should be supported, and which jettisoned?—I shall obviously need to be less ecumenical.

That said, it is not a question of opting for this or that theory—something which could only result in a doctrinaire definition—as much as one of defining an orientation for theory. I would define that orientation as materialist in the sense proposed by Brian Moon when he suggests that the term 'materialist' should now be 'deployed in a limited sense to designate a mode of analysis that grounds explanations of social phenomena in historical conditions without constructing those conditions as the expression or general effect of a more fundamental cause' (Moon, 1993: 7). Contrary to the associations of historical materialism, then, the stress here is on contingency, on the forms of social life and conduct that result from the interaction of multiple historical conditions and forces without the form of their interaction being subject to any general form of determination, and therefore explanation, arising from the effects of an underlying causal mechanism—be it that of a mode of production, the principles of structural causality, patriarchy or, for that matter, the putative unity of culture as a whole way of life. To argue for a cultural studies that would be materialist in this sense, then, is to argue for a cultural studies that will be differentiating and particularising in its focus, that will be densely historical in its attention to the specific makeup and functioning of particular relations of culture and power, understanding these as the outcomes of complexly interacting conditions and giving rise to equally dispersed and complexly organised effects.

Such, then, is the nature of the intellectual program I would propose for cultural studies. However, it will not have escaped the reader's attention that revisions of the kind I am suggesting affect the political orientations of cultural studies just as much as they do its theoretical concerns. It is to these questions that I now turn.

A PROSAIC POLITICS

In an earlier essay, I suggested that cultural studies might usefully 'envisage its role as consisting in the training of cultural technicians: that is, of intellectual workers less committed to cultural critique as an instrument for changing consciousness than to modifying the functioning of culture by means of technical adjustments to its governmental deployment' (Bennett, 1992: 406). The basis for this suggestion consisted of the argument that modern forms of cultural politics have to be seen as closely related to, and partly generated by, the ways in which the sphere of culture has been, in Foucault's sense, so deeply governmentalised that it now makes no sense—if it ever did—to think of culture as a ground situated outside the domain of government and providing the resources through which that domain might be resisted. The suggestion has provoked some disagreement, some of which has been of great value and highly productive (see, especially, O'Regan, 1992). Nonetheless, I should like to stick by it and, indeed, explore its implications further as a way of developing a more prosaic conception of the intellectual politics of cultural studies. Pierre Bourdieu has recorded, in connection with the Frankfurt School, that he felt 'a certain irritation when faced with the aristocratic demeanour of the totalising critique which retained all the features of grand theory, doubtless so as not to get its hands dirty in the kitchens of empirical research' (Bourdieu, 1990: 19). As a way of countering this traditional style of intellectual work in the cultural field, Bourdieu advises that he has sought constantly to develop a pragmatic, even barbaric, relation to culture and to work hard at 'considering the job of being an intellectual as a job like any other, eliminating everything that most aspiring intellectuals feel it necessary to do in order to feel intellectual' (1990: 29–30). In a similar way, my conception of the cultural studies intellectual as a technician who needs to think of her or his work as being related—and needing to be related—to the sphere of government is informed by a similar ambition to establish more mundane protocols for both the form and substance of intellectual work that addresses and situates itself in the cultural field.

It might help, in elaborating the implications of this view, to consider the contrasting formulations which tend to predominate when intellectuals are trying to puzzle out what cultural studies is, or ought to be, about. Frederic Jameson's essay 'On "Cultural Studies"'—a review of the collection of essays derived from the cultural studies conference held at the University of Illinois in 1990—provides a convenient counterpoint. 'The desire called Cultural Studies,' Jameson begins his essay, 'is perhaps best approached politically and socially, as the project to constitute a "historic bloc," rather than theoretically, as the floor plan for a new discipline.' (Jameson, 1993: 17) If this is so, Jameson continues, then its aspirations were most clearly expressed by Stuart Hall when he argued that the formation of cultural studies in Britain had been shaped on the model of the Gramscian notion of the organic intellectual. It was a project shaped by the will or hope that intellectual work might be aligned with an emerging historical movement and was therefore predicated, as Hall put it, on 'living with the possibility that there could be, sometime, a movement which would be larger than the movement of petit-bourgeois intellectuals' (Hall, 1992: 288). Jameson argues that this formulation entails cultural studies being thought of as a project committed 'to the forging of a heterogeneous set of "interest groups" into some larger political and social movement', although he is quick to note that the practice is often different, at least in the American context, where isolationist conceptions of identity politics often prevail over such synthesising political aspirations. Nonetheless, while clearly acknowledging its utopian aspects, the view of cultural studies as 'the expression of a projected alliance between various social groups' (Jameson, 1993: 17) is the one Jameson prefers. As a consequence, he suggests, 'its rigorous formulation as an intellectual or pedagogical enterprise may not be quite so important as some of its adherents feel', a position that renders questions relating to the form that it might take as an academic program and the position it might occupy in educational institutions relatively unimportant.

This is, I think, a fair rendering of what has been, and remains, an important tendency within cultural studies. But I think it is a seriously mistaken one in at least two respects. First, insofar as cultural studies comprises (among other things) a set of teaching and research programs located within or otherwise dependent on and related to academic institutions, it underestimates the significance of attending closely and in detail to the consequences of this, its primary institutional locale. From this perspective, questions concerning the forms of knowledge, instruction and training that are to be offered in cultural studies programs, and the kinds of future destinies for which these are envisaged to equip students, are crucial to the kinds of long-term practical effects that it will prove capable of exerting.

However, perhaps the more important question—and this brings me to my second point—concerns the kinds of practical effects cultural studies might intelligibly aspire to. The prospect that it might furnish a stratum of intellectuals who will prepare the way for an emerging historical movement to which that stratum will then attach itself in a moment of organicity seems increasingly unlikely, for a number of reasons. First, the political imaginary sustaining such expectations is now too seriously damaged and the attempts to suture it back into place—as in the writings of Ernesto Laclau and Chantal Mouffe, for example—have too evidently failed for this to be thought of as a realistic or even desirable prospect in any of the western societies in which cultural studies has developed (see Bennett, 1990a). Second, and perhaps ultimately more telling, the prospect of organicity that it offers is an incoherent one. Of course, individual figures may well—and importantly—function as organic intellectuals insofar as the positions they take up in relation to the agendas of specific social movements or groups are concerned. It is quite another matter, however, to think of cultural studies as providing a stratum of organic intellectuals for an emerging alliance of progressive social forces. For, even supposing that such an alliance were a realistic or, indeed, an intelligible political prospect, cultural studies simply is not the kind of thing that could undertake such a task. Its institutional placement does not allow it to do that kind of work, and those who work within the field—for we are all, by virtue of the social position established by our work, petit-bourgeois intellectuals no matter what our biographical backgrounds and credentials might be—do not have the qualifications or capacities for it.

This is not to argue that, in an appropriately more limited usage, the notion of the 'organic intellectual' is without its value. McKenzie Wark has argued that Marcia Langton is 'very much the image of an "organic intellectual"—someone whose knowledge grows directly out of the particular struggles and forms of organisation of the community she identifies herself with—the Aboriginal people' and notes that her work in this regard has encompassed the roles of 'administrator, advocate, actor and anthropologist' (Wark, 1994: 23). John Frow and Meaghan Morris, generalising this perspective, suggest that, if the notion of the organic intellectual is detached from 'those phantom "emergent" subjects of history', it can help clarify 'the actual practices developed by real intellectuals in Australia' in patterns of work that are partly institutionally and partly constituency-based in a country whose political traditions and limited resources allow for a good deal of cross-over and exchange between intellectuals working in different institutional fields: the academy, cultural institutions, government (Frow and Morris, 1993: xxv).

In such a context, the question of the relationship between cultural studies and organic intellectuals—which is also a question concerning the relations that might most usefully be developed between the forms of teaching and research conducted within academic institutions and the political agendas and constituencies that have been formed in relation to different fields of social conflict in society at large—can be reformulated. For, viewed in this light, it is no longer an issue of trying to coordinate different movements into a historic bloc under the banner of cultural studies, or one of each and every cultural studies intellectual trying to become organic. Rather, it would concern the development of forms of work—of cultural analysis and pedagogy—that could contribute to the development of the political and policy agendas associated with the work of organic intellectuals so defined. Of course, work produced in accordance with such an understanding would point in many directions. One of the directions in which it would point, however, would be toward the politics of the bureau. For it is often within or in relation to the bureau—that is, the machineries of government in its broadest sense—that the work of organic intellectuals is conducted.

It was considerations of this kind I had in mind when, in my contribution to the collection of essays Jameson reviewed, I suggested that intellectuals working in cultural studies needed to begin to 'talk to the ISAs'—that is Althusser's famous Ideological State Apparatuses.

My purpose was to argue that, if it aspired to any practical forms of social application, then it was imperative that cultural studies engage with the actually existing practical horizons, agendas and constituencies evident within different fields of cultural policy debate and formation comprised by the relevant sections of government and by the practices of cultural and media institutions. Jameson took issue with this suggestion, arguing that while it might 'have some relevance in a small country with socialist traditions', it could have no applicability in the United States where most readers on 'the left' (wherever that now is) would find the suggestion 'obscene' (Jameson, 1993: 43). He was similarly perturbed by Ian Hunter's suggestion that, to the degree that it is still caught up in the slipstream of aesthetic critique, cultural studies might have relatively little to offer once it goes beyond the comforting illusions of the typical arts faculty to concern itself with other cultural regions. He thus found the following passage 'truly chilling and comical' (1993: 43):

> To travel to these other regions though—to law offices, media institutions, government bureaus, corporations, advertising agencies—is to make a sobering discovery: They are already replete with their own intellectuals. And they just look up and say, 'Well, what exactly is it that you can do for us?' (Hunter, 1992: 372)

The division of opinion here is real and substantial. On the one hand, cultural studies is invited to subscribe to an understanding of the connections between intellectual work and practice through which intellectuals bypass existing forms of social administration and management in order to connect more directly with social movements of different kinds. On the other, cultural studies is urged to find a way of answering the bureaucrat's question—'What can you do for us?'—as a precondition for connecting the work of intellectuals to the fields of social administration and management in which the social and political demands of different constituencies are translated into practicable administrative options. This is, admittedly, a somewhat polarised way of posing the matter. However, these options do, I believe, clearly summarise the key issues at stake in present debates about the future directions cultural studies should take.

I shall not pursue Jameson's remarks further here except to situate them. For it is clear that what speaks through them is precisely that disjunction of the aesthetic and the worldly, of culture and the mundane concerns of the practical affairs of government, that is the legacy of Romantic aesthetics—in this case, in perhaps its most influential contemporary Marxist version. How else are we to account for a Marxist who regards work developed in 'a small country with socialist traditions' as a negative model, who regards as repugnant the prospect of 'talking to the ISAs' even though he works in one, and who can see no possible areas of interaction between the work that might be conducted in the academy and that of intellectuals in other cultural regions outside the academy? Views of this kind are, perhaps, understandable when viewed in the American context where both the sheer size of the higher education sector and the significant role of private institutions within that sector provide the kind of institutional conditions which allow critical debate to circulate in a semi-autonomous realm which might seem removed from those of government and administration. There are, however, few places outside the United States where similar conditions apply. Where this is not so, indigenous intellectual traditions are likely to prove of more service than the radical versions of American liberalism that now blight much of the debate in this area. In his review, Jameson rightly notes that Raymond Williams' work is now frequently 'appealed to for moral support for any number of sins (or virtues)' (Jameson, 1993: 22). As I have already indicated, there are many aspects of Williams' theorisation of culture in which the legacy of the Romantic tradition is clearly visible. However, his work was more complex and many-sided than such an evaluation, starkly stated, would suggest and it is from the ambivalences of Williams that I should like to take my final bearings in relation to the question of policy.

When, in *Culture and Society*, Williams began the process—never really finished—of his reckoning with the Romantic tradition, he criticised it not merely for the elitism of its selective definition of culture. He was just as alert to the powerfully anti-practical and anti-reformist tendencies which might arise from the totalising forms of critique to which Romanticism was prone. He was also at pains to dissociate himself from those forms of intellectual analysis and engagement which suggest it is possible to bypass the need for a real entanglement with those agendas of social, political and cultural reform which define the effective horizon of presently existing policy processes and concerns. He was thus terse in his disparagement of the view that the lofty heights of culture might provide a vantage point from which the mundanities of social and political life might be transcended. This was, indeed, the constitutive tension of Romanticism which Williams was concerned to argue against:

> The attachment to culture which disparages science; the attachment which writes off politics as a narrow and squalid misdirection of energy; the attachment which appears to criticise manners by the priggish

> intonation of a word: all these, of which Arnold and his successors have at times been guilty, serve to nourish and extend an opposition which is already formidable enough. The idea of culture is too important to be surrendered to this kind of failing. (Williams, 1967: 135)

It was, Williams continues, the tension between Arnold's view of culture as a process of growth and development and his failure to find adequate evidence for that process in the social conditions of his day that led to the transformation of culture into an increasingly abstract and transcendental standard of judgement. The result, Williams argues, was a wholly disabling contradiction. 'Culture,' as he put it, 'became the final critic of institutions, and the process of replacement and betterment, yet it was also, at root, beyond institutions.' (Williams, 1967: 136)

It is clear, moreover, that this was not merely a theoretical matter for Williams, not just something he said. It also affected a good deal of what he did, and in particular his engagement over a number of decades with the practical agendas and institutions of cultural policy in postwar Britain, without ever surrendering his intellectual independence or critical voice. In this regard, Williams did not just speak to 'the ISAs'; so far as his relationship to the Arts Council was concerned, he was a fully functioning member of one of the most important instruments of cultural policy formation in postwar Britain. What he had to say about this in an essay he wrote in 1981 is revealing. Reviewing four different conceptions of the objectives of cultural policy—'state patronage of fine arts; pump-priming; an intervention in the market; and expanding and changing popular culture' (Williams, 1989: 142)—that might guide the policies of a body like the Arts Council (or, we might add, the Australia Council, the Canada Council or the National Endowment for the Arts, and the whole host of related bodies which now proliferate in the cultural-governmental spheres of advanced western societies), Williams, unsurprisingly, states his preference for the last of these conceptions as providing the only valid grounds on which 'we can, in good conscience, raise money for the arts from the general revenue' (1989: 148). While recognising that this was not the prevailing view in the Arts Council, Williams is clear that 'because it [the Council] is there it is where the argument has to start':

> Thus instead of apologising for the principles of public funding of the arts, or nervously excluding or reducing those aspects of policy which either the pillared and patented or the political and commercial hangers-on disapprove of, we should get together, in such numbers as we can, and fight the real battles. (1989: 149)

Williams concludes his essay by looking to Keynes—the architect of the Arts Council—acknowledging his important contribution in 'an open and recognising spirit' (1989: 149). It is, then, this Williams that I suggest we should now look to in a similar spirit, while acknowledging that there are other aspects of his work—and in particular some of his more general theoretical formulations—from which we now need to register our distance. In his essay 'The uses of cultural theory', Williams—in a phrase that has been made much of—asks, in a chastising tone, whether there is 'never to be an end to petit-bourgeois theorists making long-term adjustments to short-term situations' (1989: 175). Andrew Milner entertains the prospect, only to dismiss it as unlikely (quite rightly) that Williams might have had myself in mind when making this remark, only to conclude (although improbably in my view) that his target was more likely to have been Stuart Hall (Milner, 1993: 88).

In fact, Williams is perfectly clear about whom he has in mind: namely, the advocates of those forms of intellectual and cultural avant-gardeism 'which are based practically only on their negations and forms of enclosure, against an undifferentiated culture and society beyond them' (Williams 1989: 175). The first part of this phrase reveals tellingly enough Williams' impatience with those who would take their stand on the purely negatively and transcendentally constituted ground of critique. It is, however, in the second part—in the notion that practical engagements within actually existing political agendas should be directed toward the creation of an 'undifferentiated culture and society' shaped by 'the acceptance and the possibility of broader common relationships' (1989: 175–76)—that the limitations of Williams' own position are evident. In the political and cultural situations which now exist in the societies where cultural studies has made some headway and where, albeit in different ways and as a result of different histories, the recognition and promotion of cultural diversity is a more pressing priority, the long-term vision that Williams proposes here loses its coherence and purchase. For this particular petit-bourgeois theorist, then, the issue is not one of making long-term adjustments to short-term situations, but of making long-term adjustments because the long-term situation itself now has to be thought in new ways.

Equally important, there are a multitude of day-to-day issues pertaining to the administration of culture and, indeed, to the use of cultural resources in a wide range of government and governmental programs whose resolution bears consequentially on all our ways of life. Only by recognising that culture is ordinary in this sense will it be possible for both theory and practice to take account of the fact that, like any other area of activity, its actual futures will be determined, in significant measure, by the ways in which such practical questions of cultural policy are routinely posed and resolved.

2 Being 'in the true' of cultural studies

In his essays on the life sciences, Georges Canguilhem proposes that a history of the sciences should be history of errors as well as a history of truth, a history of delays and setbacks as well as one of progress. With a view to accomplishing this, he proposes the concept of 'scientific ideology' as a means of relativising the distinction between truth and error by converting it into that between a science and its prehistory, and so a distinction internal to that relation rather one of a general epistemological kind. 'A scientific ideology,' as he puts it, 'comes to an end when the place that it occupied in the encyclopedia of knowledge is taken over by a discipline that operationally demonstrates the validity of its claims to scientific status, its "norms of scientificity".' (Canguilhem, 1988: 33) If a scientific ideology comes to be named as such only when a science has established itself, the errors which are thus retrospectively attributed to that ideology still constitute a part of the history of the science in question inasmuch as they form the discursive ground which simultaneously sustained and impeded its formation. Such ideologies, Canguilhem suggests, may also have an afterlife, retarding the further development of the sciences they have spawned through the influence they continue to exert on the operative norms and procedures of scientific inquiry.

The fate of Althusserianism, of course, suggests the need for caution in drawing parallels between the epistemic conditions and procedures of the natural and the human sciences. It is Foucault who reminds us that different discursive formations have their own conditions and modes of 'being in the true', and that these are not necessarily transportable across and between different fields of inquiry. There have been moments, however, when it has seemed that the relations between cultural studies and its precursors might be cast in the form of a distinction between a science and its ideological prehistory. Stuart Hall's assessment of Raymond Williams' role in the formation of cultural studies thus draws on Althusserian terminology, and thereby indirectly on Canguilhem, in interpreting *The Long Revolution* as 'a text of the break' (Hall, 1980: 101) while seeing *Culture and Society* as still 'profoundly marked by the imprint of the tradition to which it was counterposed: and nowhere so much as in its *method*' (1980: 98)—that is, its continued dependency on the techniques of practical criticism.

In the event, however, such conceptions have not had an enduring influence on the ways in which cultural studies is customarily described or on the ways in which its relations to other disciplinary formations—past and present—are characteristically viewed within the literature which has sought to define and specify its distinguishing attributes. Here, quite different forms and conditions of 'being in the true' have come to prevail. To be 'in the true' of a discursive formation, Foucault argues, is to obey 'the rules of some discursive "policy" which would have to be re-activated every time one spoke' (Foucault, cited in Lentricchia, 1983: 197). In the case of cultural studies, at least two aspects of such a discursive policy can be identified. I shall call these the rule of theoretical and methodological indeterminacy and the rule of wholeness via marginality.

The first rule is succinctly summarised by John Hartley in his observations regarding a widespread reluctance to identify cultural studies in terms of any definite set of substantive theoretical positions or procedures of inquiry:

> Cultural studies is notable for its participants' squeamishness about orthodoxy, manifested positively in a commitment to interdisciplinarity, and negatively in the avoidance of authority; it has no unified theory, textual canon, disciplinary truth, agreed methodology, common syllabus, examinable content, or professional body, no bodily integrity at all. (Hartley, 1991: 7)

Carolyn Steedman, taking an outsider's look at cultural studies from the more secure disciplinary basis of a practising historian, similarly notes a widespread reluctance to codify the knowledge base of cultural studies and an equally marked resistance to the prospect of its institutionalisation as a discipline (see Steedman, 1992: 617). Tony Dunn exemplifies the position Steedman has in mind when he writes that cultural studies 'is a whirling and quiescent and swaying mobile which continuously repositions any participating subject', a project which is destined never to arrive at a definite view of itself as its realisation is to be 'forever deferred' (Dunn, 1986: 71, cited in Steedman, 1992: 617).

The second rule offers an ethical-cum-political compensation for this theoretical and methodological indeterminacy in construing social marginality as an experiential route which allows those who travel it to achieve an integrative kind of intellectual wholeness which stands in for theoretical and methodological criteria in furnishing cultural studies with its epistemological protocols. Many social positions might be, and have been, advanced as candidates for this role—social class, gender, ethnicity, subalternality.[1] In what might be regarded as one of the founding examples of this form of being 'in the true', the marginality of the 'Celtic fringe', as exemplified by Williams' Welshness, was viewed as having allowed Williams to acquire an understanding of British culture as a whole in view of his lived experience of the relations between the culture's dominant and its resistive elements. 'Wales,' as Hall put it in his obituary appreciation of Williams, 'gave him a perspective on Cambridge—on the way a culture becomes dominant, a "central system of practices, meanings and values" and the necessary tension between that and the emergent energies and experiences which stubbornly resist it.' (Hall, 1988: 21)

While not wishing to propose that cultural studies should aspire to the status of a science or that it should develop a theoreticist obsession with identifying its defining characteristics, my purpose here *is* to suggest that cultural studies does now need to be fashioned into a disclipinary undertaking of a more conventional and recognisable kind. This need not be to gainsay its interdisciplinary status, although this should now no longer be allowed as a means of evading difficult questions of theory and method. For it is true of many systems of thought—and especially so of the disciplines which now comprise the humanities—that they begin their careers by creating some elbow room for themselves within the interstices of the existing array of disciplinary knowledges. However, the need, then, to define precisely how an emerging system of thought draws on and combines the techniques and methods of existing disciplines into distinctive new configurations cannot be indefinitely deferred. If there has been a reluctance to pursue these questions in relation to cultural studies, this is perhaps attributable to what might be regarded as the third rule of its mode of 'being in the true': the view that cultural studies offers the prospect of a knowledge which, in being 'beyond the disciplines', will also be a knowledge without limits or constraints. To propose a disciplinary future for cultural studies, by contrast, is to envisage that, in arriving at a greater degree of definiteness about itself, cultural studies will

recognise that, like all other knowledges, its domains and possibilities are circumscribed and limited by both the theoretical and the institutional conditions of its existence.

However, a brief detour through the history of cultural studies—or, more accurately, through the history of its histories—will be necessary before such a prospect can be placed on the agenda. For the reluctance to characterise cultural studies in terms of a definite set of theoretical and methodological characteristics is not a result of modesty—far from it. Nor is it because cultural studies lacks a discourse of the truth. Rather, it is a symptom of its subscription to an ethical mode of 'being in the true', a discursive policy which is itself a sign of a continued reliance on the means and forms for authorising statements which characterise many of the traditional humanities disciplines which it is often supposed cultural studies has displaced and supplanted. And it is in this respect—to recall Canguilhem—that cultural studies is still encumbered by a past that it has yet to break with in order to place its concerns on a more secure and distinctive footing. But this is to conjure with the prospect of a cultural studies whose main epistemological breaks have yet to be made—and this, in turn, is to entertain the possibility that those texts which have so far been viewed as comprising the foundations of cultural studies might still bear the impress of earlier 'scientific ideologies' of culture that now need to be jettisoned.

HISTORICISING CULTURAL STUDIES

Now that cultural studies is acquiring its historians, it is relevant to ask: what kind of history—or histories—will prove most serviceable in charting new directions for its future development? The terms in which we are to understand the relations between cultural studies and the earlier disciplinary formations from which it has sought to disentangle itself have a crucial bearing on these issues. Narratives matter and the kinds of stories we tell ourselves about cultural studies, about how it has or has not passed an epistemological, ethical or political threshold which differentiates it from its disciplinary forebears, will influence how we envisage its future trajectories and seek to contribute to their development. If these questions are to be broached productively, however, cultural studies now urgently needs to do unto itself as it would do, and has done, unto others: namely, to entertain the possibility that cultural studies intellectuals might, in significant respects, have misunderstood their relations to the conditions which have enabled their own practice and conferred on it a social functioning which might not be in accord with their intentions.

The distinction I have in mind here is that suggested by Kurt Danziger in his history of psychology: a distinction between histories written from the point of view of the inside of a discipline, resulting in an account which 'always conveys a strong sense of being "our" history', and histories written from positions that do not necessarily share the 'framework of issues and presuppositions from the field that is the object of study' (Danziger, 1990: vii). Most of the accounts of cultural studies that are so far available to us are 'insider' accounts written from within its framework of shared assumptions. Better, they are accounts which have helped forge and articulate those shared assumptions and to organise a 'we' whose members recognise the history of cultural studies as their own—the history of their trials and tribulations, setbacks and advances. As accounts which have thus been concerned to construct a particular sense of being 'in the true' that characterises and distinguishes the cultural studies enterprise, they have all (necessarily) been written from within that truth in the very process of forming it.

The questions I want to ask are: what kinds of issues do histories written in this mode occlude? And how else might we think about cultural studies' own stories and tell them back to it in ways which might prompt some reconsideration about how those who work in this field should view their practice in the context of the relations and conditions which enable it? We were once very adept at identifying the ideological processes that were going on 'behind the backs' of other social agents. A question we now need to consider is: has anything been going on 'behind the back' of cultural studies that might help identify what it is and what it does more tellingly than the conscious aspirations of its advocates?

The most influential accounts of the kind I have in mind—and whose grain I want to think against—come from, or are organised in some kind of relation to, the story of the Birmingham Centre for Cultural Studies. They include Hall's various essays (see Hall 1980, 1989, 1990, 1992), the accounts of others closely associated with the Birmingham Centre—writers like Dick Hebdige, John Clarke, and Richard Johnson—and the accounts contained in influential collections like the *Cultural Studies* anthology edited by Lawrence Grossberg, Cary Nelson and Paula Treichler (1992). There are, of course, important limitations associated with these accounts which need to be noted in advance. In spite of their disavowals to the contrary, for example, they have tended to construct a Birmingham-centred myth of origin for cultural studies which has distracted attention from the formative role of other institutions and projects, and particularly that of SEFT(the Society for Education in Film and Television), whose influence was, for me, in many ways more decisive. Difficulties also arise, as both Meaghan Morris (1992) and Graeme Turner (1992, 1992a) have noted, where a more general representative or paradigmatic status is attributed to British cultural studies in view of the distorting effects this often has on debates in other national contexts, in intruding into them issues and concerns which have no local currency or provenance. When all this is said and duly acknowledged, however, the Birmingham case remains an important and influential one, largely because, as the first fully developed and broadly circulated *account* of the development of cultural studies, it has come to function as an exemplary narrative whose rhetorical claims and maneouvres have been drawn on to help sustain and develop similar stories elsewhere. It is in this light that I shall consider these accounts: as furnishing a template from which other narratives of cultural studies and, in some respects, the story of cultural studies as a whole have been fashioned.

That the Birmingham story has been able to play this role is attributable, in good measure, to its tendency to proceed as if the history of cultural studies could be adequately represented in the form of a set of theoretical and political struggles viewed and related from the perspective of those engaged in them. Carolyn Steedman has thus noted how accounts of cultural studies tend to be cast in the heroic mould. In doing so, moreover, she draws attention to the fact that, no matter how stridently their claims to non- or even anti-disciplinary status might be pressed, these accounts are very similar to those of conventional disciplinary histories in the rhetorical strategies they deploy. She thus observes, after citing the passage from Tony Dunn discussed earlier:

> They all *start* like that, but within a few paragraphs are well into that most conventional claim for disciplinary orthodoxy—the writing of their own history. (What they are also doing, the historiographically informed observer notes, is defining themselves, finding themselves, through an act of consciousness-raising: telling their own story, reaping all the social and psychic benefits of autobiography and oral history.) (Steedman, 1992: 617)

Steedman's interest in these issues arises from her concern with the relations between history and cultural studies. As an historian who is, understandably, reluctant to see her discipline's identity entirely submerged within that of cultural studies, her main interest is in how and why the concerns of history and cultural studies have come to run so closely together. Her point—and it is surely correct—is that the conventional accounts of cultural studies are of little assistance in answering questions concerned with detailed and specific issues of this kind. To the contrary, she considers it necessary to look elsewhere—to look at what has been going on 'behind the back' of cultural studies by examining the various conditions and relations which have helped shape its development without necessarily registering themselves in the consciousness of its theorists.

In order to account for the role of history within cultural studies, therefore, Steedman looks not to the field of theory—the influence of Marxist historiography, say—but to the changing forms of history teaching and learning associated with both the secondary and tertiary sectors. Her conclusion, if viewed from the perspective of the resistive credentials which cultural studies has usually laid claim to, might seem quite scandalous—as, indeed, any genealogy of cultural studies should be if it is to generate a productive friction and so, as Foucault suggests, be a history that is 'made for cutting' (Foucault, 1980: 154). For she suggests that the extended concept of culture as 'a whole way of life' that has subtended the work of historians within cultural studies owes its influence to a reshaping of the concerns and classroom practices of both history and English secondary school curricula. In short, her argument is that ' "the culture concept" as used by historians, and in some of the models for acquiring historical knowledge within cultural studies' was 'actually invented in the schools, between about 1955 and 1975' (Steedman, 1992: 619–20). She argues that the 'virtual disappearance of history as a subject taught to children, its integration into topic and project work', combined with the influence of Piagetian theories of child development dictating 'that children should "discover" the past through a study of its artifacts (Clothes, Houses, Food) and through their identification and empathy with people living in the past' coincided with developments in the English classroom which had led to the 'breaking down of barriers between teachers and taught, common involvement in a common project, a text or groups of texts making inquirers of them all' (1992: 619).

This suggests that, however radical and innovative they might have seemed at the time, the collaborative aspects of cultural studies teaching and research—issues that have rightly been foregrounded in accounts of the Birmingham Centre—were merely the first transplantation into the humanities academy of pedagogic relations and practices that were already firmly in place in the schooling system. Steedman's view of the reasons for the close relations between history and cultural studies at the tertiary level takes this line of reasoning further in viewing the new kinds of training and shifts of emphasis that have accompanied these developments—a shift away from the expensive individual researcher-in-the-archive model of history training to a view of history as a collective, group-based process of deciphering and contextualising cultural documents—as a necessary practical response to the vast increase in the number of students entering into tertiary humanities programs.

I am not concerned to assess the specific virtues of this account here. Rather, my interest lies in the type of explanation it offers in seeking a basis for the characteristic traits of cultural studies in the conditions of culture's pedagogic deployment in the secondary school. This naturally places many of those traits in a new light: subcultural theory loses some of its radical resonances if viewed as a late echo of a transformed secondary curriculum. In this and other respects, Steedman's arguments run against the grain of conventional 'insider' accounts of cultural studies, offering a glimpse of what a subversive genealogy of cultural studies might look like—subversive because it suggests that the enabling conditions of cultural studies are located in precisely that sphere, the sphere of government and social regulation, to which cultural studies has usually supposed itself to be opposed.

Considerations of this kind, of course, have received little attention in those accounts of cultural studies which are 'in the true'. Nor could they have. Mundane institutional particularities are necessarily invisible where cultural studies is viewed as an intrinsically interdisciplinary practice, embodying a form of intellectual wholeness beyond the fragmenting effects of institutionalised divisions of academic labour. For this in turn carries with it the view (or, in some cases, the requirement) that cultural studies must remain above its institutional determinations, untouched by them, if it is to remain true to itself and avoid co-option. In a way that would usually be denied to any other intellectual or cultural practice which might furnish it with an object of analysis, cultural studies, where this view prevails, is seemingly able to make use of the educational apparatus as no more than a convenient occasion for its own projects.

The point can be illustrated via a much-quoted passage from Stuart Hall which, in accounting for the present-day location of cultural studies within the academy, does so in a manner which simultaneously explains that location away and minimises its significance in construing it as the outcome of entirely circumstantial and contingent considerations. For Hall, the moment of cultural studies' academic institutionalisation was a conjunctural expediency enjoined on it by changing political conditions and, consequently, a moment devoid of any formative significance. Arguing that originally, in Britain, 'cultural studies was not conceptualised as an academic discipline at all' but had its roots in the politics of the New Left, Hall construes its move into the university, as instanced by the establishment of the Birmingham Centre, as a convenient refuge for the politics of the New Left—and a basis from which to continue with those politics—in a changed political environment. The argument depends on viewing the extra-mural departments of British universities as a kind of midway staging post for New Left politics on their way from the more general forms of political engagement which had characterised them in the 1950s into the academy. Noting that Williams, Hoggart, Thompson and, indeed, he himself had worked in extra-mural departments (and that they were all, therefore, in direct contact with adult working-class students), Hall goes on:

> We thus came from a tradition entirely marginal to the centres of English academic life, and our engagement in the questions of cultural change—how to understand them, how to describe them, and how to theorise them, what their impact and consequences were to be, socially—were first reckoned within the dirty outside world. The Centre for Cultural Studies was the locus to which we *retreated* when that conversation in the open world could no longer be continued: it was politics by other means. Some of us—me, especially—had always planned never to return to the university, indeed, never to darken its doors again. But, then, one always has to make pragmatic adjustments to where real work, important work, can be done. (Hall, 1990: 12)

It may well be true, of course, that the experience of working in an extra-mural context was an important and formative one for Hall, Williams, Hoggart and Thompson. Yet there are grounds for caution about the degree to which extra-mural departments can intelligibly be construed as margins capable of serving as an originating locale for a radical cultural studies project.[2] As it happens, I too started my career, just a few years later, in the early 1970s, in an extra-mural department and it was clear to me then (as now) that if a centre/periphery logic is to be used to describe the relations between such departments and the remainders of their universities, then they are more accurately described as the centre's outposts than as its margins. This was, indeed, an explicit aspect of their conception within the history of the extension movement—a movement which, heir to the civilising and improving mission of the earlier 'rational recreations' movement, had been governed by a centre-to-outpost model of knowledge production and dissemination. Such conceptions, moreover, were nowhere more deeply ingrained than in extra-mural conceptions of the nature and function of the literary lesson in their commitment to some version of Leavisism or, by the late 1950s and 1960s, left-Leavisism. Then again, insofar as extra-mural literary courses recruited from the working classes—and this was usually only marginally so as, for educational and cultural reasons of the kind that Bourdieu has made us familiar with, extra-mural courses drew the majority of their students from the middle classes—this was usually via benevolent associations, like the Workers' Educational Association (WEA), which typically had few connections with the industrial or political sectors of the working classes.

My point, then, is that the view of the extra-mural department as a space on the margins of the academy capable of nourishing cultural studies in providing a direct and unmediated contact with 'the dirty outside world' of working-class experience will not withstand scrutiny. To the contrary, it provided a highly mediated form of contact with working-class culture and experience, one whose historical formation disposed it to function more as a vehicle for transmitting the dominant culture to the remoter parts of the social body than as a crucible for the development of a tradition of radical cultural critique.[3]

Questions of historical accuracy to one side, however, perhaps the more substantial point concerns the intelligibility of the argument that the university, once fully entered into, might be used as merely the convenient site for, as Hall puts it, 'politics by other means'. The argument, as Hall goes on to elaborate it, interprets the decision to take up an institutional position within the university as the outcome of a strategic adjustment within the politics of the New Left. This institutional move, Hall argues, brought about no fundamental changes in the political agendas of cultural studies. Only the envisaged means changed. As before, the aim was to form a counter-hegemony within British society. Now, however, adopting a longer political horizon, this was to be brought about by forming a stratum of intellectuals who would function as the organic intellectuals of a counter-hegemonic social movement. Indeed, for Hall, this remains the essential political project of cultural studies:

> The fact that we had no greater success than the left has had since in trying to construct a 'historical bloc' out of such heterogeneous social interests, political movements and agendas, in building a hegemonic political practice out of, and with, these differences does not negate the urgency of the task. (Hall, 1989: 33)

Of course, many questions might be asked about the viability of this project and the appropriateness of the expectation that an intellectual discipline—or, more accurately, inter-discipline—might serve as a vehicle for its development. Certainly, the notion that a cultural studies encampment in an English department might fulfil the role Gramsci had earlier envisaged for the Factory Councils now seems, with each year that passes, an increasingly unlikely scenario. To put it bluntly, the prospect of a cultural studies-led counter-hegemony is now—or certainly ought to be—as dead as a dodo. The issue I want to focus on here, however—for I think it has a crucial bearing on how we should now think about and debate the future of cultural studies—is the assumption that the institutions and spaces of public education are available in a manner that allows them to be simply used as convenient sites for the political projects which individual intellectuals choose or subscribe to, rather than being contexts which necessarily confer their own logic and social direction on the work that is conducted within them.

CULTURAL STUDIES AND PEDAGOGY

While some recognition of these considerations is embodied in conventional accounts of cultural studies, this is so only to the degree that an opposition is posited between, on the one hand, the view of cultural studies as an autonomous cultural, political and educational project which assigns itself its own objectives and, on the other, the danger that it might be institutionally co-opted. These are the terms in which Hall poses the issue in outlining what he sees as the dangers of cultural studies' successes, particularly in America (see Hall, 1992), and they organise a recent thoughtful review of the present state of cultural studies offered by Maureen McNeil (McNeil, 1992). What is wrong with such accounts, I want to suggest, is the dualism that organises them—the notion that cultural studies was first one thing, formed up outside the institutions and practices of higher education, and then another as it has come to be co-opted by them. We shall only think clearly about the present position of cultural studies and its future possibilities if we recognise that, to the contrary, it has been, from the start, a project shaped by the public education system in which it has been located and which has formed its primary (but not only) conditioning context. Moreover, if—as is commonly argued—English comprised the primary disciplinary incubator for cultural studies, we shall fully understand its role in this regard only if we follow Carolyn Steedman's lead and look to the ways in which many of what are customarily viewed as the formative and distinguishing characteristics of cultural studies were in fact prefigured in the changing norms and practices of English teaching within secondary schooling.

It is, in this connection, important to note that the texts of Williams and Hoggart which have commonly been viewed as foundational in relation to British cultural studies—*The Long Revolution*; *Culture and Society*; *The Uses of Literacy*—exerted a considerable influence on the teaching of English in secondary schools a good decade before cultural studies became an identifiable project in the tertiary sector. My own first encounter with these works was in 1962 as a student in a newly fashioned teaching context—a general studies adjunct to the fifth-form English class in a north of England state grammar school—that was governed by a pedagogic agenda which (although I did not realise it at the time) was that of a left-Leavisism in search of a broader range of texts, outside the literary canon, through which to shape the formative moral and political consciousnesses of a new generation of 'English subjects'. Obliging us to read Williams and Hoggart, that is to say, served as a means of negotiating our assent to working on and with popular texts, and with our own everyday experience, as a means of provoking classroom discussion about contemporary social, political and moral issues.

My experience in this regard was, I believe, typical; I mention it here because of the light it throws on the relations between cultural studies and English where these are viewed as practices grounded in the education system. In his estimation of the significance of the early works of Williams and Hoggart, Hall, as we have seen, describes them as 'works of the break'; he describes *The Long Revolution*, for example, as having brought the whole English culture and society tradition to 'a decisive close'. Subsequent criticisms and debates have given us ample grounds for doubting whether this is so. Ian Hunter (1988) has thus demonstrated the Romantic pedigree of Williams' conception of culture as a 'whole way of life' whilst Guari Viswanathan has called attention to the bias implicit in the method of *Culture and Society* as one 'that consistently and exclusively studies the formation of metropolitan culture from within its own boundaries' (Viswanathan, 1991: 49) at the expense of those external conditioning factors which derive from the relations of imperialism. This is said not to diminish the importance of Williams' work but, rather, to help identify the nature and register of its significance more precisely. For we shall surely misunderstand the character of Williams' contribution if we interpret it as being of an epistemological kind. It would, for example, be implausible to suggest that Williams' work opened up culture as a new continent of knowledge on the model of Althusser's reading of what

Marx did for history (see Althusser, 1973). Rather, his contribution was that of expanding the scope of the moral mission of English in giving it a new set of objects (culture as a whole way of life) to latch on to.

To say this is not to doubt that Williams' inversion of the moral and political evaluations of Leavisism resulted in a view of culture that helped form the projects of cultural and political critique connected to the New Left. To argue that the institutional underpinnings of cultural studies need to be attended to more closely, and attended to in their positivity as autonomous determinations, is not to propose that the trajectories and problematics of cultural studies can then be reduced to those underpinnings. But if this is so, it is also true to say that the significance of these early texts of cultural studies was not tied to, or limited by, their New Left mobilisation. For they had already acquired a life in the English classroom which bound them to the changing agendas of secondary schooling in a public education system that, for the first time, was on the threshold of feeding into a mass system of tertiary education—and was therefore dealing with populations which did not have access to the canonised forms of high culture which had hitherto served as the pedagogic props for forming the moral and aesthetic sensibilities of elite social cadres. This suggests a certain tension within cultural studies. For while the discovery of the realm of everyday life and culture has commonly been recounted as being fuelled by and enabling a politics of resistance, the pedagogical space within which this discovery has taken place and been put into pedagogical effect has been one that has been shaped by a governmental interest in the cultural aspects of population management and regulation. The destiny, if not the mission, of cultural studies may thus, in the long haul, prove to be that of allowing everyday life and cultural experience to be fashioned into instruments of government via their inscription in new forms of teaching and training.

It is in the light of considerations of this kind, then, that I believe it is mistaken to suggest that the positions cultural studies has occupied in the education system can be viewed merely as a set of external contingencies—simply as the contexts in which we do our work, setting our own agendas, rather than in any way significantly determining the nature and function of that work as well as the social purposes which it serves. Such views, moreover, have been harmful to the extent that they have led to a low degree of institutional self-reflexiveness on the part of much cultural studies theory and a corresponding incapacity to relate (without reducing) the theory and the practice, the politics and the pedagogy of cultural studies to the circumstances of its most immediate institutional settings.

A number of options present themselves. One would be to accept that, if the condition of being 'in the true' of cultural studies is at all as I have described it, it should properly be understood as a moral discipline which—chiefly by means of practices of textual criticism and commentary—is principally caught up in the processes of conscience and person formation. In this case, cultural studies may indeed emerge as the heir of literary studies in its English formation. This is the view Michael Pickering takes in commending cultural studies for having conducted a critique of English for its narrow elitism and thereby—in reintegrating formalist analaysis with critique on an expanded textual terrain which encompasses the popular—restoring English to itself and its true vocation. It is in this respect, Pickering concludes, that 'it is cultural studies rather than English which today approximates closest to the tradition laid down by people like Coleridge, Carlyle, Ruskin, Arnold and Morris' (Pickering, 1992: 76).

Put that way, the prospect is a depressing one. Yet this is not to dispute the usefulness of criticism. Insofar as cultural studies is inescapably involved in a practical engagement with cultural representations, criticism of one kind or another is a necessary part of its concerns. The question, if I may put it this way, is not 'to criticise or not to criticise', but how to do so and with what purpose in view. Toby Miller has suggested that any form of cultural criticism so constructs the cultural representations which it takes for its occasions as to engender a form of incompleteness, lack or fault in the reader and, thereby, open up a space in which a career of self-formation or reformation may be initiated (Miller, 1992). If this is so, the challenge that faces a cultural studies criticism consists in the development of practices of textual commentary that will be alert to both the possibilities and limitations deriving from the different pedagogical situations that will constitute the primary contexts within which those practices of textual commentary are deployed.

It is equally clear, however, that there are many aspects of the organisation and political deployment of culture in social life that could not be adequately understood or be effectively and practically engaged with if criticism were all that cultural studies had to offer—or, indeed, all that it aspired to. Additionally, then, I want to suggest that cultural studies should lay claim to a definite set of knowledge claims and methodological procedures that will be convertible (as one of the points of their application) into clearly defined skills and trainings that will prove utilisable in a range of spheres of practical life.[4]

However, this can only happen if cultural studies renounces its aspirations to being a knowledge without limits—for, as I have tried to show, this also means being a knowledge without definite characteristics—and seeks, instead, to become a discipline.

While I do not want to propose a disciplinary inventory for cultural studies here, it will prove instructive to consider why there has been, and remains, such a marked resistance to envisaging a disciplinary future for cultural studies. One thing is clear: this reticence is not explicable by any properties of the objects of knowledge or critique that cultural studies has concerned itself with. If, as a shorthand, these consist in the relations of culture and power, then these have also been a matter of concern for other intellectual and political projects which have encountered no difficulty in conducting their debates in disciplinary terms. The project of cultural history associated with the work of Roger Chartier is one example, especially in view of the way in which it has sought to define its ambit and procedures in relation to those of anthropology and sociology without opting for the cultural studies co-optive strategy of claiming to integrate and synthesise all competing knowledges into itself (see Chartier, 1988). If considered closely, however, we shall see that this aspect of the cultural studies mode of 'being in the true' is little more than a new way of enunciating a discursive space that was prepared for it by its own disciplinary forebears.

DISCIPLINING CULTURAL STUDIES

In an obituary review of Raymond Williams' work, Nicholas Garnham, commenting on the difficulty of summarising Williams' achievements, attributes this to 'the fact that no coherent theory or method of cultural analysis lies waiting simply to be abstracted from his work' (Garnham, 1988: 123). Garnham is consequently obliged to summarise Williams' accomplishments in the form of a set of quasi-personalised attributes: his refusal to separate his intellectual and creative activities from his political involvements, for example. A survey of these attributes leads Garnham to conclude that Williams' 'work was always serious, in the proper sense of that word, in a way that I think applies to no other writer in our field' (1988: 130). In short, what marks Williams out are his exemplary qualities as a person and as an intellectual.

Many other obituary appreciations were driven to the same conclusion. My own attempt to assess the nature of Williams' legacy concluded that this consisted 'not merely in his work but in having lived an exemplary political and intellectual life' (Bennett, 1989: 88). Stuart Hall, in similarly concluding that Williams 'was, simply, *exemplary*', attributes this to his capacity to overcome the alienating effects of the division of intellectual labour. Explaining why Williams' work has proved so resistant to disciplinary classification, Hall argues that this was because 'His cast of mind was intrinsically *connective*. "My own view is that we must keep trying to grasp the process as a whole." He wrote, as he himself said, "against the frame of the forms".' (Hall, 1988: 21) If this is the dream of a knowledge without limits, Williams' accomplishment was not merely to enunciate this dream; he also embodied it, giving it a form and a content in his own life. Williams' concern with 'the process as a whole' was thus not a matter of abstract theoretical principle—like the principle of the priority of the whole over the parts was for Lucien Goldmann—but was rather also integrated into the very tissue of his intellectual practice as evidenced by his concern to reach out beyond the academy 'to return everyone—critic, politician, student, general reader—to the only subject which *really mattered:* the "central processes of our common life".' (1988: 21) In these and other ways, Williams personified an anticipatory overcoming of the dualisms produced by the division of labour. 'There wasn't,' as Hall puts it, 'the usual rift between thought and feeling, idea and life, which characterises so much "politicised" intellectual work.' (1988: 21)

My purpose in identifying these traits which characterised so many of the tributary reviews written in commemoration of Williams is not to doubt that Williams was a man of exceptional personal integrity. Rather, my concern—to draw on a distinction Bourdieu proposes in *Homo Academicus*—is with Williams as an epistemic rather than as an empirical individual: that is, with the figure of Williams as constructed within and by the discourses of cultural studies. My purpose, then, is to ask what kind of a discourse of the truth enables—and, indeed, requires—the utterance of remarks of this kind. For it is clear that this discourse and the opposition which organises it—essentially that between a knowledge whose truth claims are based on criteria of technical competence and one which seeks its basis in the personal qualities of the intellectual—would have no pertinence in other spheres of intellectual inquiry: maths, engineering, economics, or political science, for example.[5] What authorises and produces such remarks, conferring on them their intelligibility and salience, is rather a specific political technology of the intellectual, peculiar to the cultural sphere, within which the exemplary qualities of the intellectual are accorded an epistemic value and status such that they play a crucial role in making the truth manifest and operationalising it. What prompts the use of this particular form of appreciation in relation to Williams, then, is the fact that his work and the ways in which it has been responded to, especially by its takeup in cultural studies, have both remained a part of, and been deeply affected by, the political technology of the intellectual associated with the disciplinary history of English in its dependence, as Hunter (1988) has argued, on the moral authority invested in the person of the exemplary teacher—a technology which is, in turn, a particular institutionalisation of the voice of prophetic authority associated with the broader discursive formation of English Romanticism (see Holloway, 1953).

There was, in this sense, nothing new about the tone struck in the obituary commemorations I have briefly summarised (and it is for this reason that I do not think they can be attributed simply to the honorific conventions of the obituary form). To the contrary, the tendency to view Williams' work through the prism of his life—to see it as an attempt to overcome in theory the oppositions and dualities which he had lived and sought to overcome experientially and practically—has been an enduring feature of Williams' criticism and commentary. Richard Hoggart, in reviewing *Culture and Society*, thus judged the book a product 'not only of a mind well-equipped and well-controlled, but of one emotionally well-nourished', a fine balance of reason, judgement and sensibility which Hoggart interprets as the result of Williams' biographical bridging of the worlds of formal education and working-class community: 'a fine intelligence,' as he puts it, 'developed through good educational opportunities; and a sense of local and communal roots which is not sentimental' (Hoggart, 1959: 172–73). This assessment set a pattern few have departed from, using the metaphor of 'border country' to read Williams' life against his work, and vice versa, to explain how Williams seems able to cohere apparently contradictory elements and to anticipate their eventual full and total reconciliation.[6]

In these respects then, to come to my point, the figure of Williams has been so fashioned as to serve as an emblem for the prospect of a knowledge which, situated on the other side of the fragmenting effects of intellectual specialisation, will not be wracked and torn by its schisms. In effect, Williams has thus served as a kind of symbolic precursor of the intellectual consequences of the condition of a common culture into which the historical process has yet to deliver us.[7] The difficulty this gives rise to, however, is that disciplines become undefinable except in negative terms—except, that is, in terms of the respects in which they fall short of, or fail to contribute to, the holistic and integrative forms of cognition that will characterise inquiry once the limitations of disciplinary boundaries have been surpassed. It is for this reason that cultural studies, insofar as it is heir to such conceptions, has usually proved unable to define itself as a discipline in terms of definite traits and characteristics. Instead, attempts to define cultural studies usually result in an evasion of this task in favour of an anticipatory dissolution of other disciplinary specificities into the cultural studies cauldron.

Richard Johnson's essay 'What is cultural studies anyway?' is a case in point—and an instructive one in that, although one of the most taut and constructive definitional discussions of cultural studies yet to be offered, it is ultimately diverted from identifying a set of disciplinary attributes that are specific to it in favour of adumbrating its aspirations toward a form of intellectual completeness. Johnson's purpose, he states, is to consider 'arguments for and against the academic codification of cultural studies' and especially to ask: 'should cultural studies aspire to the status of an academic discipline?' However, the question is put from a perspective which, echoing the cultural studies discourse of the true, favours an answer in the negative:

> A codification of methods or knowledges (instituting them, for example, in formal curricula or in courses on 'methodology') runs against some of the main features of cultural studies as a tradition: its openness and theoretical versatility, its reflexive even self-conscious mood, and, especially, the importance of critique. I mean critique in the fullest sense: not criticism merely, nor even polemic, but procedures by which other traditions are approached both for what they may yield and for what they inhibit. Critique involves stealing away the more useful elements and rejecting the rest. From this point of view cultural studies is a process, a kind of alchemy for producing useful knowledge; codify it and you might halt its reactions. (Johnson, 1986/87: 38)

Defined in these terms, the issue revolves around an opposition between the academicisation of cultural studies and its capacity to produce 'useful knowledge'—a term which, in Johnson's own historical work, recalls the opposition between self-provided forms of working-class education and the mystifying and ideologically misleading forms of education provided by the state (see Johnson, 1979). Broached in this way, Johnson deflects the question of the definition of cultural studies into a familiar double-bind according to which, the more it succeeds, the more it fails. How, he asks, can students who encounter cultural studies as an orthodoxy—an administered curriculum with its own textbooks, etc.—be expected to inhabit it critically? And if they are unable to do this, is what they do adequately described as cultural studies? Yet Johnson is quick to recognise the other side of this dilemma (dilemmas are like that!) in contending that, without a clear sense of its own disciplinary integrity, cultural studies runs the practical risk that its graduates will prove unemployable, just as it entertains the theoretical risk that its identity will be pulled hither and thither by the different disciplines (literature, sociology, history) on which it draws, thus reproducing disciplinary differences within itself in the form of rivalries between a literary and a sociological cultural studies, etc. The difficulties this prospect of disciplinary divisions within cultural studies occasions for Johnson are instructive:

> This would not matter if any one discipline or problematic could grasp the objects of culture as a whole, but this is not, in my opinion, the case. Each approach tells us about a tiny aspect. If this is right, we need a particular kind of defining activity: one which reviews existing approaches, identifies their characteristic objects and their good sense, but also the limits of their competence. Actually it is not definition or codification that we need, but *pointers* to further transformations. This is not a question of aggregating existing approaches (a bit of sociology here, a spot of linguistics there) but of reforming the elements of different approaches in their relations to each other. (Johnson 1979: 41)

Viewed in this light, the task of defining cultural studies is reinterpreted as the need to devise ways of integrating different disciplinary perspectives into a moving method which will achieve greater forms of completeness from the point of view of understanding the cultural process as a whole. There is much of value to be learned from the details of Johnson's proposals on this matter. Here, however, I want to focus on the assumption which forms the backdrop to these: that disciplinary specialisation—or, indeed, any specialising kind of intellectual perspective or focus—must be judged wanting from the perspective of the whole. In reviewing a range of customary oppositions—between culturalism and structuralism, between text-based studies, production studies and the study of lived-cultures—Johnson thus concludes that each approach 'has a rationality in relation to that moment it has most closely in view, but is quite evidently inadequate, even "ideological", as an account of the whole' (1979: 72–73). However, unless the ways in which the shortcomings of other disciplinary perspectives are to be overcome are specified in terms of definite rules of transformation through which their methods are to be either supplanted by, or integrated into, those of cultural studies, statements of this kind are either platitudinous or evasive. What performs this role instead for Johnson is an implicit epistemological norm of totality in which the aspiration toward greater forms of completeness always and necessarily overrides the partialising effects of disciplinary divisions.

Of course, it may well be that a fully hard and fast definition of cultural studies is not possible and, certainly, the matter is not one that either needs or merits obsessive attention. However, if we are to recognise the position that cultural studies now occupies within educational institutions, and if we are to take our bearings from this in order to chart possible paths for its future development, a greater degree of definitional clarity and definiteness would not go amiss. This, however, will only be possible on the condition that we abandon the existing forms of being 'in the true' of cultural studies in order to fashion new ones. For the problem has not been any lack of definitional discussion within cultural studies, but rather the ways in which such discussions have been conducted. In his valuable proselytising for and on behalf of cultural studies, Stuart Hall has always insisted that cultural studies can't be just *anything*. However, as I have argued elsewhere, when he then tries to define its boundaries, the result has often been an identification of a certain style of intellectual work which, in its appeal to the personal qualities of the intellectual, borders on, but without quite becoming, a system of charismatic authority (see Bennett, 1992). It is the contention of this chapter that the definition of cultural studies in terms of a set of disciplinary attributes that can be learned and applied is, now, a better means of ensuring its continued useful and productive development than its conception as an intellectual style to be emulated.

It might be objected that to abandon the claim to an inherent interdisciplinariness is, at the same time, to sacrifice the virtues of intellectual mobility and flexibility that have been claimed for, and on behalf of, cultural studies. No doubt there are risks of real losses here. In the final analysis, however, the objection cannot be sustained, mainly because of the static, reified and unhistorical view of disciplines on which it rests. This is not merely to reiterate the historical truism that today's disciplines are yesterday's interdisciplines. Rather, the more important point is that, within the social sciences and humanities, most disciplines—of history, sociology, economics, literary studies, art history, etc.—have, in recent decades, proved remarkably mobile and flexible, constantly generating new objects of concern and attention within and between themselves without any necessary reference or indebtedness to cultural studies.

The tendency to overlook the historical mobility of disciplines is not entirely accidental. For there is a sense in which the cultural studies discourse of the true both requires and perpetuates a misleadingly petrified account of the disciplines it sees itself as transcending. That other knowledges should be viewed as partial and incomplete is a necessary counter-foil to cultural studies' own claims to embody an integrative kind of intellectual wholeness; the constant demonstration of such incompleteness is, indeed, the means by which the case for wholeness is advanced. But then this too often means that cultural studies fails to offer any accounts of other humanities disciplines which assess them in their positivity. One might say that cultural studies needs the disciplines, in that it is only with reference to their one-sided partialities that its own claims to transcendence can be advanced. A consequence of this, however, is that cultural studies never says anything about those disciplines except to point out their incompleteness from the point of view of the principle of epistemic wholeness it itself aspires to. This is, indeed, a different process from that which Canguilhem argued ought to characterise the history of scientific thought. Here, it will be recalled, new truths establish themselves in and through the process of producing new objects of knowledge whose characteristics allow previous statements to be classified as error. This is quite a different process from discounting disciplines on the grounds of their incompleteness in relation to a yet-to-be-achieved norm of cognitive wholeness. Cultural studies will acquire a better understanding of both its own concerns and practices as well as of their relations to those of adjacent disciplines—whose practical as distinct from rhetorical transcendence is by no means in sight—if it abandons its present discourse of the truth and focuses, instead, on proposing a more definite and limited set of disciplinary attributes for itself, viewing these, more modestly, as existing alongside other disciplinary norms and paradigms rather then auguring their dissolution into its own totalising ambition.

3 Cultural studies: The Foucault effect

The range of uses and meanings associated with the term 'cultural studies' is now so large that venturing any definition is risky. Nonetheless, I shall offer one. If we wish to find, or to produce, some common ground between the different national and theoretical schools of cultural studies that are now available, we shall best do so if we say, simply, that cultural studies is concerned with the analysis of cultural forms and activities in the context of the relations of power which condition their production, circulation, deployment and, of course, effects. We might, however, also add that its inquiries into such matters are guided by a practical interest in the ways in which culture functions or operates within, and as a part of, those relations of culture and power.

That, though, is about as far as it is possible to go in defining cultural studies without introducing contentious aspects into the definition that will close the shutters on debate. For there are many different ways in which relations of culture and power might be theorised, and just as many views regarding the kinds of practical interests that should guide the analysis of those relations. I shall, then, stick with this relatively open definition and, by way of stimulating debate, draw on Foucault's work to outline one way of interpreting this definition. This, naturally enough, is the interpretation I favour—or, I should say, have come to favour—in view both of the new theoretical insights it offers into the makeup and functioning of relations of culture and power and of the kinds of practical orientations towards these that it suggests and enables. This is what I mean by 'the Foucault effect': the influence Foucault's work has exerted in problematising the understandings of the relations of culture and power associated with earlier phases in the development of cultural studies and in proposing useable alternatives.

If, however, 'cultural studies' is now a floating signifier that has been cut loose from its 'original' moorings in Birmingham (although I doubt it can accurately be described as ever having had a single anchorage of that kind), the same is true of the signifier 'Foucault'. There are many Foucaults and, as he would be the first to argue, we should not seek to meld these into one in subjecting the name 'Foucault' to the unifying impulse of 'the author effect'. To be clear about which Foucault I have in mind, I have borrowed my title from the collection of essays on and by Foucault edited by Graham Burchell, Colin Gordon and Peter Miller under the title *The Foucault Effect: Studies in Governmentality*. This is not the Foucault much loved by libertarian thinkers. To the contrary, the essays collected in this volume share an acceptance of those aspects of Foucault's work which point to the increasing governmentalisation of social relations as a necessary and inescapable horizon of contemporary social and political life which, as such, conditions both the kind of practical influence intellectuals can reasonably expect to have and the manner in which that influence can be exercised. The implications of this for cultural studies, I shall argue, are, first, to suggest that the relations of culture and power which most typically characterise modern societies are best understood in the light of the respects in which the field of culture is now increasingly governmentally organised and constructed. This entails recognising that changing how cultural resources function in the context of relations of power usually involves modifying the ways in which cultural forms and activities are governmentally deployed as parts of programs of social management. This, in turn, requires that intellectuals lower the threshold of their political vistas in a manner that will enable them to connect with the debates and practices through which reformist adjustments to the administration of culture are actually brought about.

To conjure with such mundane prospects as the end-points of cultural politics is, of course, a long way from some of the better known clarion-calls of cultural studies: the call to a politics of resistance, for example; the commitment to organising an alliance of popular forces in opposition to the state; or the strategy of forming affective alliances around changing cultural nodal points. Yet these—or at least some of them—are positions associated with the traditions of cultural studies which have been important in the development of my own work but which now seem increasingly vulnerable to criticism—and which are certainly quite limited in their capacity to be translated from one national context to another. With this in mind, my purpose in addressing Foucault's influence on cultural studies is to indicate why it now seems to me important that work in cultural studies should be unravelled from the positions with which it has earlier been associated and to outline how this might be done. I shall do so by showing why, from the point of view of understanding how culture works in the service of power—or, better, how culture works *as* power—Foucault is better to 'think with' than Gramsci.

This will involve consideration of three issues. First, by comparing Gramsci's arguments concerning the role of the ethical state with the Foucaultian perspective of liberal government, I shall argue the respects in which the latter offers a more useable characterisation of the functioning of culture–power relations in modern societies. This will prepare the way for a contrastive analysis of the implications of these two different analytical perspectives for our understanding of state–civil society relations and the place and role of culture within such relations. Finally, I shall illustrate these theoretical and historical concerns by comparing and contrasting the implications of the two perspectives for the terms in which the roles accorded women in the emergence of modern forms of cultural governance might be accounted for.

It is not just that Foucault is better to 'think with' than Gramsci; he is also better to 'do with'—better, that is, in enabling intellectual work to be rendered appropriately and practically relevant to the circumstances in which it is produced. For, at the end of the day, my own passage from Gramsci to Foucault has been prompted as much by practical concerns as by theoretical ones: by Foucault's much greater 'useability' in the contexts in which, today, intellectual work has and needs to be done.

THE ETHICAL STATE, LIBERAL GOVERNMENT AND CULTURAL MANAGEMENT

My argument so far has perhaps been misleading in suggesting that it is only recently that cultural studies has been subjected to a 'Foucault effect'. Many would dispute this. In his now classic essay 'Cultural studies: Two paradigms', for example, Stuart Hall cites Foucault's work as one of the founding sources of inspiration for British cultural studies. Indeed, writing in 1981, Hall went so far as to say that 'Foucault and Gramsci between them account for much of the most productive work on concrete analysis now being undertaken in the field' (Hall, 1981: 35). Having said that, however, Hall goes on to chastise Foucault for failing to see how the various transitions he had been concerned to chart in the fields of penality, sexuality, psychiatry, language and political economy 'all appear to converge around exactly that point where industrial capitalism and the bourgeoisie make their fateful, historical rendezvous' (1981: 36). Foucault, in other words, was in error in failing to see how the economic relations of capitalism constituted a unifying principle of the social formation such that these different historical transitions could be seen as corresponding to one another as parts of a connected set of processes occasioned by the development of capitalism. He was also in error in not seeing how the forms of power that were exerted in the spheres of the economy, penality and sexuality were derived from, or in some way related to, the class power of the bourgeoisie.

In truth, the issues here are somewhat clouded since, in Hall's work at this time, discussions of Foucault often served as a coded reference to what was widely regarded, within cultural studies, as the baleful influence of the uses to which Foucault was put in the work of Barry Hindess and Paul Hirst. This was especially true of their polemical contention, which Hall rightly took issue with, regarding the necessary non-correspondence of the different levels of a social formation. Although his target was thus somewhat skewed, Hall's arguments were nonetheless typical of the ways in which, in the 1970s, the more influential tendencies within British cultural studies sought to deal with the troubling grit of Foucault's work. Taken one by one, it was suggested, Foucault's accounts of contemporary forms of power could be admitted as useful, but with the then crippling rider that they had first to be dissociated from those theoretical positions which most marked Foucault's work as distinctive. Foucault was 'OK'—but he had no theory of the state; his substitution of the couplet knowledge/power for the distinction between truth and ideology committed him to a politically paralysing epistemological agnosticism; his conception of the micro-physics of power allowed no way in which little struggles might be connected to form the basis for a society-wide struggle with revolutionary potential. In short, all those aspects of Foucault's work which he had directed, polemically and strategically, against Marxism were directed back at him as criticisms because they were not Marxist! In effect, Foucault was admitted into the cultural studies roll-call only on the condition that he brought no troublesome Foucaultian arguments with him. The role accorded his work was not that of reformulating received problems so much as being tagged on to arguments framed by the very formulations he questioned, lending them a spurious Foucaultian pedigree. Quoted extensively, he was used very little.

The reasons for this are not difficult to fathom. For what this strategy amounted to was an attempt to fashion a Foucault who could be fitted into a Gramscian mould. If, at the time Hall was writing, Foucault and Gramsci could be allowed to share the field of 'concrete analysis', no similar division of the field was contemplated at the theoretical level where the formulations of Gramsci were granted more or less undisputed sway. This is neither surprising nor reprehensible. The 'Gramscian moment' in British cultural studies was an important and remarkably productive one and the process of distinguishing its concerns and formulations from those of contending theoretical positions was, as is always true of intellectual movements, central to its formation. The difficulty, however, was that enlisting Foucault for this project was made possible only by erasing from his work all those historical and theoretical arguments which made it distinctive—and distinctive precisely because it called into question much of the theoretical apparatus on which the Gramscian theory of hegemony depends. This much, perhaps, may be easily conceded. What I also want to argue, however, is that it is precisely those aspects of Foucault's work which were thus exorcised in favour of Gramsci that give us a better understanding of the mechanisms of culture and power in modern western societies than do the Gramscian concepts to which they were obliged to defer.

It will be helpful, in the first instance, to approach these matters historically. For both Foucault and Gramsci, the early modern period in western Europe sees a significant transformation in the ways in which relations of culture and power were organised. In Gramsci's case, this is expressed in his account of the emergence of what he variously describes as the ethical, cultural or educative functions of the modern state. In the case of Foucault, the argument takes the form of a more general account of the transition from juridico-discursive to disciplinary and, in his later writings, governmental forms of power. On the face of it, these two accounts have much in common. Both agree that the period from the late eighteenth through to the mid-nineteenth centuries witnessed the development of new institutions and practices which embodied a more detailed interest in the cultural activities and values of the population as a whole as well as more effective—in the sense of more detailed and regular—ways of directing and regulating those activities. However, while these similarities are important, it is, I shall suggest, the differences that matter more.

In the case of Gramsci, the key to this historical transformation consists in the historical peculiarity of the bourgeoisie as a class which, obliged to govern by and with the consent of the governed, must dedicate its energies and resources to the ongoing task of organising that consent. It is this that provides the basis for his view that 'the State has become an "educator" ' (Gramsci, 1971: 260), dedicated to the task of raising 'the great mass of the population to a particular cultural and moral level which corresponds to the needs of the productive forces for development, and hence to the interests of the ruling class' (1971: 258). It is worth noting the historical contrast Gramsci draws in introducing this conception of the state:

> The previous ruling classes were essentially conservative in the sense that they did not tend to construct an organic passage from the other classes into their own, i.e. to enlarge their class sphere 'technically' and ideologically: their conception was that of a closed caste. The bourgeois class poses itself as an organism in continuous movement, capable of absorbing the entire society, assimilating it to its own cultural and economic level. (1971: 260)

This was, for Gramsci, a crucial historical divide. Unlike other ruling classes before it, the bourgeoisie has need of an active interest in the culture of subordinate classes in view of the requirement that it recruit active popular support for the incessantly expansive projects to which the imperatives of accumulation commit it. Active leadership of society rather than coercive rule becomes the hallmark of the bourgeoisie's aspirations, if not always of its achievements. For the ruling classes of earlier modes of production, by contrast, the cultural values, standards and practices of the population at large—while fully capable of provoking political alarm and intrusive forms of regulation—were not matters requiring the kind of sustained, systematic and, above all, developmental attention that Gramsci attributes to the bourgeoisie.

The historical contrasts which organise Foucault's account of the emergence of modern western forms of government are, at first sight, quite similar. The absolutist systems of rule which had prevailed in most of Europe prior to the French Revolution were, Foucault argues, in what is certainly a vast over-generalisation, characterised by a form of power which he calls the juridico-discursive. In this conception of power, Foucault argues, everything is given over to a singular function: the maintenance and extension of the prince's power as an end in itself. There is, accordingly, little interest in the conditions of life or culture of the population, or in carrying the power of the state into these except insofar as doing so might contribute to the pursuit of the singular end of extending the prince's power. It is for this reason, Eugene Weber notes, that the French crown exhibited little concern with the languages spoken in the regions under its administration.

'Language,' as he puts it, 'was relevant merely as an instrument of rule.' (Weber, 1976: 70) Although French was enforced as the language to be used at court and for the administration of state affairs, no attempt was made to establish it as a national language shared by all regions and all classes:

> The King's speech had precedence over those of his subjects, and all who engaged in public affairs were bound to use it or pay others to use it on their behalf. But linguistic unity hobbled far behind even the incomplete administrative unity of the Ancien Régime; nor does it seem to have been a policy goal. (Weber, 1976: 70)

Indeed, the disjunction between the language of power and that of everyday usage had a distinctive political value of its own. In the ascending set of power–knowledge relations associated with juridico-discursive systems of rule, Foucault argues, power is exercised with a view to magnifying and enlarging the distinctions between classes, and especially to exaggerate the differences between king and populace. In such a regime, power exercises its sway in being symbolised and magnified before the populace in ways that are calculated to allow the populace to acquire a knowledge of power via an exhibition of its effects—in the form of palaces, royal entries and the scene of punishment or, less spectacularly, the distinctive sumptuary and linguistic codes of the court. The reverse, however, is not true. For if, in juridico-discursive systems of rule, it is important that the populace should acquire a knowledge of power, there is no equivalent stress placed on the need for a knowledge of the populace on the part of government. The subordinate classes—their conditions of life and culture—do not, at this stage, constitute an object of knowledge.

It is in reversing the axis of individuation produced by this earlier set of power–knowledge relations, Foucault argues, that the historical distinctiveness of governmental forms of power is most clearly discerned. In late eighteenth century cameralist conceptions of the functions of the state; in the formulations of the science of police from the same period; and in nineteenth century programs of liberal government—in all of these formulations, the art of governing is seen to be more and more dependent on the acquisition of an increasingly close and detailed knowledge of the conditions of life of the population. There are, of course, important differences between the roles accorded this knowledge within these different conceptions of government. In the formulations of police, the need to acquire a knowledge of the conditions of life of the population is connected to the fantasy of a totally administered society, and a society which has therefore to be known in its every detail. Liberal government, by contrast, posits the existence of spheres of life and freedom which are, and are to remain, autonomous of itself but which still need to be rendered knowable in order that government 'will not be arbitrary government, but will be based upon intelligence concerning those whose well-being it is mandated to enhance' (Rose, 1993: 290). That said, there is a common tendency between these conceptions of government. The exercise of power is now thought of as being as closely tied up with the process of knowing as it is with that of making known; power is dispersed and applied through mechanisms which make the population an object as well as a subject of knowledge; and power itself, rather then being blazoned forth in an attempt to augment its effects in making them manifest, now also hides behind, or within, the processes of its own exercise.

For both Foucault and Gramsci, then, modern systems of rule are distinguished from their predecessors in terms of the degree and kind of interest they display in the conditions of life of the population. There is the further consideration that both attribute to modern systems of rule a new kind of concern with, and attentiveness to, the subjective lives of the subordinate classes. Foucault's concept of liberal government thus shares some affinities with Gramsci's concept of consent in the stress it places on the need for governmental objectives to be accomplished by developing these in the form of self-acting imperatives which individuals will voluntarily follow in pursuing their own ends rather than via the impositional logic of rule *d'état*. Both thus see the way in which power is exercised being subjected to a fundamental change in the early modern period in view of the degree to which it comes to be caught up in a more thorough and extensive set of relations and practices aimed at bringing about a more extensive knowledge of, and voluntary transformations within, popular forms of thought, feeling and behaviour by inscribing these in new contexts and apparatuses. It is for this reason that both accord culture an enhanced role in the structure and functioning of modern systems of rule.

However, that is about as far as the similarities go. For the nature of the transformations in popular forms of belief and conduct that are to be effected via new mechanisms of cultural governance, and the actual nature of such mechanisms themselves, are viewed quite differently between the two cases.

In Gramsci's case, for example, the crucial change concerns the degree to which the exercise of power in bourgeois-democratic forms of rule aims not merely at exacting the obedience of the popular classes but further aspires to win their active support for, and participation in, the projects of the ruling classes. It is to this singular end, Gramsci argues, that all of the major ideological apparatuses of both state and civil society—from popular schooling through the media to the institutions of art and culture—are dedicated. 'The school as a positive educative function, and the courts as a repressive and negative educative function, are the most important State activities in this sense,' Gramsci argues. But, he continues, 'in reality, a multitude of other so-called private initiatives and activities tend to the same end—initiatives and activities which form the apparatus of the political and cultural hegemony of the ruling classes' (Gramsci, 1971: 258). Moreover, and insofar as this is so, this end is to be accomplished by means of an invariant mechanism whose operative principles are, in the final analysis, psychological ones. For consent is a psychological state and the means through which such consent is to be organised are, for Gramsci, primarily mental ones. Inducing the popular classes to consent to bourgeois forms of rule and leadership is to be accomplished by exposing those classes, regularly and routinely, to bourgeois ideologies and values whose capacity to command popular support depends on their ability to acquire a greater degree of social weight, influence and persuasiveness than the contending class ideologies and values with which they must compete.

It may be true, as Renate Holub has suggested, that Foucault and Gramsci share an understanding of how power operates 'within the systems and subsystems of social relations, in the interactions, in the microstructures that inform the practices of everyday life' (Holub, 1992: 200). However, it would be misleading to see the Gramscian position as a variant of Foucault's understanding of 'the microphysics of power' in view of the degree to which, in the former, power is understood as arising from a highly unified and centralised origin rather than being dispersed in its operation and constitution. Positing a centre of and for power in the ruling class or power bloc, the Gramscian theory of hegemony is concerned to analyse the descending flows of cultural and ideological power and the degree to which these are successfully countered by countervailing cultural and ideological influences arising from the conditions of life of the popular classes. The field of culture is thus viewed as being structured by the bipolar contest between, on the one hand, the descending flows of hegemonic ideologies as they are transmitted from the organising centres of bourgeois cultural power and relayed through society via the ideological apparatuses of the state and civil society and, on the other, the putatively ascending flows of counter-hegemonic ideologies arising out of the situation of the subordinate classes.

It is also typically the case that Gramscian analysis tends to look *through* rather than *at* the ideological apparatuses of the state and civil society. Moreover, the essential function of those apparatuses—that of serving as vehicles for carrying bourgeois ideologies to the subordinate classes—is taken as pre-given. The family, the media, popular schooling, the art and culture industries: these tend to be viewed, in the Gramscian tradition, very much as neutral carriers of ideologies with the result that the analysis focuses less on the properties of these institutions as institutions than on the content of the ideologies they relay. Given the stress the theory of hegemony places on the psychological mechanism of consent—on the winning of hearts and minds—it is the battle of ideas that matters most and, given that ideas are viewed as deriving their provenance and currency from their position and role in relation to the conflict between the two fundamental classes in society, this battle of ideas is viewed as taking much the same form and posing much the same issues for analysis no matter what the fields of its occurrence. The Gramscian tradition within cultural studies has accordingly been little concerned with the specific properties of particular cultural institutions, technologies or apparatuses, preferring to look through these to analyse a process (the organisation of hegemony) which is seen as taking place in an invariant manner (the psychological mechanism of consent) within, across and between these apparatuses in spite of what their manifold differences in other regards might be. It is this that explains the marked importance accorded the theorisation of generalised forms of linguistic, ideological or discursive articulation within Gramscian cultural studies as part of an attempt to provide a generalised theory of consent whose mechanisms remain the same across the whole of the cultural field.

Foucault's work differs from this analytical program in almost all particulars. Those modern forms of rule which Foucault calls governmental are thus characterised by the multiplicity of the ends which they pursue and the diversity of the instruments that are developed in the pursuit of such ends. In his discussion of Machiavellian conceptions of the art of governing, Foucault argues that the prince constitutes a transcendental principle which gives to the state and governing a singular and circular function such that all acts are dedicated to securing political obedience as a necessary condition of the exercise and extension of the prince's sovereignty as an end in itself. By extension, of course, the same is true of Marxist theories of the state, since these interpret the state as embodying a singular principle of power—albeit one derived from outside itself in the sphere of class relations—and view the activities of all branches of the state and, in Gramsci's case, of civil society too as contributing to the reproduction and extension of that power. Governmental power, by contrast, has no such singular anchorage, authorisation or function, but is rather characterised by the diversity of the objectives which it pursues, objectives which derive from and are specific to differentiated fields of social management rather than resting on some unifying principle of central power (the sovereign, the state).

For Gramsci, as we have seen, the singular and circular problematic of political obedience is replaced, in bourgeois-democratic societies, by the equally singular problematic of consent. For Foucault, by contrast, the development of modern forms of government—which, it is important to remember, can be evident in the procedures of private associations and organisations just as much as in those of the state—goes beyond the problematic of political obedience to replace it with a concern with knowing, regulating and changing the conditions of the population in potentially limitless ways, the logics of which, depending on the circumstances, may or may not tend in the same direction, may or may not correspond to and further class interests, and so on.

Perhaps more important, however, are the respects in which the Foucaultian optic focuses on precisely those matters which tend to be neglected within the Gramscian paradigm. As Colin Gordon has argued, Foucault's main criticism of legitimation theory—of which I take the Gramscian account of consent to be a variant—is that it 'cannot be relied upon as a means of describing the ways in which power is actually exercised under such a sovereignty' (Gordon, 1991: 7). It is, so to speak, too 'heady' in its approach to power, sees it in terms that are too intellectual, and so fails to take adequate account of the more mundane and technical means through which power is routinely exercised. Foucault's interest has accordingly focused more on the technological aspects of the mechanisms of power where these are understood to include the field of subjectivity but in ways which (i) do not attribute any necessary or invariant form (consent) to the relations between individuals and power, and (ii) do not equate the field of subjectivity with that of consciousness.

In his essay 'Technologies of the self', Foucault defines governmentality as the 'contact between the technologies of domination of others and those of the self' where technologies of domination are defined as concerned to 'determine the conduct of individuals and submit them to certain ends or domination' and technologies of the self are defined as permitting 'individuals to effect by their own means or with the help of others a certain number of operations on their own bodies and souls, thoughts, conduct, and way of being, so as to transform themselves in order to attain a certain state of happiness, purity, wisdom, perfection, or immortality' (Foucault, 1988: 18–19). This conception directs our attention to the ways in which the relations between persons and cultural resources are organised within the context of particular cultural technologies, and to the variable forms of work on the self, or practices of subjectification, which such relations support. In their turn, such practices have as their product not the subject of a consciousness so much as the operators of particular forms of life which constitute particular zones of a person's existence.

The implications of this perspective for cultural studies are to suggest that its attention should concentrate on the variable relations to different forms of power that are produced for individuals within the contexts of such technologies. From such a perspective, the Gramscian emphasis placed on the content of ideologies-in-struggle emerges as of less importance than the institutional mechanisms which provide for a particular organisation of the relations between persons, positions, symbolic resources, architectural contexts, etc. within the framework of a particular technology. Foucaultian work on the history of schooling is thus typically concerned to stress the similarities between the pedagogical and technological environments of the popular school and those envisaged by the alternative schemas of radical working-class education, seeing in these a basis for grouping them together as parts of a technology of culture and power in spite of the different curricula arising from their different educational philosophies (see Hunter, 1994). This, in turn, leads to a quite different way of framing political issues and priorities within the sphere of culture. 'The problem,' as Foucault put it, 'is not changing people's consciousness—or what's in their heads—but the political, economic, institutional régime of the production of truth.' (Foucault, 1980: 133)

I shall return to these considerations later. For a fuller understanding of the contrasting implications of the Foucaultian and Gramscian paradigms for the role played by culture in modern forms of governance, however, we need to look more closely at Gramsci's and Foucault's conceptions of civil society and of its relations to, in the first case, the state and, in the second, government. Again, at first sight, there seems to be much in common between their positions on this matter inasmuch as both introduce a certain fluidity into the state–civil society relationship, transforming it from a categorical distinction into a more permeable divide. On further inspection, however, this apparent similarity serves only to mask the radical incommensurability of their approaches.

CIVIL SOCIETY, CULTURE AND 'THE STATE'

Most commentators are agreed that the view of the state as educator which Gramsci advanced as a part of his theory of hegemony significantly revised the Hegelian construction of the state–civil society relation—on which Marxist theories of the state depended—while still remaining within its orbit. The significance of the Hegelian conception of civil society compared with the earlier tradition of social contract theory, which had included the family in its conception of civil society, consists in its limitation of civil society to the sphere of private and clashing interests arising out of the field of economic relations (see Pateman, 1989). When translated into Marxist terms, the divisions of interest which arise from the organisation of civil society give rise to class divisions. These, in turn, are governed by an immanent dynamic of power arising from the structure of the relations of production. The role accorded the state within this conception is to reinforce those relations of power which arise spontaneously from and are immanent to the organisation of class relations in civil society. In this conception, as Graham Burchell summarises it, 'the state's exercise of governmental power can be seen as in continuity with, or as grafted on to, society's immanent relations of power' (Burchell, 1991: 140).

Gramsci's innovation concerns less his conception of the state's function (he was by no means the first to think of the state as combining coercive and educative functions) than where and how he sees that function being performed. For he sees the state as itself a part of society's immanent relations of power, as inserted within these in a manner which helps to form and constitute them rather than being simply grafted onto pre-existing relations of class power. This was what Christine Buci-Glucksmann had in mind when she referred to the 'methodological duplication of the superstructures' associated with Gramsci's expansion of the state concept. In the elasticity he introduced into the conception of the state—an elasticity that is fully stretched in his most expansive formulation of the state as 'the entire complex of practical and theoretical activities with which the ruling class not only justifies and maintains its dominance, but manages to win the active consent of those over whom it rules' (Gramsci, 1971:

244)—Gramsci sought to disentangle the concept of the state from that of 'the government' or 'political society'. He did so by producing for the state an enlarged sphere of operations which trespassed significantly, if not entirely, on the fields of activity normally associated with the separated domain of civil society. The state, he argues, has to be understood as 'not only the apparatus of government' but also 'the "private" apparatus of "hegemony" or civil society' (1971: 261). If this formulation extends the state's reach into the ideological and cultural apparatuses of hegemony, other formulations extend it into the constitution of the social relations of economic production. Fordism is thus, for Gramsci, simultaneously an economic, a political, an ideological and a cultural phenomenon, thus overcoming any essentialist state/civil society division in its complex combination of productive and educative functions.

What consequences follow from this expansion of the state concept? The main ones, as Buci-Glucksmann glosses them, consist in the replacement of the rigid hierarchies of determination associated with the base–superstructure conceptions of classical Marxism by a more fluid and interactive conception of the relations within and between economic, political, ideological and cultural relationships. The state, in its educative role, comprises the totality of those activities that are involved in the production of consent. As such, it straddles the economic, political, ideological and cultural spheres of social activity in a manner which renders incoherent their conception as separate realms. This permeability of the state–civil society relation is paralleled by a double splitting as the functions of the state are split into two (coercion plus consent) while, at the same time, the state itself is divided into two parts (political society and the cultural and ideological apparatuses). In moments of crisis, this double splitting gives way to a more simple form of bipolar opposition as the state acts coercively in relation to a civil society which it locates outside of itself. In more normal times, however, the mediating and connecting role that is allowed to the cultural and ideological apparatuses means that the state's role in the organisation of consent is targeted, in good measure, at itself owing to its capacity to 'pop up' again, as an object of its own strategies, in the sphere of civil society. The way in which the state thus operates on the relations between its own constituent parts, however, is a matter that is itself specified by the immanent relations of power from which the state arises and in which it is embedded. As Gramsci puts it, the educative and formative role of the state is always that 'of adapting the "civilisation" and morality of the broadest masses to the necessities of the continuous development of the economic apparatus of production' (1971: 242). The restriction Gramsci places on the social forces which can aspire to become hegemonic has much the same consequence. His contention here is that only a fundamental class exercising a 'decisive function' in the 'decisive nucleus of economic activity' (1971: 161) can realistically aspire to recruit the support of other social forces for its hegemonic projects. This is because only fundamental classes—the proletariat and the bourgeoisie in capitalist societies—are able to construct totalising social programs that are rooted in the immanent relations of economic power.

No matter how much Gramsci thus reserves what Hindess and Hirst (1975) usefully call a matrix role of determination for the economy, his writings on the state, civil society and hegemony entail an enormous expansion of the importance accorded the role of culture in the organisation of social life owing to the degree to which, so to speak, culture seems to crop up everywhere. As a consequence of the expansiveness of Gramsci's concepts and of his tendency to blur the boundary lines between them in providing for their overlapping and merging into one another, culture is not, for Gramsci, a separate realm (a superstructure) but an element in the constitution of each and every realm (the state, civil society, the economy). It is in this way, if I may be allowed a clumsy neologism, that Gramsci effects a 'culturalisation' of social relations. He does so, however, not in the sense of inverting the hierarchies of determination of classical Marxism in making the economy an effect of a determining cultural superstructure. Rather, culture for Gramsci functions more as a connective salve which, as a consequence of its dispersal, of its capacity to crop up everywhere, bestows a cohesiveness on the social in interconnecting its diverse parts. At the same time, of course, the construction or contestation of hegemony is, for Gramsci, mainly a cultural matter depending on the suasive capacity of different class-based hegemonic projects whose form is, essentially, that of different rhetorical constructions of the social pitted against one another in their competition to recruit popular consent.

If we turn, now, to Foucault's writings on governmentality, we find that none of these concepts is in the same place or performs the same function. For while these also call into question the dichotomous constructions of the relations between state and civil society inherited from social contract theory, the manner in which they overcome these is quite different. This is not done, as in Gramsci, by blurring the state–civil society distinction. Rather, Foucault's step is the (to my mind) more interesting one of arguing for the historical and artefactual nature of the distinction, seeing it as an effect of particular strategies of government which have organised civil society as an interface between the projects of government and the objects which those projects construct. Graham Burchell puts the point succinctly when, glossing Foucault, he argues that civil society should be viewed neither as an aboriginal reality, 'a natural given standing in opposition to the timeless essential nature of the state', nor as 'an ideological construct or something fabricated by the state'. Rather, he suggests, civil society should be regarded as the 'correlate of a particular technology of government'. He continues:

> The distinction between civil society and the state is a form of 'schematism' for the exercise of political power. Foucault describes civil society as in this sense a 'transactional reality' existing at the mutable interface of political power and everything which permanently outstrips its reach. (Burchell, 1991: 141)

The context for these remarks is a discussion of Foucault's concept of liberal government and its construction of civil society as a realm of individuals with independent interests whose autonomy has to be recognised as both setting limits to government as well as ordaining the means through which its objectives must be pursued. These comprise those techniques of 'governing at a distance' which, eschewing the impositional logic of rule *d'état*, aim to induct individuals into programs of self-management through which specific governmental objectives will be realised or carried through in and by the voluntary activities of individuals who are thus conscripted as agents for the exercise of power on and through themselves.

Yet, to return to an earlier point, the similarity between this position and the Gramscian conception of consent in the stress both place on the need for modern forms of government to organise and work through the voluntary compliance of the governed is more apparent than real. This is partly because, in the Foucaultian case, the mechanisms of liberal government do not depend on the production of a generalised form of consent through the mechanisms of ideological articulation via which, in an expansive hegemony, the ideologies and beliefs of subordinate classes are connected to those of the ruling bloc as represented by the state. The state, as we have seen, does not possess any such general class character or unity. Nor, for Foucault, are the realms of government and the state coterminous. However, the manner in which he disentangles these differs quite markedly from that proposed by Gramsci.

As we have seen, Gramsci's methodological duplication of the superstructures extends the state back into civil society. Foucault speaks, instead, of a 'governmentalisation of the state' through which techniques of governing aimed at shaping and directing the conduct of individuals that were initially developed in a range of non-state organisations (professional bodies, cultural institutions, voluntary associations) come to form a part of state-based programs of government. In an earlier phase of his work, Foucault argued—discussing the nineteenth century swarming of disciplinary projects that occurred throughout the social body—that the state rarely initiated these projects which, to the contrary, rested on highly dispersed conditions of existence and operated in an uncoordinated manner. However, he did suggest that the state functioned to codify and cohere those disciplinary projects so as to lend to them a class character. By the time of his writings on governmentality, this residual influence of the Marxist problematic had disappeared. The 'governmentalisation of the state' does not produce any essential or even articulated class (or any other kind of) unity for the forms of government which thus find a place in the programs and operating procedures of state institutions any more than it entails the equation of government with the state. Rather, the stress on what Colin Gordon calls the '*modes of pluralisation* of modern government' directs attention to the diversity of the ends to which government is directed, the diversity of the means it employs and of the forms of voluntary involvement it aims to organise, as well as to the dispersal of these varied practices of governing across the state–civil society relation which thus emerges as a permeable and fluid boundary line rather than an essential divide.

Government, viewed from this perspective, is, as Peter Miller and Nikolas Rose put it, 'the historically constituted matrix within which are articulated all those dreams, schemes, strategies and manoeuvres of authorities that seek to shape the beliefs and conduct of others in desired directions by acting upon their will, their circumstances or their environment' (Miller and Rose, 1992: 175). As such, Miller and Rose suggest, the dualisms of earlier political vocabularies—state–civil society, public–private, government–market—lose their force as descriptions of separated realms and come to function, instead, as discursive elements in programs of government which, in spanning these divides, nonetheless continue to mobilise their currency in the processes through which they specify their aims, delimit their fields of application and identify their targets.

This system of concepts does not support any places that culture might occupy or any functions that it can perform that are analogous to the places and functions it has been accorded within Gramscian cultural studies. The role of connective salve mediating between and interconnecting the different levels of a social formation into a cohesive whole is not a function which, in the problematic of governmentality, needs to be performed. Equally, there is no role for culture to play as part of a set of broader ideological processes through which generalised forms of consent to the hegemonic projects of a ruling bloc are to be organised. This much is, perhaps, evident. What matters rather more, however, are the respects in which the deeper structure of the analytical topographies of the two positions differ. For there is nowhere in the Foucaultian position where immanent relations of power might be located from which cultural divisions expressive of different class positions and values might first emerge and then, through the state, be hierarchically organised in a manner which will subordinate one part of an already divided cultural field (the culture of the subordinate classes) to another (the culture of the ruling bloc) through the general mechanisms of social control, legitimation or consent. Rather, culture emerges as a pluralised and dispersed field of government which, far from mediating the relations between civil society and the state or connecting the different levels of a social formation, operates through, between and across these in inscribing cultural resources into a diversity of programs aimed at directing the conduct of individuals toward an array of different ends, for a variety of purposes, and by a plurality of means.

What distinguishes this sphere of government from others? The answer, in part, consists in the way in which it organises distinctive fields and instruments of action by means of the discursive antinomies which are peculiar to it. Robert Young has argued that the concept of culture 'must paradoxically always take part in an antithetical pair or itself be divided into two'. He illustrates this splitting that is inherent in the structure of the concept by means of the following oppositions which have constituted the organisation of the concept in the modern period:

> *culture* versus *nature*;
> *culture* versus *civilisation*;
> *culture* versus *anarchy*;
> *high culture* versus *low* culture (in rough historical sequence: folk/working-class/mass/popular culture). (Young, 1995: 29)

For Young, writing from the perspective of postcolonial theory, this antithetical structure of the concept is part of a general historical process through which 'the externality of the category against which culture is defined is gradually turned inwards and becomes part of culture itself' (1995: 30). It is for this reason, he suggests, that 'culture is always a dialectical process, inscribing and expelling its own alterity' as the concept 'does not so much progress as constantly reform itself around conflictual divisions, participating in, and always a part of, a complex, hybridised economy that is never at ease with itself' (1995: 30). From this perspective, culture is to be understood as a crucial conceptual operator in the history of difference, endlessly caught up in practices of othering by defining itself against what it constructs as outside itself only, later, to absorb that excluded as a part of its own internal tensions. As he puts the point later in the same essay:

> Culture never stands alone but always participates in a conflictual economy acting out the tension between sameness and difference, comparison and differentiation, unity and diversity, cohesion and dispersion, containment and subversion. Culture is never liable to fall into fixity, stasis or organic totalisation: the constant construction and reconstruction of cultures and cultural differences is fuelled by an unending internal dissension in the imbalances in the capitalist economies that produce them. (1995: 53)

Young's primary concern in developing this argument is to insist on the role that the dynamics of colonialism have played in the formation of the concept of culture. Culture, he argues, 'has always marked cultural difference by producing the other' in a historical and, following Homi Bhaba, psychoanalytic dialectic in which racism has both played an integral role and been a model for other (class and gender) kinds of othering. His conclusion is that the modern concept of culture has always 'carried within it an antagonism between culture as a universal and as cultural difference, forming a resistance to Western culture within Western culture itself' (1995: 54).

There is, however, another way of looking at the matter, one which—rather than rooting the antithetical structure of the concept of culture in a general historical dialectic of othering and integration characterising the relations between 'the west and the rest'—would see it as the result of a number of different histories in which the 'splitting' of culture emerges from the construction of a number of different fields of government and the relations these establish between, on the one hand, culture as a set of resources for governing and, on the other, culture as the domain(s) to which those resources are to be applied with a view to enacting some change of conduct. There need not, from this point of view, be any general kind of historical-cum-psychoanalytic dialectic rooted in the dynamics of western civilisation to account for the different oppositions or antagonisms which have governed the construction of this field. These rather result from the establishment of different targets for different programs of government and from the different ways in which cultural resources are deployed in pursuit of those programs. What matters most about these antagonisms, viewed from this perspective, is that they group together, within the same field, the object of government (working-class culture, the colonised) and its means (high culture, western culture). Indeed, what the antithetical structure of culture—when looked at as a field of government—establishes is not the separation of different kinds of culture into categorially or ontologically distinct spheres so much as a way of connecting them within a particular field of government. The relations that are established between the different parts of this field, moreover, more typically take the form of a gradient which allows the cultural means of government to function as parts of a program through which the object will be progressively adjusted to the norm which those means of government represent. Rather, for example, than speaking of a contest of high culture *versus* low culture, the logic of culture, viewed governmentally, organises a means for high culture to reach into low culture in order to provide a route from one set of norms for conduct to another.

GENDER, CULTURE, GOVERNMENT

To let the argument rest here would be to leave it somewhat abstractly stated. It will therefore be useful to consider the role that was accorded women in the part that specifically cultural concepts and rhetorics were called on to play in mid-nineteenth century programs of liberal government. The literature on this subject is both rich and considerable. Much of it has been written in the context of feminist engagements with debates concerning the relations between the public and the private spheres (see, for example, Ryan, 1990; Landes, 1992) while the work of Leonore Davidoff and Catherine Hall integrates feminist perspectives with a Gramscian account of the role of gendered norms of conduct in the formation of a middle-class hegemony (Davidoff and Hall, 1987). Fortunately, however, Nancy Armstrong's account of the role of conduct books in the formation of particular gendered capacities for moral self-regulation suggests a perspective that resonates well with the arguments sketched in above, as well as offering a convenient point of connection with our earlier discussion of Gramsci's and Foucault's contrasting accounts of the new modalities of power and its exercise associated with the development of modern western societies.

Armstrong's concern is with the part played by conduct books in shaping new norms of conduct for women in Britain over the period from 1760 to 1820. The model of the domestic woman which these conduct books fashioned provided a basis for shifting moral authority from the aristocracy to the formative middle classes long before that was accomplished, in the public realm of economic life, by the emergence of *homo economicus*. In aristocratic culture, Armstrong argues, images of femininity were articulated to power through sumptuary codes regulating the display of the body of the aristocratic woman. Within these codes, the aristocratic woman was to function as 'an ornamental body representing the family's place in an intricately precise set of kinship relations determined by the metaphysics of blood' (Armstrong, 1987: 108). The construction of the new ideal of the domestic woman entailed a critique of 'the ornamental body of the aristocrat' while, at the same time, organising a new norm of femininity that was divorced from that embodied in the image of the labouring woman. Whereas the value of both the aristocratic woman and the labouring woman resided in the surfaces of their material bodies—the one valuable as the ornamental body, the other as the labouring body—the new ideal of domestic woman fashioned by the conduct books resided in a newly sculpted, self-regulating interiority. As Armstrong puts it:

> Conduct books attacked these two traditional notions of the female body in order to suggest that the female had depths far more valuable than her surface. By implying that the essence of the woman lay inside or underneath her surface, the invention of depths in the self entailed making the material body of the woman appear superficial. The invention of depth also provided the rationale for an educational program designed specifically for women, for these programs strove to subordinate the body to a set of mental processes that guaranteed domesticity. (1987: 114)

For Armstrong, the new forms of moral self-inspection promoted by the conduct books helped bring about a 'cultural change from an earlier form of power based on sumptuary display to a modern form that works through the production of subjectivity' (1987: 120). Christine Barker-Benfield's discussion of the culture of sensibility points in a similar direction in showing how the gendered aesthetic discourses of the mid-eighteenth century which, still in thrall to the politics of display, attributed to women a naturally more delicate taste for the ornaments of life subsequently gave way to a more spiritualised sensibility in which woman's value consisted in her power as an agent for the moral reformation of self and others. For both Armstrong and Barker-Benfield, however, this new woman's sphere of moral operation is initially confined to the home where her role is to regulate and restrain the desires of economic man and to convert the results of his labour into an aesthetically and morally desirable form of domestic life. 'If "his" aim is "to accumulate",' Armstrong says of economic man, 'then "hers" is "to regulate", and on "her conduct in these concerns" depends the success of all "his labours".' (1987: 120)

In summary, then, the domestic woman of the late eighteenth and early nineteenth centuries functioned as a moral-cum-aesthetic reformatory apparatus whose sphere of operation was restricted largely to the domestic sphere. In the mid-century period, by contrast, as a clear example of the processes Foucault has in mind when he speaks of 'the governmentalisation of the state', this reformatory apparatus is relocated into the public realm via a series of programs which seek to enlist the gendered and, of course, classed virtues of the domestic woman as a means for the moral reformation of men in general and of the workingman in particular. In museums, art galleries, public parks, gardens and promenades, women were, in the schemes of cultural reformers, portrayed as aesthetic-cum-moral exemplars whose presence and influence would help transform the codes of male conduct. The domestic woman was, in short, the very model of the auto-inspecting, self-regulating forms of individuality required by liberal forms of government. The intelligibility of her functioning in this regard, however, depended precisely on her placement at the intersections of a series of overlapping antinomies (female–male; high–low; private–public; state–civil society) and her ability, in relation to each of these, to function as part of a reformatory gradient through which that which lies outside the sphere of culture and government (male boisterousness) is to be brought into it and refashioned.

These conditions, of course, were highly specific ones depending on a number of conjunctions which, although they have had long-term effects, were soon to fly apart. The waning influence of Romanticism in the late nineteenth century was to prove critical in this regard. As Ursula Vogel has shown, the gendered aspects of Romantic aesthetic discourse enabled women to be represented as exemplars for the processes of self-harmonisation which the Romantic aesthetic project required. This was because women were regarded as being naturally, by their very disposition, closer to the forms of wholeness and completion which it was the obligation of every person to strive to achieve (Vogel, 1987). The emerging ascendancy of modernism from the 1870s, however, witnessed an increasing attenuation of women's role as aesthetic-cum-moral exemplars in view of modernism's critiques of both Romanticism and the earlier culture of sensibility, and its construction of a significantly more masculinised canon of high culture in their place (see Sparke, 1995). Even so, it is no accident that public cultural and educational institutions—like libraries (see Garrison, 1976)—should have proved among the more significant fields for the employment of women in professional roles in view of the continuing aesthetic-cum-moral functions that it was expected—by both women and men—they would be able to perform by virtue of their gendered constitution.

THE FOUCAULT EFFECT

The distinctive aspects of the ways in which gendered attributes were deployed in nineteenth century programs of cultural management, then, consist in their close association with the development of new governmental forms of power. These achieved their effects much less spectacularly than the forms of power they displaced through the attention they accorded the studied manipulation of the relations between social agents in specific institutional contexts. This is what I mean by 'the Foucault effect' in cultural studies: the way in which Foucault's perspectives, in encouraging us to focus on the detailed routines and operating procedures of cultural institutions, allow us to see how cultural resources are always caught up in, and function as parts of, cultural technologies which, through the ordering and shaping of social relations which they effect, play an important role in organising different fields of human conduct. The business which culture is caught up in, looked at in these terms, goes beyond the influence of representations on forms of consciousness to include the influence of institutional practices, administrative routines and spatial arrangements on the available repertoires of human conduct and patterns of social interaction.

However, it is equally important—and this brings us to the second aspect of 'the Foucault effect' in cultural studies—that the role of culture in the organisation and regulation of different fields of conduct is seen to be disaggregated from those kinds of singular politics which see all fields of cultural struggle as being connected to a generalised struggle of the subordinate against a single source of power (the state, the ruling class, patriarchy) or an agglomerated source of power (the patriarchal imperialist state). Let me go back to Stuart Hall for a moment. It was, in Hall's view, impossible for Foucault to theorise a social formation or the state adequately since his view that the relations between practices are contingent meant that he was 'deeply committed to the necessary non-correspondence of all practices to one another' (Hall, 1981: 36). It is difficult to see why this would be so: to say that practices do not necessarily correspond with one another is not to say that they necessarily do not correspond. My interest here, however, is less in the accuracy of Hall's criticism (this is where his merging of Foucault and Hindess and Hirst shows through most clearly) than in the fact that, over the period since Hall offered this assessment, the balance of opinion within cultural studies—including Hall's own views—has shifted so that this aspect of Foucault's work is now more likely to be cited as a positive asset rather than a disadvantage. A stress on the fluidity of social relations and practices, and on the contingent ordering of their connectedness as, now, necessary ways of theorising the social has become something of a commonplace within cultural studies as its earlier formulations have been adjusted in the light of what have been variously described as post-structuralist, postmodernist or post-Marxist critiques.

A key issue for cultural studies concerns how this contingency of the social is to be theorised. One tendency—and it is the tendency that has emerged out of the dialogue between the Gramscian tradition within cultural studies and, as Dick Hebdige puts it, the world of 'the posts' (Hebdige, 1988), as well as being the position with which Hall's later work has been most closely aligned—views the processes through which social relations acquire a degree of provisional fixity as being primarily discursive: a result of the ways in which social actors are induced to view their relations to one another as a consequence of the conduct of ideological struggle. This, in rough summary, is the position that the politics of articulation has now arrived at: a position in which the effective forms of social alliance and division are held to derive from the forms of connectedness, or articulations, that have been established, by discursive means, between different ideological and cultural values. If this produces a practical role for the intellectual, this is achieved at the price of only being able to conceive cultural politics as taking a discursive form, a struggle waged solely on the field of representations. Where all that was once solid has 'melted into air', it is not surprising that, where this view prevails, conceptions of both the ends that intellectuals should pursue in the cultural sphere and the means by which to pursue them should have become increasingly 'airy' in tone.

For Foucault, by contrast, the order of relations that is contingently established between practices can only be discerned through the application of a dense materialism which charts the relations, similarities and migrations between different fields of practice. By the same token, the Foucaultian perspective suggests that any effective involvement of intellectuals in the cultural sphere must rest on a 'politics of detail' that entails ways of addressing and acting effectively in relation to the governmental programs through which particular fields of conduct are organised and regulated. In these ways, the 'Foucault effect' I have sought to identify should serve, at the levels of both theory and practice, as an effective antidote to the headier forms of thought and action that now too often go under the label of cultural studies.

PART II

History

4 Culture: A reformer's science

Intellectual disciplines, George Stocking Jr has argued, are just as likely as other social projects to develop creation myths to account for the origins of their most sacred beliefs and concepts. The case he has in mind is that of the role accorded Edward Burnett Tylor in early accounts of the history of social anthropology. In such accounts, Tylor emerges as the author of the anthropological concept of culture as a way of life and, more particularly, is seen as responsible for the stress that this definition now places on the view that cultures are plural and that their standards—of belief, behaviour and value—are relative to particular human communities. Tylor's role within this 'anthropological creation story' (Stocking, 1968: 72), Stocking argues, is that of having wrested this plural and relativising view of culture from the Eurocentric and absolutist concept of culture associated with the humanist tradition which, at the time Tylor was writing, was most influentially represented by Matthew Arnold. Stocking's purpose, however, is to suggest that, when looked at more carefully, Tylor's concept of culture as a way of life is incapable of playing the founding disciplinary role which convention attributes to it. In probing more closely the relations between Tylor's concept of culture and that of Arnold, Stocking shows how Tylor's usage in fact depended upon, rather than providing an alternative to, the hierarchical and absolutist standards of judgement associated with the Arnoldian usage. Far from having leapt 'full-blown from Tylor's brow in 1871' (1968: 73), the modern relativist meaning of the anthropological concept of culture was, Stocking suggests, in fact rendered impossible by the definition Tylor proposed.

The point is now largely conceded within the history of anthropology where Franz Boas—with a good deal more plausibility, but still not without ambivalence (see Liss, 1995)—is now usually credited with responsibility for the cultural relativism which characterises contemporary anthropological practice. The question I want to ask here, however, is whether the significance that has been accorded Raymond Williams' concept of culture as a way of life within conventional accounts of cultural studies has been similarly misplaced? Is this now part of a 'cultural studies creation story' which both exaggerates the degree to which, in Williams' own work, this concept involved a break with the Arnoldian heritage just as it also obscures other pedigrees which might be claimed for this key concept of cultural studies? Is it part of a Just-So story of cultural studies which has now to be assessed as concealing more than it reveals? All of the signs required to support such a view are there. Reference to the founding role of this concept is now more or less wholly routinised within cultural studies, where it plays just as much of an honorific and ritualistic role as references to Tylor used to do within earlier histories of anthropology. This has meant that there have been few extended critical discussions of the concept within cultural studies and few, if any, attempts to provide a genealogy for the concept that would step outside or provide a counter to its accepted status as the founding concept of a new discipline (or anti-discipline). There are, then, good reasons for supposing that approaching the concept with a little more critical suspicion might yield some unexpected dividends.

My purpose here, then, is to play doubting Thomas to see if this might help in 'sniffing out' some aspects of the concept that have hitherto received little attention. In doing so, however, I have no wish to deny that Williams' concept of culture as a way of life has played a positive and enabling role in the development of cultural studies. Its value in this regard will, I trust, be evident from my earlier discussion of Williams' work in Chapter 1. What I do want to suggest is that, when considered in relation to Williams' oeuvre as a whole, that concept is far more complex—and far more fraught with contradictions and ambiguities—than conventional accounts have allowed. I shall further suggest that, when its roots are considered more closely and when the actual patterns of its use within Williams' work are carefully attended to, the concept will prove incapable of carrying the radical freight which the perceived wisdom within cultural studies has customarily attributed to it. Instead, by looking at Williams' concept of culture as a way of life in the light of Stocking's critical discussion of Tylor's 'anthropological' concept of culture, I shall suggest that the concept remains inescapably normative. My purpose in so contending, however, is not to condemn the concept for that reason. Rather, I shall argue that a strategic normativity—a term I shall define shortly—has to be regarded as an essential component of the concept of culture in enabling the study of culture to function, as Tylor envisaged it should, as a 'reformer's science' which inescapably involves difficult and sometimes intractable normative questions.

However, to come to my second set of concerns, I also want to relate my discussion of the part that the concept of culture as a way of life has played in cultural studies to the roles it has performed in the rhetorics and practices of cultural policy. A full account of its career in this regard cannot be entered into here. I shall, instead, take my bearings mainly from its influence on a number of the agenda-setting reports, statements and discussion papers issued by the Australian Commonwealth government in recent years. In 1986, the McLeay Report, *Patronage, Power and the Muse*, endorsing the view that 'cultural value is not limited to any narrow range of activities', declared its support for a broad definition of culture that would include all activities 'which involve the interpretation or perception of existence' irrespective of how those activities are socially classified and valued: whether as art, entertainment, the media or heritage (McLeay Report, 1986: 23). In the 1992 discussion paper released by the Department of Arts, Sport, Environment, Tourism and Territories (DASETT), under the title *The Role of the Commonwealth in Australia's Cultural Development*, the spirit of Raymond Williams is explicitly invoked to sustain the importance of two senses of culture—culture as intellectual and artistic activity and culture as 'a whole way of life in both its material and spiritual dimensions'—the interaction of which provides the discussion paper with its distinctive policy signature:

> The Government encourages and supports culture in its more specific sense (the practice and appreciation of music, the visual arts, literature, theatre, cinema, the preservation of our history and heritage) because of its fundamental importance to culture in a broader sense—that is, because of its importance to our whole way of life. (DASETT, 1992: 1)

Creative Nation—the cultural policy statement issued by the then Prime Minister, Paul Keating, in 1994—is more sparing in its discussion of definitional issues. Yet the influence of an anthropological view of culture is evident in the references to Australian culture as 'the work of Australians themselves through what they do in their everyday lives, as communities and as individuals (whether it be as writers, workers in industry, farmers, parents or citizens)' (DOCA, 1994: 9).

Similar definitions have informed the process of cultural policy development in post-apartheid South Africa. In its draft cultural policy, for example, the African National Congress stated:

> Arts and cultural policy deals with custom and tradition, belief, religion, language, identity, popular history, crafts, as well as all the art forms including music, theatre, dance, creative writing, the fine arts, the plastic arts, photography, film, and, in general is the sum of the results of human endeavour. (African National Congress, 1996: 1)

A similarly expansive definition is found in *All Our Legacies, All Our Futures*, the draft White Paper on arts, culture and heritage issued in June, 1996:

> *Culture* refers to the dynamic totality of distinctive spiritual, material, intellectual and emotional features which characterise a society or social group. It includes the arts and letters, but also modes of life, the fundamental rights of the human being, value systems, traditions, heritage and beliefs developed over time and subject to change. (Department of Arts, Culture, Science and Technology, 1996: 10)

The role of definitional statements of this kind is, of course, debatable. Their function is often honorific, according definitional issues their due in the first few paragraphs only to lose sight of them when coming to the more meaty business of establishing specific policy priorities or horse-trading between competing policy agendas. The degree of significance accorded them in the administrative processes through which cultural policies are put into effect may also prove highly variable. Even so, it would be a mistake to view such statements as purely discursive events with no further consequences. The cumulative weight of citation of these and related definitions in a wide range of national contexts (the policy rhetorics in the United States, Canada and the United Kingdom are very similar) has signalled and, in good measure, brought about a shift in policy priorities. Their primary role in this regard has been to extend the ambit of cultural policy in authorising a democratic expansion of the fields of activity that can be brought within its compass.

In this sense, at least at first sight, the uses to which the concept of culture as a way of life have been put within the discourses of cultural policy echo those which have characterised its usage within cultural studies. If, in the latter, its main effect has been to establish both the legitimacy and importance of studying those forms of culture which fall outside the officially valorised forms of high culture, then so its usage within cultural policy has provided a definitional means of negotiating an enlargement of the fields of cultural activity which it is thought relevant to bring together and address as parts of the same policy field. Its role, in effect, has been that of discursively managing the transition from an arts to a cultural policy framework.

So far, so good. In advocating what, at first sight, seems to be a non-hierarchical and value-neutral understanding of culture, the anthropological definition appears to bring about a democratic and egalitarian plenitude in its construction of the policy field: everything is included, and on equal terms. However, while not wishing to dispute that this is so, this is not the only or, from a cultural policy perspective, necessarily the most important work that the concept performs. Its role in securing a more even spread of funding and other forms of government support across the cultural divides of class, gender and ethnicity has, to be sure, proved crucial in weakening the policy stranglehold of elitist concepts of art. By the same token, however, this process has brought about a parallel expansion of the fields of activity which are now encompassed as objects of cultural administration. It has also done so, I suggest, in ways which are inescapably normative in the sense of effecting a governmental construction of the fields of cultural activity that are thus brought within the purview of policy to the degree that these are constructed as vehicles for in some way bringing about a reformation of habits, beliefs, values—in short, of ways of life.

To bring my two concerns together, then, I want, by considering aspects of its usage in the writings of Tylor and Williams as well as in cultural policy discourse, to take issue with the view which sees the concept of culture as 'a way of life' as an inherently even-handed one which neither accepts nor makes distinctions of value—be they political or aesthetic—between different kinds of culture. Far from being agnostic in such matters in accepting the equal value of all forms of culture, the strategic normativity which characterises the concept has meant that it has functioned to lay open the ways of life of different sections of the populace to reformist programs of government. For Robert Young, as I have noted, culture is usually thought of as opposed to something outside itself (nature, anarchy) or as itself being internally divided (high culture versus mass culture or national versus regional culture) (see Young, 1995: 29). These divisions, however, are rarely neutral. To the contrary, the splittings they propose typically result in a hierarchical ordering of the relations between different components of the cultural field, one part of which is defined as a lack, an insufficiency, a problem, while the other is viewed as offering the means of overcoming that lack, meeting the insufficiency, resolving the problem. Culture thus, so to speak, always stands on both sides of a normative divide and the work in which it is engaged consists in the movements it initiates and is caught up in across the opposing realms which that divide establishes.

It is this hierarchical ordering of the relations between different spheres of culture that results in a strategic normativity in which one component of the cultural field is strategically mobilised in relation to another as offering the means of overcoming whatever shortcomings (moral, political or aesthetic) are attributed to the latter. This results in the establishment of a normative gradient down which the flow of culture is directed in reformist programs through which cultural resources are brought to bear on whatever might be the task to hand: improving the morals and manners of the workingman; civilising the 'savage'; empowering communities; promoting cultural diversity; or, in the case of Williams' own writings, eradicating the corroding effects of capitalist individualism by mobilising the virtues of working-class community. It is, moreover, through the interiorisation of such normative gradients that reformist programs are able to be translated into techniques of cultural self-management through the organisation of a culturally stratified self in which one level is pitted against another in an unending process of self-inspection and self-reform.[1]

This, at any rate, is the view I want to develop in showing how these normative aspects of the concept have supplied the discursive coordinates for the functioning of culture—understood as an historically specific system—as a means of acting on the social. My purpose in so arguing, however, is not to engage in a recondite exercise in the history of ideas for its own sake. To the contrary, the purpose of my archaeological excavations will be, in recovering the normative aspect of the concept of culture as a way of life, to argue for its retention in view of its capacity to lend a degree of definitional coherence to the concerns of cultural policy studies in proposing a way of understanding the concept of culture that can both, as the anthropological usage proposes, span an expanded range of cultural activities, as well as including the arts of governing that are applied to them. To put the point another way: my purpose is to detach the concept of culture as a way of life from the resistive credentials it has accumulated through its use within cultural studies and to attach it to ones which accentuate both the governmental component which inevitably enters into the constitution of the cultural field and the reformist disposition which this brings with it.

CULTURE, PERFECTIBILITY AND REFORM

Let me look first a little more closely at the early history of the concept. Williams, its most influential contemporary advocate, argues, in *Keywords*, that the concept of culture as 'a particular way of life, whether of a people, a period or a group' was 'decisively introduced into English' by Tylor in his 1871 text *Primitive Culture*.[2] Here is how Tylor introduces the concept in the opening sentence of that book:

> Culture or Civilisation, taken in its wide ethnographic sense, is that complex whole which includes knowledge, belief, art, morals, law, custom, and any other capabilities and habits acquired by man as a member of society. (Tylor, 1874: 1)

In grouping art together with morals, law and customs rather than separating it out as a special realm invested with a unique value and significance, and in proposing that all of these activities be considered from the point of view of their role in the formation of particular capabilities and habits, this definition would indeed seem to be quite radically relativistic in its implications. This impression is a misleading one. Stocking argues that, in the stress he places on *culture*, in the singular, and in proposing culture as a synonym for the concept of civilisation, Tylor remained very much under the influence of hierarchical conceptions of culture. Far from offering a criticism of, or alternative to, aesthetic definitions of culture, Tylor put these to work within an evolutionary problematic. In grafting the Arnoldian conception of culture as 'a conscious striving toward progress or perfection' (Stocking, 1968: 84) on to an evolutionary conception of social development, Stocking argues, Tylor attributed a unity to culture as the overall evolutionary process through which human capacities are developed. From this perspective, far from according equal value to the cultures of different social groups or societies, Tylor's concern was to rank them in an evolutionary hierarchy. 'When he spoke of "the culture" of a group . . .,' as Stocking puts it, 'it is clear that in almost every instance that he meant "the culture-*stage*" or the "*degree* of culture" of that group' (1968: 81).

Not surprisingly, the evolutionary ranking of cultures that Tylor proposed was markedly Eurocentric. By the second chapter of *Primitive Culture*, any appearance of cultural relativism is abandoned when Tylor asks whether, amidst all the evidence of cultural variability between different societies, it might be possible to rank different cultures in a hierarchy of development. From his perspective as an English gentleman, he has little difficulty in determining how this might be done:

> The educated world of Europe and America practically settles a standard by simply placing its own nations at one end of the social series and savage tribes at the other, arranging the rest of mankind between these limits according [sic] as they correspond more closely to savage or to cultured life. (Tylor, 1874: 26)

Although Tylor rehearses a number of possible theoretical objections to this position, he is eventually driven to the conclusion that this practical resolution of the matter is not far off the mark. My interest here, however, is less concerned with Tylor's Eurocentrism *per se* than with the role which this plays in allowing him to hitch the reforming mechanism that is at the heart of Arnold's concept of culture to the assumptions of progressive social evolutionism. For Arnold, the proper business of the study of culture consisted in identifying ideal norms of human perfection and, in holding these up as ideals to be emulated, encouraging individuals to adjust their behaviour so as to conform more closely to those norms. 'But culture indefatigably tries,' Arnold says in his 1882 text *Culture and Anarchy*, 'not to make what each raw person may like, the rule by which he fashions himself; but to draw ever nearer to a sense of what is indeed beautiful, graceful, and becoming, and to get the raw person to like that.' (Arnold, 1971: 39) Stocking suggests that a similar reforming mechanism is at work in Tylor, but with the important difference that it is articulated to historical and evolutionary rather than to aesthetic norms of human perfection. This mechanism, Stocking suggests, is made especially clear when Tylor argues that the primary practical purpose to be served by the study of culture consists in the role that such analysis can play in aiding the evolutionary tendencies of social development so as to help mankind raise itself to progressively higher levels of culture and civilisation. It is on this note that Tylor concludes his study by suggesting that the study of culture should be regarded as 'a reformer's science' in view of the fact that its role is 'to expose the remains of the old crude culture which have passed into harmful superstition, and to mark these out for destruction' and so be 'active at once in aiding progress and in removing hindrance' (Tylor, 1874: 410).

If, then, as Williams argues, it is indeed with Tylor that the concept of culture as a way of life first enters into English, that moment is characterised by a strategic normativity inscribed in the heart of the concept through which particular ways of life—of colonised peoples, of the working classes—were constructed as the objects of reformist governmental programs: reformist in the sense that they aimed to bring about regulated transformations in the ways of life to which they were applied. 'One might say,' Stocking notes of Tylor, 'that he made Matthew Arnold's culture evolutionary', and he goes on to add that to 'do so was no small contribution' (Stocking, 1968: 87). It also proved to be a lasting contribution, one which has remained tangled up with the subsequent usage of the concept, and nowhere more clearly so than in Williams' own work. In most available accounts, Williams' use of the concept of culture as a way of life is said to have ended the stranglehold of the Arnoldian or selective definition of culture in according an equal value and significance to the cultural beliefs and practices which make up the everyday life of all social groups and classes. In his first extended discussion of the term in *The Long Revolution*, however, Williams does not so much replace the Arnoldian definition of culture with the anthropological one as insert the latter within an historicised variant of the former. For the function Williams attributes to the anthropological (or, as he calls it, the social) definition of culture is determined by the way he situates that definition within a social evolutionary version of the view that culture constitutes a norm of human perfection.

Throughout his discussion, it is culture as a whole that Williams is concerned with and, although he argues that the concept can be broken down into three general categories, it is the patterns of interaction between these that most engage his attention. He begins with the 'ideal' definition of culture which, after Matthew Arnold, he summarises as 'a state or process of human perfection, in terms of certain absolute or universal values'. He then introduces the documentary definition of culture as one in which culture is viewed as 'the body of intellectual and imaginative work, in which, in a detailed way, human thought and experience are variously recorded'. It is only then that he introduces 'the "social" definition of culture, in which culture is a description of a particular way of life, which expresses certain meanings and values not only in art and learning but also in institutions and ordinary behaviour' (Williams, 1965: 57). In no way, however, does Williams suggest that this social definition of culture should displace the documentary or ideal definitions. To the contrary, he insists that each definition has its value and that each has a role to play in the analysis of culture as a whole. This is made clear when he discusses how the ways of life which are brought under the anthropological or social definition of culture might be studied and the purpose to be served by their analysis:

> Again, such analysis ranges from an 'ideal' emphasis, the discovery of certain absolute or universal, or at least higher and lower, meanings and values, through the 'documentary' emphasis, in which clarification of a particular way of life is the main end in view, to an emphasis which, from studying particular meanings and values, seeks not so much to compare these, as a way of establishing a scale, but by discovering their modes of change to discover certain general 'laws' or 'trends', by which social and cultural development as a whole can be better understood. (1965: 58)

Aware of the difficult ground he is treading here, Williams is careful to distance himself from the view that the process of social and cultural development can be equated with the development and realisation of absolute values of human perfection. Recognising that such values are relative to place and to time, he suggests that the process of social and cultural development needs to be thought of not as 'human perfection, which implies a known ideal towards which we can move, but human evolution, to mean a process of general growth of man as a kind' (1965: 59). In doing so, however, he gets out of bed with Arnold only to get back into it again with Tylor. For the role which he proposes for cultural analysis is that of identifying those meanings and values which, although 'discovered in particular societies and by particular individuals, and kept alive by social inheritance and by embodiment in particular kinds of work, have proved to be universal in the sense that when they are learned, in any particular situation, they can contribute radically to the growth of man's powers to enrich his life, to regulate his society, and to control his environment' (1965: 59). As with Tylor, a dialectic of culture, perfectibility and reform is inscribed at the heart of Williams' understanding of the purpose of cultural analysis as that of helping to identify those cultural tendencies and processes which ought to be nourished and encouraged from the point of view of their capacity to contribute to the 'general growth of man as a whole' (1965: 59).

This remains true of Williams' later work: a very similar, but not identical, dialectic animates his depiction of the relations between what he calls dominant, residual and emergent forms of culture and of the parts these play in his account of the mechanisms of cultural development. The procedures Williams deploys in defining these terms, and the kinds of differentiations he seeks to establish by their use bear a striking resemblance to the terms used by Tylor to identify which forms of culture contribute to, or stand in the way of, the progressive evolution of culture as a whole. When, in *Marxism and Literature*, Williams introduces the concept of residual cultures, he does so by distinguishing the residual from the archaic. Although both are remnants of earlier phases of cultural development, Williams sees their relations to contemporary cultural processes as being essentially different to the degree that the archaic is seen as being wholly disconnected from the active culture of the present where its existence, if any, assumes increasingly artificial and contrived forms:

> I would call the 'archaic' that which is wholly recognised as an element of the past, to be observed, to be examined, or even on occasion to be consciously 'revived', in a deliberately specialising way. What I mean by the 'residual' is very different. The residual, by definition, has been

> effectively formed in the past, but is still active in the cultural process, not only and often not at all as an element of the past, but as an effective element of the present. (Williams, 1977: 122)

The distinction is structurally the same as that which Tylor proposes between survivals and revivals. By revivals, he has in mind 'old thoughts and practices' which sometimes 'burst out afresh, to the amazement of a world that thought them long since dead or dying' (Tylor, 1874: 16–17). If this echoes Williams' concept of the archaic, what Tylor means by survivals is close to Williams' concept of the residual. He defines the term as follows:

> These are processes, customs, opinions, and so forth, which have been carried on by force of habit into a new state of society different from that in which they had their original home, and they thus remain as proofs and examples of an older condition of culture out of which a newer has been evolved. (1874: 16)

Revivals, like the archaic for Williams, comprise cultural forms and practices which, having fallen into disuse, are subsequently reactivated in a consciously imitative way.[3] As such, their cultural impetus derives solely from the present rather than from any tradition of effective cultural continuity linking past and present in a seamless line of development. Survivals, by contrast, are like Williams' residual culture to the degree that both comprise forms and practices which have been carried on from the past into the present as parts of continuing and active cultural traditions. There is, however, an equally important difference between the two. In Tylor's case, it is 'force of habit' or cultural inertia which accounts for the continuing existence of survivals.[4] As such, survivals attest to the existence of what are essentially two discontinuous cultural times within the present—the time of the primitive and that of modernity—while at the same time realigning those times into a singular time in the construction of survivals as being, finally, ripe for demolition now that they have connected with modernity. For Williams, by contrast, the residual refers to traditions and practices which have had a continuing active existence within the same culture rather than to customs which have survived from one cultural time (the primitive) to allow for their discovery and annexation by another.

There are also important differences in the analytical perspectives from which these two sets of definitional contrasts are approached. For Tylor, the concept of survivals allowed the cultures of colonised peoples—savages, he called them—to be treated as a form of past in the present, as 'survivals' of prehistoric forms of life which had elsewhere been obliterated by the progress of civilisation, which could then be interpreted as evidence of what the past of European human prehistory must have been like. The concept thus allowed cultures existing in the present to be interpreted as both a past that had survived into the present unmodified from an earlier age and as a means of imaginatively reconstructing other pasts. Such cultures, of course, also represented a past in the present that, through colonial projects of improvement, needed to be removed—that is, to be effectively assigned to the past as past—to the degree that they constituted an impediment to the advance of progress. This, as we have seen, was the political sting—and it has proved a long and effective one—informing Tylor's concept of culture as a reformer's science.

For Williams, by contrast, the concept of residual cultures serves the purpose of identifying sources and resources of cultural innovation that can help to push and prod a culture beyond the ossifying grip of what is, at any particular point in time, its dominant mode. To understand the historical dynamism of a culture, Williams argues, it is necessary to realise that the composition of any culture is always marked by a tension between the different temporalities of its constituent elements. The hegemony of the dominant culture can, Williams suggests, be partly undone from the perspective of the residual or the emergent—from the point of view, that is, of a time which precedes it or of a time which goes beyond it—since each rests on a creative force—an ascendant social class in the case of emergent cultures; a once influential but now declining force in the case of residual cultures—which can have an alternative or even oppositional relation to the dominant culture. Yet, in all of this, the task of identifying the truly residual and the genuinely emergent remains a difficult one, since not all forms of culture which seem to fall outside the temporality of the dominant culture actually do so.

The truly residual, Williams thus argues, embodies 'certain experiences, meanings, and values which cannot be expressed or substantially verified in terms of the dominant culture' but which 'are nevertheless lived and practised on the basis of the residue . . . of some previous social and cultural institution or formation.' (1977: 122) However, this is not to be confused with those imposter forms of the residual—the archaic—whose distinction from the genuinely residual consists in the fact that they have been 'wholly or largely incorporated into the dominant culture' (1977: 122). The distinction between different versions of community illustrates the point Williams is trying to make here:

> Again, the idea of rural community is predominantly residual, but is in some limited respects alternative or oppositional to urban industrial capitalism, though for the most part is incorporated, as idealisation or fantasy, or as an exotic—residential or escape—leisure function of the dominant order itself. (1977: 122)

Similarly, the genuinely emergent is not to be confused with the novel, since this reflects simply the spur to the production of new cultural product that is inherent in the dominant forms of capitalist cultural production rather than any creative force capable of leading beyond the dominant culture. It is, as Williams puts it, 'exceptionally difficult to distinguish' between those new values, practices and relationships 'which are really elements of some new phase of the dominant culture (and in this sense "species specific") and those which are substantially alternative or oppositional to it: emergent in the strict sense, rather than merely novel' (1977: 123). It is so difficult, in fact, that the task has to be redefined. Emergent culture, before it is detectable as such, has to pass through a twilight zone before it achieves adequate and recognisable forms of expression. In such cases 'what we have to observe is in effect a *pre*-emergence, active and pressing but not yet fully articulated, rather than the evident emergence which could be more confidently named' (1977: 126). The emergent, in this sense, is an embryonic new structure of feeling in the phase before it has crystallised into a form that allows it to be named: it is the ineffable, unsayable, unsorted complexity of a new form of '*presence*' which, even though it cannot yet be classified, exerts 'palpable pressures' and sets 'effective limits on experience and on action' (1977: 132).[5]

Tylor, of course, had no need of a concept of emergent culture in order to identify mechanisms that would keep the processes of cultural development on the go by unfixing the ossifications of the dominant culture since, for him, writing from a self-confident bourgeois and colonial perspective, the dominant culture was itself inherently dynamic. Nonetheless, he did face the same problem as Williams in needing to distinguish the different ways in which past forms of culture continue to exist in the present. Indeed, his task here was more complex than Williams'. For whereas Williams needed only to distinguish the residual from the archaic, the late nineteenth century currency of degenerationist conceptions meant that the Tylorean reformer had to sift the signs of his times more carefully in order to distinguish between true survivals, cultural revivals and cultural degenerations if he were to discern where and how the evolution of culture as a whole were to be aided and assisted by correctly identifying its different temporal trajectories. This is clear in his sharp remarks on the slack reasoning that placed the dangerous classes of London and Oceanic or African savagery in the same category:

> If we have to strike a balance between the Papuans of New Caledonia and the communities of European beggars and thieves, we may sadly acknowledge that we have in our midst something worse than savagery. But it is not savagery; it is broken down civilisation. Negatively, the inmates of a Whitechapel casualty ward and of a Hottentot kraal agree in their want of the knowledge and virtue of the higher culture. But positively, their mental and moral characteristics are utterly different. Thus, the savage life is essentially devoted to gaining subsistence from nature, which is just what the proletarian life is not. Their relations to civilised life—the one of independence, the other of dependence—are absolutely opposite. To my mind the popular phrases about 'city savages' and 'street Arabs' seem like comparing a ruined house to a builder's yard. (1874: 42–43)

To juxtapose Williams' comments on the relations between the dominant, residual and emergent elements of a culture with Tylor's comments on the differences between the dangerous classes and primitive savagery in this way might seem wilfully provocative. That is not my intention. The differences in the cultural and political perspectives which motivate their respective analyses are clear enough to require no further comment. Yet this should not prevent us from recognising the homology between the structure of the categories that each uses and the striking similarity of the intellectual procedures which this involves. For both Williams and Tylor, the concept of culture forms part of an account of a general process of human growth and development; for both of them, a necessary part of cultural analysis consists in the identification of those particular forms of culture which contribute to or impede this general process. This involves, in both cases, the development of a set of concepts whose function is to account for the process of cultural development by construing this as the result of a complex pattern of interaction between cultural elements belonging to and marked by different temporalities; and for both, finally, this involves the application of a particular normative grid through which some ways of life were to be actively developed and supported while others were marked for passage into history. Both were reformers working with an essentially similar reforming apparatus. Where they differ has to do mainly with the modernist narratives within which that apparatus was set and put to work: a relatively straightforward evolutionism in the case of Tylor and Williams' more complex account of history as the unfolding of the aesthetic and moral conditions for a common culture.

When *The Long Revolution* was first published, E.P. Thompson wrote a long review of the book for *New Left Review*. The gist of Thompson's argument (I have since been unable to obtain a copy to verify its details) was that Williams had gone into the heart of enemy territory in seizing the concept of culture from the monopolistic clutch of the likes of Arnold and Eliot and so redefining it that it could serve as the basis for a new intellectual and political project. This, as we have seen, is also the status it has been accorded within cultural studies. Now that the dust has settled a bit, however, a more cautious verdict might be in order. Indeed, if there is any merit to my analysis, we might rather have to see Williams' approach to culture as a complex combination of a range of nineteenth century traditions in which an Arnoldian aesthetic is mixed with elements of a Tylorian evolutionism within the context of a Marxist historicism.

A FIELD OF GOVERNMENT

There are, then, reasons for doubting that, when we speak of culture as a way of life, we are taking our stand on clear and firm relativist ground. This is not to suggest that the concept of culture as a way of life must somehow always bring with it the spirit of Arnold or, perhaps worse, the imprint of Tylor's evolutionism or even the organic wholeness of Williams' conception of the historical overcoming of social divisions as a condition for the creation of a common culture. My contention, rather, is that, even if these particular normative paradigms fall away, the concept nonetheless remains caught up in and helps to constitute a normative grid through which the areas of social life to which it is applied are constructed as objects and practices to be acted upon. This is no less true of the usage of the concept within contemporary discourses of cultural policy than it is of the role it plays in the work of Tylor and Williams. For while, on the one hand, such uses have democratically extended the range of activities which might qualify for support under the heading of culture, this same process has enlarged the range of activities which are brought into the sphere of culture as a field of government and which, as such, are laid open to reforming administrative programs. Such programs are now very rarely universalist ones of the kind associated with Arnold and Tylor, whose long historical reach still held Williams in its pincer grip. Indeed, the kinds of reformist objectives which characterise contemporary forms of cultural policy are more typically orientated toward detaching the administration of cultural life from the universalist reforming agendas of these earlier, nineteenth century positions. Even so, culture—in its broad sense, as ways of life, customs, morals, and habits—remains caught in—constituted and defined by—a reforming apparatus whose structure remains unaltered.

A brief consideration of Zygmunt Bauman's essay 'Legislators and interpreters: Culture as the ideology of intellectuals' will help make the point I am after here, even though the position Bauman ends up advocating is sharply different from the one I am proposing. For Bauman, in an argument that is rich in historical insight, the reforming disposition inherent within the extended definition of culture was closely tied up with the narratives of modernism. It was, he suggests, a disposition which gave rise to a legislative orientation to culture in which all those forms of life which seemed immature, backward, imperfect, primitive, vulgar, or merely local and limited from the perspective of the grand narratives of modernism could be reformed or legislated out of existence. In his own words:

> The intellectual ideology of culture was launched as a militant, uncompromising and self-confident manifesto of universally binding principles of social organisation and individual conduct. It expressed not only the exuberant administrative vigour of the time, but also a resounding certainty as to the direction of anticipated social change. Indeed, forms of life conceived as obstacles to change and thus condemned to destruction had been relativised; the form of life that was called to replace them was seen, however, as universal, inscribed in the essence and the destination of the human species as a whole. (Bauman, 1992: 11)

If, then, the narratives of modernism and the reforming programs these engendered typically placed the intellectual in the position of a legislator, Bauman argues that the more pluralised and relativised normative environment of postmodernism has transformed the intellectual into an interpreter. 'Without universal standards,' he argues in another essay, 'the problem of the postmodern world is not how to globalise superior culture, but how to secure communication and mutual understanding between cultures' (1992: 102).

I have few problems with this formulation or the many like it—in the writings of James Clifford (1988) and of Mary Louise Pratt (1992) on the subject of transculturation, for example—which now enjoin tolerance of diversity and cross-cultural understanding as the primary cultural challenge of our time. However, it is when Bauman goes on to speak of culture now as 'a spontaneous process devoid of administrative or managerial centres' and to argue that 'from the perspective of the present-day intellectuals, culture does not appear as something to be "made" or "remade" as an object for practice; it is indeed a reality in its own right and beyond control, an object for study, something to be mastered only cognitively, as a meaning, and not practically, as a task' (1992: 23) that I think he goes astray. What this neglects are the respects in which securing 'communication and mutual understanding between cultures' is not, and cannot be, merely an interpretative matter. To the contrary, while notions of 'mastery' can easily be dispensed with, such objectives remain dependent on precisely that reforming or legislative orientation to culture that Bauman would forgo in order to secure the institutional spaces and organisational frameworks within which the mutual interpretation of cultures he advocates can take place. At least this is so if the processes of communication and mutual understanding he has in mind are to involve and concern the majority of the population rather than just the cloistered exchanges of the seminar.

There could be few illusions in present-day Australia, for example, that the development of appropriately respectful and tolerant relations of cross-cultural understanding between white and indigenous Australians is presented to us precisely as a task to be accomplished and one requiring the development of its own distinctive forms of management and administration. Legislative mechanisms allowing the repatriation of cultural materials to indigenous custody; training programs to provide museums, art galleries and libraries with indigenous staff who can be responsible for managing their indigenous collections; liaison mechanisms to connect the work of such staff to input and direction from indigenous communities; training programs for indigenous film-makers and broadcasters; training for white cultural workers regarding the appropriate protocols to be observed in relationships with indigenous communities; special legal protocols for negotiating the relationships between Australian systems of intellectual property and Aboriginal customary law; the different rules that white cultural workers have to learn regarding the relationships between photography and the image that obtain within Aboriginal culture; the development of agreed conventions regarding the depiction of indigenous Australians on film and television; the provision of special systems and guides for managing the relationships between tourists and Aboriginal sacred sites; setting limits to inter-cultural communication through special provisions for the maintenance of indigenous rights to secrecy; rules for managing the past in regulating the relationships between archaeologists and indigenous communities insofar as these concern burial and sacred sites: in all of these ways, the process of recognising where cultural values differ and then of promoting forms of exchange between them that have the mutual support of both parties has presented itself, and still does, as, among other things, a task of cultural management which requires a degree of administrative inventiveness and an utterly sedulous attention to questions of administrative detail that would have been well beyond the reach of Bauman's nineteenth century cultural legislators.[6] The same is true of multicultural policies. The development of programs of cultural maintenance for non-English-speaking Australians and the promotion, on the part of mainstream Australia, of respect and tolerance for the cultural diversity of Australia's multi-ethnic communities depend, in good measure, on a range of programs that are concerned explicitly with managing cultural resources in ways calculated to achieve these outcomes: guidelines to correct the Anglophone bias of collecting institutions to make sure that their collections represent the true cultural diversity and multilingual composition of Australia; the multicultural charter of Special Broadcasting Services; and the development of multicultural guidelines for school curricula, for example.[7] To cite these various administrative and policy mechanisms is, of course, no reason to be complacent regarding their actual outcomes. There is still a good way to go before satisfactory frameworks, customs and procedures will have been devised that will prove capable of managing the complex and highly different forms of cultural diversity which characterise the relations between the Anglo-Celtic, multicultural and indigenous populations of Australia. Moreover, as the race debate unleashed in the aftermath of the 1996 election has shown, there is a good deal further still to go before an acceptance of such goals will be firmly secured in 'mainstream' Australia. My point, however, is that the forms of cross-cultural communication and understanding Bauman advocates are wholly unachievable without the kinds of cultural management and administration he disparages. In doing so, to recall a phrase of Adorno's, he forgets himself out of sheer open-mindedness—mainly, I suspect, because, like most postmodernists, he sees history setting out on a new chapter even when, objectively speaking, it may have only turned a page.

For in all of the programs I have summarised—and there are similar ones in most countries—the management of cultural resources in ways intended to reform ways of life remains very much a part of the active politics and policy of culture in contemporary societies. This might, in some cases, as with cultural maintenance programs, for example, involve developing and extending existing patterns of thought, feeling and behaviour. In other cases—racist beliefs and colonial practices, for example—it might involve targeting particular ways of life for transformation and their replacement by new ones. In either case, a normative mechanism remains at the heart of what is still a reforming endeavour. Indeed, we might, paraphrasing Arnold, say that culture still indefatigably tries not to make what each raw person may like, the rule by which they fashion themselves; but to draw ever nearer to a sense of what is indeed a liberal, plural, multicultural, non-sexist tolerance of diversity and to get the raw person to like this. The objectives, of course, are different, but the mechanism remains very much the same.

That mechanism, moreover, remains dependent upon—indeed, is inscribed within—the normative structure of the concept of culture that has been bequeathed to us by Arnold and Tylor and which, through a complex process of inheritance, has entered into contemporary policy discourse via the work of Williams. *Our Creative Diversity*, the recent report of the World Commission on Culture and Development, offers clear and compelling confirmation that this is so. Following the lead of *Creative Nation* in its assertion that culture 'encompasses our entire mode of life, our ethics, our institutions, our manners and our routines, not only interpreting our world but shaping it' (cited in World Commission, 1995: 233), *Our Creative Diversity* proposes to expand 'the concept of cultural policy from a narrow focus on the arts' and suggests instead that it 'should be directed at encouraging multi-cultural activities' (1995: 18). Here, then, in the promotion of creative diversity in our ways of life, is a reformist program for cultural policy that is wholly at odds with the universalist aspirations of Tylor and other advocates of nineteenth century modernist programs of civilisation. Yet the mechanism on which this program depends is exactly the same as that proposed by Tylor in that it rests on a normative splitting of culture into two spheres and the organisation of a hierarchical gradient between the two to specify the directions in which the reforming impetus of culture must flow. The splitting, in this case, takes the form of a division between tolerant and intolerant cultures which identifies which cultural values and ways of life are to be allotted a reforming role in both national and transnational cultural policies and which ways of life are to be targeted as objects of reform:

> the need for people to live and work together peacefully should result in respect for all cultures, or at least for those cultures that value tolerance and respect for others. There are some cultures that may not be worthy of respect because they themselves have been shown to be intolerant, exclusive, exploitative, cruel and repressive. Whatever we may be told about the importance of 'not interfering with local customs', such repulsive practices, whether aimed at people from different cultures or at other members of the same culture, should be condemned, not tolerated . . .
>
> But for the rest, more than tolerance for other cultures is required. We should rejoice at cultural differences and attempt to learn from them, not to regard them as alien, unacceptable or hateful. Governments cannot prescribe such attitudes and behaviour as respect and rejoicing, but they

> can prohibit attacks on people from different cultures and their practices and they can set the legal stage for mutual tolerance and accommodation. They can outlaw some of the outward manifestations of xenophobia and racism. (1995: 54)

The values espoused here are significantly different from those endorsed by Tylor in terms of their content. But the functioning of culture as a reforming apparatus remains the same. Like Tylor, the World Commission on Culture and Development is concerned to mark out for destruction the remains of those older cultures which stand in the way of cultural development. The only difference—although, of course, it is a crucial one—concerns the content of the norms which animate this reforming apparatus: a shift from a view of cultural development which sought to erase cultural diversity to one dedicated to (within limits) the promotion and celebration of diversity.

If, then, culture is a reformer's science, it is hardly an exact one and it is certainly not neutral. The content of the norms which are to animate the machineries of cultural reform and so specify the logic and direction of their functioning is a matter for contestation. There are no absolutes here, no matter how often they might be asserted. In its splitting of the sphere of culture into two along the axis tolerance–intolerance, the World Commission on Culture and Development piously universalises its condemnation of intolerance in the name of 'absolute standards of judging what is right, good and true' (1995: 55). Real life is more complicated, consisting in the political interplay between different constructions of the right, the good and the true. The particular kinds of strategic normativity that will characterise particular programs of cultural reform will depend, essentially, on how these interplays between the spheres of culture and politics are conducted.

My concern here, however, has been a more limited one. Policy, like the terms administration and management, some have argued, is alien to culture. My purpose, to the contrary, has been to suggest that it is central to its constitution; and that—quite in spite of its appearances to the contrary—the historical role played by the anthropological definition of culture has been that of extending the cultural reach of the arts of governing. This should not be a matter for regret. To the contrary, it is precisely this junction of the fields of culture, policy and administration which constitutes, so to speak, our inheritance and provides the conditions for our activities as intellectuals (whether as theorists, policy-makers or administrators) in the cultural sphere.

5 The multiplication of culture's utility

In his *Principles of Museum Administration*, published in 1895, George Brown Goode, Director of the U.S. National Museum at the Smithsonian Institution, argued that the furtherance of what he referred to as 'the . . . Museum idea' would be inseparable from the museum's ongoing association:

> with the continuance of modern civilisation, by means of which those sources of enjoyment which were formerly accessible to the rich only, are now, more and more, placed in the possession and ownership of all the people (an adaptation of what Jevons has called 'the principle of the multiplication of utility'), with the result that objects which were formerly accessible only to the wealthy, and seen by a very small number of people each year, are now held in common ownership and enjoyed by hundreds of thousands. (Goode, 1895: 72)

In thus proposing a program for the museum's future development, Goode also provided that program with a philosophical anchorage in that tradition of radical social reform which had its roots in English utilitarianism.

He thus attributed the authorship of 'the . . . Museum idea'—in brief, the view that museums should serve as instruments of public instruction—to Sir Henry Cole. Closely associated with the Philosophical Radicals, and personally acquainted with John Stuart Mill, Cole was well versed in the principles of Benthamism and, through his roles as architect of the Great Exhibition, founder of the South Kensington Museum and the first effective head of the Department of Art and Science, he sought strenuously to put these principles into practical effect.[1] For Cole, the primary guiding principle of government policy in the spheres of art and education was to enhance the usefulness of culture by multiplying the circuits through which its objects and practices might be distributed and hence to increase, without limits or restrictions, the public benefit which might be derived from their extended circulation.

The Jevons to whom Goode referred is William Stanley Jevons, author of *The Theory of Political Economy*, who, in first propounding the theory of marginal utility, played a significant role in putting David Ricardo's theories to rest in favour of the emerging orthodoxies of neo-classical economics.[2] However, if Jevons' theory of marginal utility provided a more precise and progressive way of making Bentham's hedonic calculus operational, his purview was not limited to the distributional arrangements which might result from the egoistical calculations of utility of individuals in the marketplace (White, 1992a).[3] There might also be areas of social life where, for social, political or moral reasons, calculations of a public utility might be made and asserted in face of those arising from the play of market forces. The public ownership of cultural resources as a means of securing what he referred to as 'the vulgarisation of pleasures' was, for Jevons, a case in point. Here is the passage from the 1883 text *Methods of Social Reform* in which Jevons introduced the principle of the multiplication of utility to which Goode referred:

> The main *raison d'être* of Free Public Libraries, as indeed of public museums, art-galleries, parks, halls, public clocks, and many other kinds of public works, is the enormous increase of utility which is thereby acquired for the community at a trifling cost. If a beautiful picture be hung in the dining-room of a private house, it may perhaps be gazed at by a few guests a score or two of times in the year. Its real utility is too often that of ministering to the selfish pride of its owner. If it be hung in the National Gallery, it will be enjoyed by hundreds of thousands of persons, whose glances, it need hardly be said, do not tend to wear out the canvas. The same principle applies to books in common ownership. If a man possesses a library of a few thousand volumes, by far the greater part of them must lie for years untouched upon the shelves; he cannot possibly use more than a fraction of the whole in any one year. But a library of five or ten thousand volumes opened free to the population of a town may be used a thousand times as much. It is a striking case of what I propose to call *the principle of the multiplication of utility*. (Jevons, 1965: 28–29)

Goode's reference to 'the Museum idea' establishes a link not merely to Cole and Jevons—both of whom he names—but also to Sir James Kay-Shuttleworth, the prominent public servant whose work, in spanning diverse fields of nineteenth century public administration, stood, as Mitchell Dean puts it, 'at the intersection of the "statistical" idea with the "educational" idea and the "sanitary" idea' (Dean, 1991: 204). That the term 'the Museum idea' was understood as a shorthand expression for the view that museums and other cultural institutions should serve as instruments of public instruction suggests that this view of museums and their function was seen as belonging to the same class as the educational, statistical and sanitary programs associated with the work of Kay-Shuttleworth. Nor is this wholly surprising: the relations between museums and education are discernible readily enough. But what are we to make of an equation that places museums side by side with programs of public sanitation?

Let me come at the question from a different tack by considering the institutional series in which, today, museums are typically placed. Ivan Karp draws on Gramsci's distinction between civil society and political society for this purpose. If for Gramsci, Karp writes, 'the institutions of political society exercise coercion and control, while civil society creates hegemony through the production of cultural and moral systems that legitimate the existing social order' (Karp, 1992: 4), then Karp is in no doubt that museums belong wholly within the field of civil society. Museums, he says, might be run by local, state or national governments, but 'they remain agents of civil society' and, as such, 'as places for defining who people are and how they should act and as places for challenging those definitions . . . [They] can be thought about separately from the agencies of government specifically charged with social control, such as the police and the courts' (1992: 4).

Well, so it might seem today. In the nineteenth century, however, the most ardent advocates of public museums, free libraries and the like typically spoke of them in connection with courts, prisons, poor-houses and, more mundanely, the provision of public sanitation and fresh water. For Jevons, free libraries were merely one among many engines 'for operating upon the poorer portions of the population' and, as such, could be compared with the post office savings bank as 'an engine for teaching thrift', as well as being 'classed with town-halls, police-courts, prisons, and poor-houses as necessary adjuncts of our stage of civilisation' (Jevons, 1965: 32, 28). Thomas Greenwood, writing in 1888, similarly placed public museums and free libraries alongside the provision of police forces and street cleansing arrangements as indices of the degree of self-reliance shown by the citizenry of Britain's main municipalities. Those municipalities in which 'the most has been done for the education of the people, either in the way of Board Schools, Museums, or Free Libraries', he noted, are also those with 'the best street lighting and street cleansing arrangements' as well as being the ones in which 'the Police Force are under the most perfect control' (Greenwood, 1888: 18).

What are we to make of this? In what follows, I shall try to throw some light on this question by considering the concern to multiply culture's utility in the light of the endeavour to make populations self-regulating that was associated with the development of liberal forms of government. By 'liberal' here I do not have in mind the philosophical or political party meaning of the term. Rather, following Foucault, I refer to the development of new forms of social management and regulation which, predicated on the supposition that the citizen possesses a degree of freedom and autonomy (and thus is a citizen and not a subject), aim to 'govern at a distance' by creating frameworks in which individuals will voluntarily regulate their own behaviour to achieve specific social ends rather than needing to be subjected to forced direction. My purpose will be to uncover the grid of relations which made it intelligible to suppose that the development of new capillary systems for the distribution of culture would help cultivate a capacity for voluntary self-regulation in the general population.

CULTURE'S CIVILISING EFFECT

Let me go back to Jevons again. For while he wanted the circuits through which culture was distributed to be significantly expanded, he was also concerned that institutions provided with a view to maximising culture's utility might be misused. Perhaps even more worrying, however, was the difficulty of establishing whether or not this was so:

> At the South Kensington Art Museum they make a great point of setting up turnstiles to record the precise numbers of visitors, and they can tell you to a unit the exact amount of civilising effect produced in any day, week, month, or year. But these turnstiles hardly take account of the fact that the neighbouring wealthy residents are in the habit, on a wet day, of packing their children off in a cab to the so-called Brompton Boilers, in order that they may have a good run through the galleries. (Jevons 1965: 55–56)

Concerns of this kind regarding how these new engines of public instruction might be used or abused were endemic.[4] The most extended instance of such complaints I have come across came from Thomas Unwins, Keeper of the National Gallery, in the evidence which—somewhat incredulously—he gave to an 1850 parliamentary committee appointed to inquire into the Gallery's operations. Asked whether the crowds who were attracted into the Gallery in inclement weather might have been tempted indoors 'without reference to seeing pictures of high art', Unwins replied:

> Scarcely a day passes that I do not visit the Gallery myself, and I have observed a great many things which show that many persons who come, do not come really to see the pictures. On one occasion, I saw a school of boys, imagine 20, taking their satchels from their backs with their bread and cheese, sitting down and making themselves very comfortable, and eating their luncheon . . . On another occasion, I saw some people, who seemed to be country people, who had a basket of provisions, and who drew their chairs round and sat down, and seemed to make themselves very comfortable; they had meat and drink; and when I suggested to them the impropriety of such a proceeding in such a place, they were very good-humoured, and a lady offered me a glass of gin, and wished me to partake of what they provided; I represented to them that those things could not be tolerated . . . On another occasion, I witnessed what appeared to me to evidence anything but a desire to see the pictures; a man and a woman had got their child, teaching it its first steps; they were making it run from one place to another, backwards and forwards; on receiving it on one side, they made it run to the other side; it seemed to be just the place that was sought for such an amusement. (Report, 1850: minute 82)

These difficulties were regarded as being closely associated with the Gallery's city-centre location. This presented something of a dilemma, for while that location was ideal because it maximised the Gallery's public utility, it also increased the risk that the Gallery might be abused by the passing urban throng. When a commission was appointed in 1857 to consider whether the National Gallery should retain its Trafalgar Square site or be moved out to the suburbs at Kensington Gore, its deliberations were dominated by the attempt to discover a calculus which could weigh and reconcile the relative costs and benefits of these competing locations.[5]

Ruskin proposed one such calculus in suggesting that there should be two collections with different functions. When he was asked whether it was not advantageous for art, viewed in terms of the effect it might have on the public mind, to be located in central London in view of the ease and cheapness of access this would afford, Ruskin agreed but went on to note that, on the debit side, 'a central situation involves the crowding of the room with parties wholly uninterested in the matter'. The difficulty is that, while art needs to reach the crowd in order to civilise it, that same crowd spoils the pleasure of art for 'the real student' for whom, Ruskin argued, 'a situation more retired will generally be serviceable enough' (Report, 1857: para 2456). Posed in this way, the issue can be resolved by disaggregating the unity of art, splitting it into two kinds of collection in such a manner that the crowd's access to art comes to be differentiated from elite access and hierarchically organised. Ruskin thus suggested:

> But it would seem to me that all that is necessary for a noble Museum of the best art should be more or less removed, and that a collection, solely for the purpose of education, and for the purpose of interesting people who do not care much about art, should be provided in the very heart of the population, if possible, that pictures not of great value, but of sufficient value to interest the public, and of merit enough to form the basis of early education, and to give examples of all art, should be collected in the popular Gallery, but that all the precious things should be removed and put into the great Gallery, where they would be safest, irrespectively altogether of accessibility. (Report, 1857: para 2458)

Ruskin, of course, was an opponent of reforms which aimed to make art more easily accessible, especially to the unwashed masses. The advice he offered in relation to an art gallery planned for Leicester was unequivocal:

> You must not make your Museum a refuge against either rain or ennui, nor let into perfectly well-furnished, and even, in the true sense, palatial, rooms, the utterly squalid and ill-bred portion of the people. (cit. Koven, 1994: 26)

Even so, his proposal for two separate galleries with separate functions shares a good deal of ground with the ideas of reformers like Cole and Jevons in testifying to Ruskin's preparedness to maximise the uses to which art might be put by breaking it down into its component parts and assigning each a different function within a pedagogic itinerary conceived as an ascent of art's hierarchical organisation. When quizzed as to whether it was desirable to establish a gallery that contained no first-rate works of art, Ruskin was thus quite equable at the prospect of using second- and even third-rate art for the early stages of art education, provided only that nothing be admitted to the popular Gallery 'which was not good or true of its kind, but only inferior in value to the others' (Report, 1857: para 2464).

That the commission was interested in Ruskin's proposal is clear from the number of times it resurfaced during the course of its deliberations. Yet there were many practical difficulties to be surmounted if the virtues of the proposal were to be properly assessed. For if art galleries were to be differentiated so as to serve different purposes for different publics, it was first necessary to know who used them so that some calculations might be made as to which sections of the population would be most likely to visit them if they were located in such and such a place or given such and such a character. Yet it was difficult to arrive at any definite conclusions about these matters, given the rudimentary nature of the available statistics. Francis Place had anticipated these difficulties when, in the 1830s, he attempted to calculate how much 'civilising effect' might be attributed to art galleries. Noting that there had been a decline in public drunkenness and debauchery at fairs and gardens in and around London, he set out to establish how much this might be attributed to the influence of greater working-class participation in art galleries. Reproducing the numbers visiting the Adelaide Gallery over the Easter and Whitsuntide holidays in 1835 and 1836, and remarking the increase in visits from the one year to the next, Place based his conclusion that the Gallery was proving successful in spreading civilising pursuits to the popular classes less on the raw data available to him than on the ancillary evidence that it had been as 'carefully ascertained as it could be that three fourths of the visitors were working people, almost all of them young men with their wives and sweethearts or alone and apprentices' (Place, n.d.).

The 1857 commission was obliged to rely on evidence of a similar kind in its endeavours, in the wake of Ruskin's suggestion that the National Gallery should be split into two, to ascertain whether art might be divided into different classes and be deployed in different contexts in order that it might be rendered useful in different ways, and to different degrees, with different publics. These concerns were particularly to the fore in the evidence taken from James Fergusson, the general manager of the Crystal Palace. Having asserted that the substantial majority of the Palace's visitors were from the labouring classes, Fergusson justified this view by appealing to the same kinds of evidence that Place had cited. He thus advised the commission that visitor numbers were largest on Mondays at about 10 000 and declined progressively through the week to a low of 2000 on Saturdays. 'We go gradually down from the beginning of the week, which is the poor man's holiday, to the end of the week, which is appropriated almost exclusively to the more wealthy . . .' (Report, 1857: para 2692). That those who attended on Mondays were indeed working people was confirmed by observation: the labourers in attendance were identified through the fustian jackets they wore. However, although the number of visitors varied for each day of the week, Fergusson calculated that the educational benefit derived from the art on display was much the same. This conclusion involved a calculus for the measurement of culture's utility in which the low average amount of benefit derived from the mass of working-class visitors in the early parts of the week might be matched by the higher intensity of the benefit derived by the smaller numbers of better-class visitors later in the week. In Fergusson's words:

> I should say there is about the same amount of information or education present on each of the days. Very much diluted in the earlier days, concentrated in the latter days of the week. (Report, 1857: para 2692)

The remark was in the same vein as Fergusson's earlier reply to the commission's inquiries as it probed whether the experience of the Crystal Palace might provide a basis for bifurcating the collections of the National Gallery along the lines suggested by Ruskin. A question regarding the tastes exhibited by the labouring classes in the Picture Gallery, and the kinds of art that were provided to cater to those tastes, thus led to the following exchange:

> Their opinion of painting differs very much from mine. What I would admire as fine art that class of people would not admire. What you, or I, or anybody else would perhaps call vulgar painting, an imitation of life, a smuggler, a bull-fight, a grand battle, anything very illustrative, they understand and admire; but the purer class of art seems to be above them.
>
> Is the effect such as you consider instructive to the minds of the multitude that go to observe these things, instructive in art education, in leading the taste of the people?—I have not the least doubt of it; I think that the people have hitherto had so little opportunity of observing pictures that they require to begin at the rudiments before they can appreciate the higher things, and I think that the collection of the Crystal Palace Gallery being not of the highest class has been a great step towards teaching them the rudiments, and so giving them an interest in the things before attempting to teach them to appreciate a higher class. (Report, 1857: paras 2634–5)

As it happens, the commission, which interpreted Fergusson's testimony as favouring Ruskin's proposals, was later presented with contradictory evidence—and a different theory of working-class leisure interests—which suggested that moving the National Gallery outside London would serve only to make it more popular with the working classes. When Edgar Alfred Bowring was called before the commission, he advised that he had conducted statistical inquiries which showed—as indeed they did—that while attendance at collecting institutions located in central London (the British Museum, the National Gallery and so on) had declined over the period 1851 to 1856, the Zoological Gardens, Hampton Court Palace and Kew Gardens—all located in the outer suburbs—had all experienced a dramatic increase in visitors. In attempting to explain this data, Bowring suggested that moving the National Gallery outside London would increase its popularity, given his observations of the significance and cultural meaning that was attributed to visiting such institutions within the changing patterns of working-class leisure:

> Those classes do not visit places of this character without first making

> themselves clean, and probably taking half a day's holiday for the purpose, while they take their wives and families with them and, in short, attempt to make such an occasion a source of rational enjoyment and improvement. So far from their objecting to the National Gallery being removed to Kensington, the enjoyment of the half holiday taken by them for the purpose of visiting it with its accessories of ornamental gardens, fountains, &c., would be greatly increased by the walk across the green sward of the parks, where they breathe a purer and more exhilarating air than they are accustomed to in their everyday life; whereas a visit to a National Gallery in the midst of the smoke of London does not afford them this desirable relief. (Report, 1857: para 2848)

My interest, however, is not in the commission's final recommendations (as we know, the Gallery remained in Trafalgar Square), but rather in the new logic of culture that motivated its concerns, framing the direction of its inquiries and the kinds of answers it sought. In the commission's relentless exploration of the possibility—indeed desirability—of breaking the unity of culture down into its component parts—of distinguishing the first- from the second-rate and assigning them different spheres of distribution, and of determining just how much culture to make available to different publics in view of estimates of how much and what kinds of benefit they might derive from it: it is clear that culture is thought of as something that might be parcelled into different quantities, broken down into units of different value, in such a way that the utility, the civilising effect, to be derived from making available large amounts of relatively low-quality art to the masses might be weighed and balanced against the value to be derived from reserving the very best art for more exclusive forms of consumption by the educated classes.

The same logic is discernible in the debates accompanying the development of 'outreach' systems. From its foundation in the 1850s, the South Kensington Museum was conceived as a central repository from which specimen objects could be circulated to provincial museums in order to spread the improving influence of culture more evenly throughout the land. Its effectiveness in this regard was subject to periodic monitoring. In 1864, for example, the House of Commons established a Select Committee to inquire into the Schools of Art; its report included an assessment of the South Kensington Museum's system:

> There can be no doubt that the fine collection at South Kensington is calculated to raise the taste of the country, or, at all events, of those persons who are able to visit it; but it is equally certain that it is only a small proportion of the provincial public which has the opportunity of doing so, and it appears that the arrangements made for circulating

> portions of the collection to the provincial towns are as yet far from perfection. That the collection of works of Art, and the library attached to it, are not made as useful to the country schools as they might be, is due, perhaps, in part to the fact that the local committees are but imperfectly aware of the advantages which the Department offers them, but partly also to some defects in the arrangements of the Department itself. Mr Cole . . . throws out some valuable suggestions as to the formation of local museums, to be supported in great part by a system of circulating some of the works of Art belonging, not only to the South Kensington, but also to the National Gallery, and the British Museum. These suggestions are well worthy of consideration. (Report, 1881: para 780)

Reporting in 1881, a further committee established to look more thoroughly into this system of distribution recorded that 1346 examples of industrial art and 1286 paintings and drawings had been loaned to seven museums in 1880. Noting how this had been an increase on earlier years, the report went on to identify ways in which the utility to be derived from this method of distribution might be still further increased.

The language of these reports is comfortingly familiar in its recognisable continuity with contemporary bureaucratic procedures in the field of cultural administration, so much so that it is easy to overlook and therefore worth underscoring their historical novelty. For the conception of the South Kensington Museum as a central repository from which art might be circulated, in a capillary fashion, throughout the nation was not without precedent. Indeed, in the establishment and progressive monitoring of this arrangement, reference was frequently made to the *envoi* system developed in Napoleonic France through which works of art from the national collections in Paris were loaned to provincial art museums. Yet that is about as far as the similarities go. In his detailed survey and assessment of the *envoi* system, Daniel Sherman argues that, viewed in the light of the centralising ambitions of the Napoleonic period, the system's primary purpose was to embody and circulate an image of state power throughout the nation. It was for this reason, he contends, that less importance was attached to the pictures selected for this purpose than to the labels accompanying them, which indicated that they were the gift of the Emperor or of the state (see Sherman, 1989: 14). The circulation of art, in other words, was undertaken in accordance with a logic that remained, at least in part, juridico-discursive.[6] In this logic, as Foucault defines it, art serves princely power by symbolising it and making it publicly manifest. The *envoi* system was thus continuous with those earlier forms which promoted the power of the sovereign by circulating his image throughout the nation—as imprinted on coinage and medals, for example (see Burke, 1992).

By contrast, when Cole and others schooled in the tradition of utilitarianism spoke of the benefits to be derived from art's distribution throughout the realm, they constantly stressed art's divisibility, its capacity to be broken down into different quantities from which different degrees and kinds of benefit might be derived. This interest in assessing art's utility through a graduated calculus was evident in the line of questioning of the committee appointed to report on the lessons of the Paris Exhibition of 1867. The committee asked:

> Instead of spending very large sums upon very costly objects, would it not be better to distribute that large sum upon a number of objects, which are cheap in production, and at the same time of good taste, which might produce a really beneficial effect upon our own manufacture? (Report, 1867: minute 173)

Some of the experts who testified refused to accept that there might be such a calculus. For J.C. Robinson, expenditure on second-rate art could not be justified because 'second-rate things do not instruct; they rather tend to lower and vitiate the public taste' (1867: minute 656). However, the testimony of Richard Redgrave, the Inspector General for Art at the South Kensington Museum, displayed a clear commitment to a graduated calculus for assessing art's useful effects in his rejection of those forms of pure aestheticism which insisted—as did Ruskin—that only the original work of art will do.[7] While admitting a connection between utility and rarity in contending that art's usefulness is greater, the more original and singular the object, Redgrave argued that a reproduction, while not so good, is better than nothing: 'there is no doubt that the objects themselves are much finer than the reproduction; but if you cannot give them one thing, you must give them another' (1867: minute 64). Henry Cole's evidence tended in the same direction in his defence of 'democratic art' as 'art of the cheapest kind that circulates among the people'. Taken to task by the committee as to whether the circulation of second-rate art might do more harm than good, Cole gave an extended reply—developed through a number of exchanges with the committee—which equivocated between two positions: an aesthetic relativism which would see all art as equally good ('what is the object of art, but to please people? I do not know any other standard of art than that'—1867: para 848) and a position which accepts an aesthetic hierarchy while insisting that, although the effect of art might be most concentrated and intense at the peak of that hierarchy, its effect will be simultaneously of a lower intensity but more diffuse and capable of being spread more widely through the social body the lower down that hierarchy one goes.[8] The homilies through which he states his position indicate not only that art of inferior quality is better than nothing ('You cannot feed everybody with wheaten bread; rather than let them starve, I would give them rye bread'—1867: para 850) but also that such art may most usefully serve the purpose of introducing art to novitiates ('You must begin teaching a child with such books as primers and "Little Red Riding Hood" before you can get to the higher series'—1867: para 849).

In contrast to the *envoi* system, art was not, in this school of thought, envisaged as a means of representing or staging power, and the purpose of multiplying the circuits of its distribution was not to impress the populace by circulating art as a form of power-spectacle. Instead, its circulation was conceived in accordance with a governmental logic in which art, rather than representing power, *is* a power—a power susceptible to multiple subdivisions in a program which has as its end not the exertion of a specular dominance over the populace but the development of its capacities. As such, no effort was to be spared in ensuring the removal of all blockages which might impede culture's capillary distribution. The new kinds of administrative attention this entailed were nicely summarised by Edward Edwards, one of the most influential mid-century advocates of public libraries, in his criticisms of earlier library provisions. The 1709 *Act for the Better Preservation of Parochial Libraries in that part of Great Britain called England* was thus assessed as ineffectual because it provided 'no means of increase' and made 'no provision, whatever, for parochial use or accessibility' (Edwards, 1869: 10). It was, Edwards argued, not until the 1840s, when legislation was passed enabling the establishment of municipal libraries, that any effective steps were taken 'towards the diffusion of books over the length and breadth of England' (1869: 13).

Ensuring this capillary flow of culture, however, was not just an administrative or legislative matter. As James Fergusson noted, it was also an architectural question. Chastising architects for their failure to provide museums that were specifically designed for their new function of public instruction and for preferring, instead, replicas of Renaissance palaces, Fergusson viewed the resulting buildings as positive obstacles to the capillary flow of culture and knowledge:

> the architectural question is the rock that now diverts the waters of knowledge from flowing where their fertilising instruments are so much needed . . . We have thirsted for knowledge, and our architects have given us nothing but stones. (Fergusson, 1849: 8)

It will therefore be worthwhile to spend a little time considering the care and attention which were given to providing a custom-built environment for art's display, one calculated to maximise the benefit which might be derived from it by the art gallery or museum visitor.

THE CATALOGUE VERSUS THE TOUR: ART AND THE SELF-REGULATING SUBJECT

In 1841, the House of Commons appointed a committee to inquire into the administration of London's national monuments and works of art. One of the primary concerns of the committee was to determine the best ways of maintaining order in institutions which admitted all-comers without any mechanisms for screening out desirable from undesirable visitors. The evidence considered included reference to institutions of three different types, each characterised by different forms of visitor surveillance and regulation. Churches and cathedrals were of substantial interest in view of the requirement that, at least during service hours, they admit all and sundry but whose architecture—often full of nooks and crannies—prohibited any effective form of overall surveillance except for the vigilance of their priests and vergers. Second, there were institutions like the Tower of London where conduct was regulated via the technology of the tour through which visitors were obliged to go round in groups under the direction of a guide. Third and finally, there were the new institutions which had, in some measure, been designed for public visiting—like the National Gallery—where the needs of visitor surveillance and regulation were provided for in a number of ways: the calculated partitioning of space in the National Gallery and the provision of two inspectors per room; the organisation of the visitor's itinerary in the form of a one-way route, allowing no return to rooms already visited; and the organisation of open and clear spaces in which the public might exercise a permanent surveillance over itself.

The committee's clear preference was for the last of these regulative technologies. This was partly because the balance of the evidence presented suggested it was the most efficient, as one witness after another testified to the value of allowing the public unrestricted entry so as to provide for a sufficient quantity of visitors to watch over and so, effectively, police one another. The guided tour was judged ineffective in comparison, owing to its inability to provide for an adequate number of watchers. As for the latter, when asked about the arrangements prevailing in cathedrals, John Britton testified:

> Do you mean that as the practice now exists of small parties going in under the direction of one guide, there is more opportunity if the parties are inclined to do mischief, than would arise if the public were generally admitted?—I think so; for I have seen sad instances of it when I have been in cathedrals for hours together, and when I have noticed various parties come in, two in one party, five in another, and six in another, and only one servant girl of the verger superintending the whole: in consequence of which, they become scattered about the cathedral, and they can with the greatest impunity break off fingers, toes or even heads, if they are so inclined . . . (Report, 1841: para 2002)

The committee's preferences in this matter, however, were not based solely on calculations of efficiency. The more streamlined ways of managing the visitors via organised routes and impersonalised forms of surveillance also seemed preferable to the guided tour in view of their capacity to allow the individual to go at his or her own speed and thus, in being able to contemplate the cultural artefacts on display, be rendered more receptive to their improving influence. To be herded round a collection to a set time schedule, in a group with different interests and competences, and be subjected to the set patter of the warden: all these aspects of the tour were judged inimical to the civilising effect art and culture might have. Robert Porrett, chief clerk to the principal storekeeper in the Tower armouries, was fulsome in defence of the guided tour: 'nothing can be more satisfactory than it is now; I think persons seem to be exceedingly gratified; they are entertained with the very curious and valuable collection for an hour; they have the attendance of a person to answer every question that may be put, and they are conducted all round' (Report, 1841: para 2702). However, the committee's attention was more engaged by William Buss, an artist, who complained that the guided tours diminished the potential use and educational value of the collection. Asked whether the existing system of exhibiting the armouries was effective or might in any way be improved, Buss replied:

> at that time it appeared to me to be very defective; the people were hurried through in gangs of from 20 to 30, and there was no time allowed for the investigation of any thing whatever; in fact, they were obliged to attend to the warder, and if the people had catalogues they might as well have kept them in their pockets; when they wanted to read them in conjunction with the object they saw, of course, they lagged behind, and then the warder would say, 'You must not do that; the catalogues are to be read at home; you must follow me, or you will lose a great deal;' and I was particularly struck by that, for I thought it a very odd mode of exhibiting national property. (Report, 1841: para 2805)

Buss went on to sing the virtues of the British Museum and the

National Gallery for safeguarding their treasures very effectively while also allowing the visitor to develop a more individualised relation to them. He then proceeded to illustrate how the guided tour diminished the value that the visitor might obtain from the new forms of historical classification governing the armoury, especially if provided with an appropriate catalogue containing the requisite historical information:

> Is it your opinion, then, that a catalogue ought to be prepared under the public authority, with a view of being sold cheaper to visitors, and of giving more general information?—I should say it would be very desirable; but, then, if those catalogues were published, they would be useless under the present system; the warders must cease to go round with visitors, or the catalogues would be of no use.
>
> In point of fact, it is your opinion that much of the gratification that might be derived from the armouries is lost, from the hurried manner in which visitors are obliged to go through them, and by their being prevented from deliberately examining the different curiosities?—Certainly, it prevents a proper examination; if the knowledge expended by Sir Samuel Meyrick on the arrangement of the armoury was of any value, it is rendered unavailable; for you cannot trace the changes or varieties of the periods, owing to the hurried mode in which it is adopted . . .
>
> Your opinion is, that the arrangement is highly useful; but that the present mode of exhibition deprives the public of much of its advantage?—That is exactly my meaning. (Report 1841: paras 2830–33)

The exhibitions that were organised for the poor of London's East End in the 1880s and 1890s were similarly accompanied by a battery of techniques—catalogues, trained attendants, appropriately descriptive labels—designed to ensure that the poor took the correct messages from the art on display (see Koven, 1994). Joy Kasson has likewise detailed the attention paid to such matters in mid-nineteenth century America, but with the useful qualification that the new technologies of visiting developed over this period were often aimed as much at the couple as at the individual. As a consequence, women's relations to art were often mediated through their husbands as—or so the evidence of contemporary engravings suggests—it was men's role, assisted by the catalogue, to expound on the significance of the art displayed, and women's role to listen (Kasson, 1990).

My point, then, is that the concern that was evident in the establishment of public museums, art galleries and libraries to make the resources of culture available to the whole population was accompanied by an equally meticulous attention to organising an environment in which the museum or gallery visitor, or the library user, might derive as much benefit as possible from the experience. But what kind of benefit? And what kind of benefit might be expected to accrue to the state in return for its efforts and expenditures in this area? Jevons provides a route into these questions in his suggestion that the multiplication of culture's utility always brought with it an added value in the ancillary benefits to which the broadened distribution of cultural resources would give rise. Investment in libraries, museums and public concert halls would, Jevons suggested, secure a cash as well as a cultural and political return:

> Now, this small cost is not only repaid many times over by the multiplication of utility of the books, newspapers, and magazines on which it is expended, but it is likely, after the lapse of years, to come back fully in the reduction of poor-rates and Government expenditure on crime. We are fully warranted in looking upon Free Libraries as an engine for operating upon the poorer portions of the population. (Jevons, 1965: 32)

The civilising influence of culture, in other words, was expected to give rise to social benefits in view of the changed forms of behaviour that it was expected would result from exposure to it. But why should this have been so? What assumptions made this expectation—which, in hindsight, seems rather unlikely—an intelligible one? A part of the answer to these questions consists in the increasing influence of new conceptions of art associated with the rise of bourgeois, and especially Romantic, aesthetics. Viewed throughout much of the seventeenth and eighteenth centuries as a form of aristocratic diversion, the sphere of art was not, in this period, regarded as a realm possessing any special moral or aesthetic qualities. Under the influence of the *philosophes*, Kant, Schiller and Romanticism more generally, however, the spheres of art and culture came to be regarded as a special realm providing a set of resources which, in allowing the conduct of various kinds of work on the self, would result in a harmonisation of the diverse aspects of the individual's personality (see Saisselin, 1970). The fusion of these ideas with the late eighteenth and early nineteenth century culture of sensibility led to the view that frequent contact with art would result in more refined codes of personal conduct. It would help knock the rough edges off an individual's behaviour, promoting a softness and gentleness of manners. We can see the entry of such conceptions into the governmental sphere in the tasks to which art was summonsed by George Godwin, the head of the committee responsible for the affairs of the Art Union of London:

> Not merely every Irishman, but every philanthropic spirit, who feels . . . that the cultivation of taste . . . softens men's manners and suffers them not to be brutal, must rejoice at this latter circumstance and be anxious to lend his utmost aid . . . The influence of the fine arts in humanising

> and refining, in purifying the thoughts and raising the sources of gratification in man, is so universally felt and admitted that it is hardly necessary now to urge it. By abstracting him from the gratification of the senses, teaching him to appreciate physical beauty and to find delight in the contemplation of the admirable accordance of nature, the mind is carried forward to higher aims, and becomes insensibly opened to a conviction of the force of moral worth and the harmony of virtue. (cit. in King, 1964: 109)

However, this is only half the answer. For these changing conceptions of art do not explain why it was thought that the social reach of art might usefully be extended beyond the middle classes to include the population as a whole. Indeed, these conceptions could well be, and were, combined with active opposition to such a proposition. The writings of Sir Joshua Reynolds, while investing art with an exemplary status which allowed it to be thought of as a refining and civilising agent, simultaneously restricted its sphere of influence to elite social strata given Reynolds' conviction that the position of the poor was divinely ordained and not to be disturbed. The poor, for Reynolds, are inflicted with an unchanging sensuality; only the higher social ranks have the ability and, in their freedom from the exigencies of labour, the opportunity to use art as a means of facilitating their transition from a life of brute sensuality to one of civilised reason (see Borzello, 1980: 39). There can be no doubt of the continuing influence of these essentially pre-governmental conceptions of art in which art's social efficacy and function are regarded as being connected to limiting rather than expanding its social distribution. Frances Borzello cites the evidence of a witness before the 1835–36 select committee appointed to inquire into the best means of extending a knowledge of art among the people in which this view is perfectly encapsulated. Asked whether it was 'desirable to encourage a knowledge of the correct principles of design, perspective and proportion in the mind of the artisan in so far as they are artists', Charles Robert Cockerell replied:

> I do not think such knowledge compatible with the occupations of artisans, and the encouragements to it would mislead them, and interfere with their proper callings, and right division of labour, in which excellence already requires all their ability. (cited in Borzello, 1980: 11)

However, what we witness in the various nineteenth century parliamentary commissions and inquiries that concerned themselves with the spheres of art and culture is the emerging ascendancy of the view that art and culture might be governmentally deployed as civilising agencies directed at the population as a whole. Yet this was not just because the assumptions of Romanticism somehow became more plausible. Rather, the crucial changes took place in another compartment of social existence altogether. For it was the emerging ascendency of new ways of thinking about the population which made it intelligible to expect that general benefits might result from culture's more extended distribution.

CULTURE, LIBERAL GOVERNMENT AND THE PRUDENTIAL SUBJECT

The account Mitchell Dean offers, in his *The Constitution of Poverty*, of the changing moral aims and precepts which accompanied the development of new forms for the administration of the poor provides some bearings from which to explore these issues. Dean's primary concern is to take issue with the view, exemplified by the work of E.P. Thompson, that eighteenth century forms of pauper relief rested on a 'moral economy'—that is, a system of mutual obligations between rich and poor—whereas those instituted by the *Poor Law Amendment Act 1834* reflected a purely economic set of concerns, a wholly market-driven and amoral utilitarianism. Instead, he proposes that such differences are best understood in terms of the contrasting practical reasonings of two forms of government, each of which had its moral dimension. Eighteenth century forms of poor law administration thus rested on a conception of the population associated with the notion of police: that is, as a resource to be managed for the benefit of the national wealth. They accordingly sought to set the poor to work so that, in providing for their own sustenance, they might increase the wealth and strength of the nation. In dismantling many of the earlier forms of poor relief, however, the 1834 Act embodied a concern with making the poor responsible in accordance with the moral imperatives of Malthusianism in ways that reflected the newly emerging forms of liberal government.

The issues I want to focus on here concern less the contrasting ways in which the poor were materially provided for in these two systems of relief than the forms of moral regulation that accompanied them. The crucial distinction between the two, Dean suggests, is that, whereas the former system exhorted and educated the poor to engage in an 'industrious course of life', it did not, as did the post-1834 system, aspire to have them *choose* such a course of life for themselves as a matter of personal responsibility or self-regulation. There are two main points here relevant to my present interests. The first concerns the fact that, while eighteenth century forms of poor relief had been accompanied by attacks on popular recreations, and especially against alehouses, these attacks sought simply to outlaw such recreations because of the fear that the taint of slothfulness and drunkenness would, when imported into the family via the male head of household, lead to a wastage of the national resource of population. Such campaigns, in other words—like the forms of poor relief they accompanied—were aimed simply at transforming the idle poor into the industrious poor, but without such a transformation proceeding through or being dependent on any mechanism of inner or moral transformation. When Patrick Colquhoun discusses the role of alehouses in destroying morals and breeding crime, his attention focuses on the systems of inspection available to magistrates for watching over publicans and thereby regulating public houses so as to secure 'the essential interests of the State, as regards the morals and health of the lower ranks, in checking their prevailing propensity to drunkenness, gaming and idleness' (Colquhoun, 1796: 38). Similarly, Bentham's famous contention that 'Pushpin is morality in so far as it keeps out drunkenness' (cit. Bahmueller, 1981: 165) simply sees pushpin as a diversion which might keep the workingman away from drink. It does not produce an interior transformation that will make the workingman *not want* to drink.

By contrast, the influence of Malthus and the need for prudential restraint as a check to the threat of overpopulation leads, as one of the primary tactics of liberal government, to the need for precisely such an inner transformation to serve as the mechanism through which economic laws might be translated into an imperative of moral conduct. It is in this respect, Dean argues, that the Malthusian theory of population proved critical in specifying a new form of life for the poor:

> The Malthusian intervention must figure prominently in accounting for the additional virtues demanded of the poor in the nineteenth century. They were not only to be docile, industrious and sober, as in the previous century, but also to be frugal in domestic economy, avoid pauperism at all costs, practice proper restraint from unconsidered marriage and improvident breeding, join a friendly society, and make regular deposits in a savings bank. (Dean, 1991: 83–84)

It was, then, this new construction of the poor that made it intelligible to think of art and culture as resources that might be enlisted in the service of governing. If the eighteenth century poses the workhouse as a disciplinary alternative to the alehouse in a stark and unmediated opposition, the nineteenth century places the museum, the gallery and the library between the two and assigns them the task of producing the worker who will not only not frequent the public house, but who will also no longer wish to do so and who will voluntarily practise moral restraint in his conjugal relationships.[9] It is thus a fairly constant trope in the literature of cultural reform, evident from the 1830s to the 1880s, to find the art gallery, the museum and the library ranged against the public-house as agents deemed capable of transforming the workingman into a new 'prudential subject'. The 1834 Select Committee of Inquiry into Drunkenness, for example, was advised that providing reading matter through libraries would help induce sobriety in the working classes by leading to better habits (Report, 1834: para 2858). In 1867, on the eve of the extension of the male suffrage to, as he put it, 'the residuum of the English people', Henry Cole urged that it was 'the positive duty of Parliament to try and get these people who are going to be voters, out of the public-house, and I know no better mode of doing it than to open museums freely to them' (Report 1867: para 808). A few years later, in 1875, Cole conjured up the spectre of male drunkenness that culture was meant to banish:

> Then there appears to be a class of people that actually seem turned from human beings into no better than brutes: people that spend all their money in drink, and leave their children to go to the workhouse or to die—who starve their wives, beat them, and after having drunk themselves into a state of insanity, habitually sleep without clothes, lying on the straw! (Cole, 1884: 364)

The answer—or, at least, a part of the answer—Cole suggested was to open museums on Sundays so that, rather than being left 'to find his recreation in bed first, and in the public-house afterwards' (1864: 368), the workingman would be able to recreate himself together with his wife and children. And finally, to recall my point of departure, when, in 1883, William Stanley Jevons posed what he saw as some of the central cultural polarities of his day, he included that of 'the Free Library and the newsroom *versus* the Public-house' (Jevons, 1965: 7).

The 'prudential subject' in whose fashioning culture was thus to assist, however, is to be understood not as the subject of a set of beliefs who helps to perpetuate existing forms of power by consenting to them, but rather as an agent who functions as an operator for power through his conduct in practising a new form of life. For—and it is in this light that we can best understand why the provision of public museums and art galleries was so frequently placed in the same bracket as the provision of public sanitation and water supplies—taking culture to the workingman was only one of the means by which he was to be led to be both sober and prudent. This tactic was to be complemented by the distribution of purified water to houses, or via public drinking fountains, to provide an alternative to beer, just as public lavatories were envisaged as an alternative to the facilities which public-houses offered as an inducement to their customers (see Harrison, 1971). Edward Edwards, referring to the *Public Libraries Act 1850*, thus described it as a measure empowering local councils 'to build libraries, as well as build sewers; and to levy a local rate for bringing books into the sitting-room of the handicraftsman or the tradesman, as well as one for bringing water into his kitchen' (Edwards, 1869: 16) because these were all envisaged as parts of new systems of capillary distribution which, in spreading art and culture, fresh water and public sanitation, all worked towards the same end: the reform of the workingman.

My stress, here, on the working*man* is not accidental for, as will be clear from the foregoing, the 'prudential subject' these various initiatives aimed at producing was always envisaged as male. There are a number of reasons for this. The fact that married women's civic rights were held to be subsumed within those of their husbands meant that transactional relations between government and the family were usually routed via the male head of household. The moral schemas derived from Malthusianism were also important in this regard. Just as eighteenth century forms of poor relief had aimed to save women and children from distress by providing work for the male head of household, so the moral schema of the post-1834 poor laws operated through the requirements of prudential restraint which bore uniquely on the male head of household. For, it was argued, only the male head of household was able, from his position in the market, to experience and interpret the effects of nature's scarcity and the threat of starvation that would result from overpopulation so that he could translate nature's imperatives into a self-imposed morality. 'Morality,' as Dean puts it, 'becomes a matter for each individual, here understood as each adult male, confronted with an economic necessity inscribed in his relation to nature.' (Dean, 1991: 154)

Culture's target is, accordingly, always male: the museum, the reading-room, the art gallery, the library—it is always changes in the behaviour of working-class men that are aimed for when the virtues of these institutions are extolled. Where the working-class woman appears, it is not in her own right but as the potential beneficiary of reformed male conduct. The situation in regard to the middle-class woman was different. The eighteenth century 'culture of sensibility', which had attributed to women a natural delicacy and softness, an inherent gentleness of manners, sought also to deploy these virtues as ways of civilising elite male conduct through the construction of new heterosocial spaces of pleasure—spa baths and public promenades, for example—where the presence of women meant that the raucous excesses of male conduct had to be curbed (see Barker-Benfield, 1992).

In the reforming strategies of the nineteenth century, the new public cultural spaces of the museum, the art gallery and the library provided an enlarged, cross-class sphere of operation for this 'culture of sensibility' in the expectation that the presence of middle-class women would provide a model for working-class women to imitate while also enjoining on the working-class man more refined and gentle manners.[10]

THE BUREAUCRATISATION OF ART

Let me draw together the various threads of my argument so far. I have suggested that the changed discursive coordinates governing nineteenth century conceptions of the poor and the appropriate forms of their administration form a necessary aspect of any account concerned to trace the relations between the emerging forms of liberal government and the role accorded culture as a resource that might be used to induct the population into new, more prudential forms of conduct. By the same token, however, it is also clear that the sphere of culture, far from being regarded as tailor-made for this purpose, was seen as in need of a degree of refashioning if it was to fulfil the function it was thus called on to perform. That function, moreover, was inextricably caught up with a particular patterning of gender relations. Finally, this governmental utilisation of culture entailed a contradictory set of relations to aesthetic conceptions of culture. On the one hand, such conceptions were essential to governmental programs insofar as it was by virtue of its aesthetic properties that it was thought culture could serve as a civilising agent. At the same time, the mechanisms through which culture was distributed entailed both its bureaucratisation and its subordination to a utilitarian calculus.

But what hinges on these arguments? What is their more general significance? A part of my concern has been to suggest how the history of culture might be written in ways that would see its modern constitution as inherently governmental, as a field of social management in which culture is deployed as a resource intended to help 'lift' the population by making it self-civilising. There are, of course, many moments in such a history: the French Revolution is one in the importance it accorded culture as an instrument for forming a civic morality. The mid-nineteenth century period of utilitarian cultural reform is another such moment, distinct from that of the French Revolution in that its concern was less to fashion a new civic morality or ethos of citizenship than to produce a new kind of self-reforming person. Two things had happened in between: first, the history of

Romantic aesthetics had warrened out an interior within the subject and programmed the work of art in such a way as to make the transaction between the two a process of self-civilising. Second, the new conceptions of the poor associated with Malthusianism and the notion of the prudential subject provided a discursive construction of the poor, and of the field of the social more generally, which made it intelligible to think of using culture as an instrument of social management. As a consequence, the 'multiplication of culture's utility' extended the reach of culture's governmental deployment in two ways. First, it carried that reach beyond the public surface of civic conduct and into the interior of the person in the expectation that culture would serve to fashion new forms of self-reflexiveness and reformed codes of personal conduct. Second, it developed new capillary systems for the distribution of culture that were calculated to extend its reach throughout the social body without any impediment or restriction.

Moreover, the currency of this 'utilitarianisation' of culture, as it was sometimes called, was a broadly based international one. It played a significant role in the establishment of Australia's major public cultural institutions over the mid- to late nineteenth century. Central to the ethos of the major state museums and art galleries, and a major subject of concern in the affairs of literary and debating societies, it played just as important a role in the Mechanics' Institutes and Schools of Art that blossomed in country towns throughout the length and breadth of Australia over the same period (see Candy and Laurent, 1994). Indeed, it was while Jevons was in Australia—where he worked, from 1854 to 1859, as the Assayor for the Mint in Sydney and was also an active participant in the affairs of the Philosophical Society of New South Wales and the Sydney Mechanics School of Arts—that Jevons first became interested in the possibility of fusing economic theory and utilitarian philosophy that was to prove so crucial to his later work. And, as I indicated at the outset, the 'utilitarianisation' of culture was later to acquire, in the 1890s, the influential support of George Brown Goode in the United States.

By the turn of the century, then, a concern with the multiplication of culture's utility was thoroughly embedded within the vocabularies and operational routines of collecting institutions. It became the shared lexicon of a sphere of cultural administration which, in becoming increasingly professionalised, also witnessed the more rapid transfer and sharing of practices across national boundaries. When, in 1880, Archibald Livingstone visited Britain and Europe on behalf of the Australian Museum in Sydney to report on relations between museums and the development of new systems of instruction, he urged the Australian Museum to follow the example of the South Kensington Museum in circulating specimen collections throughout the land by loaning them to local museums and galleries. In doing so, he estimated that, between 1855 and 1877, the system put into place by the South Kensington Museum had allowed 65 000 objects to be seen by 8 600 000 persons—clearly a fabulous multiplication of their utility (see Livingstone, 1880: xi). When, in 1913, the Australian Museum sent Charles Hedley to visit natural history museums in the United States, he came back with a similarly vivid description of the respects in which the system for circulating specimen collections to New York secondary schools that had been introduced at the American Museum of Natural History (AMNH) had allowed that Museum to extend its 'sphere of usefulness . . . beyond the galleries to the lecture hall and beyond the lecture hall to the suburban school' (Hedley, 1913: 7). That he should have been so impressed by the AMNH's success in this matter is not surprising. Throughout the period of Henry Fairfield Osborn's presidency, the public discourse of the AMNH was dominated by an 'avalanche of numbers' as, in one annual report after another and in various other official museum publications, the Museum's success in extending the usefulness of the collections through public lecture programs and the circulation of specimen collection boxes to schools was accorded pride of place. In a 1913 text, Osborn and George Sherwood, the curator of the AMNH's Department of Public Education, reported that the number of pupils reached by the Museum's circulating collections had increased from 375 000 in 1905 to 1 275 890 in 1912. They attributed to this increase a key role in extending the Museum's influence and usefulness both quantitatively and qualititatively to the degree that many of the children who benefited from those collections were of 'foreign parentage' (Osborn and Sherwood, 1913: 6).

In the course of its international migrations, however, the principle of the multiplication of culture's utility was subject to different interpretations and, depending on the context, implemented in varying ways. Certainly, the specific combination of factors which, in the mid-nineteenth century British context, resulted in this principle being viewed as a possible panacea for a range of social problems did not travel well, either in space or time. By the turn of the century, William Henry Beveridge dismissed the view that the diffusion of culture might serve as a remedy for 'colossal evils', a tendency that was generally shared as reforming opinion moved toward social-welfarist and away from cultural and philanthropic conceptions of social problems and their possible solutions (see Koven, 1994: 44).

In other contexts, the benefits expected to result from culture's expanded distribution were significantly different in kind from those envisaged by the likes of Cole and Edwards. The writings of John Cotton Dana, the Director of the Newark Museum in New Jersey, provide a telling instance of such a changing horizon of expectations. In a couple of pamphlets he wrote in the 1920s, Dana's language positively bristles with the vocabulary of utility. In *A Plan for a New Museum*, he stigmatises old-fashioned art museums as mere 'gazing museums' which had degenerated into little more than fashion centres for elite society. In their place, he proposes the establishment of 'institutes of visual instruction' which, through the use of social science surveys, will seek to achieve 'returns for their cost' that are 'in good degree positive, definite, visible, measurable' (Dana, 1920: 13). A good museum and a useful museum are, for Dana, one and the same thing, and its usefulness is to be measured by its success in 'moving its community toward greater skill in all the arts of living' (Dana, 1927: 2). By 'arts of living', Dana is at pains to stress, he means all the techniques of modern civilisation. The phrase, as he puts it, 'extends its meaning from clean streets to clean air, from knowing the alphabet to a feeling for high poetry' (1920: 2). But if the art museum is to fulfil its role within this scheme, if it is to serve a truly useful function as an 'institute of visual instruction' (1920: 13)—or, in another formulation, if it is to be 'a new museum of the definitely useful, teaching type' (1920: 28)—then it must turn its back on its concern with art of 'approved excellence and unquestioned authenticity' (1920: 36), a concern which is now, Dana suggests, a limiting factor on the art museum's potential usefulness. Instead, in early advocacy of what would nowadays be classified as 'art and working life' programs, Dana urges that the museum must seek to expand its usefulness by exhibiting and contributing to the artistic and economic activities of ordinary people in the community which surrounds it.

Here, then, is a conception of the art gallery's function that is quite different from, and even hostile to, that championed by Cole and the English utilitarian school of cultural reform. Yet there is still a common grammar underlying their different positions, and it is a grammar which has had significant long-term consequences for the positions of art and culture in modern societies.

Walter Benjamin, it may be recalled, argued that the development, over the nineteenth century, of techniques of mechanical reproduction deprived the work of art of the aura associated with the uniqueness and singularity of its authentic individual presence (Benjamin, 1970). The truth is, however, that, side by side with the development of such techniques, art also came to be inscribed in new administrative processes through which its singularity and uniqueness were subjected to a far more thoroughgoing dismemberment as its unity was disaggregated in a manner that would allow artistic products to be deployed in varying and flexible ways as parts of governmental programs aimed at civilising the population. It was art's existence in an age of mass instruction that was primarily responsible for, not the loss of its aura, as if by accident, but the calculated detachment of art's power and effectiveness from any dependence on the auratic qualities of its singular presence. No longer serving power by representing it or embodying it, culture—as envisaged in the programs of public museums and art galleries—emerges, instead, as an infinitely divisible and pliable resource to be harnessed, depending on the circumstances, to a variety of social purposes: self-improvement, community development, improving the standards of industrial art and design.

Yet, if this is so, we shall have to review the terms in which the history of the public art gallery is most commonly understood. The account which has proved most influential here has been that offered by Theodor Adorno in his conception of art galleries as family sepulchres for works of art which, in abstracting art from real-life contexts and thereby nullifying its utility, convert its faded aura into a fetish which serves only to maintain its exchange value (Adorno, 1967). The critique is, in fact, a venerable one: it was first voiced by Quatremère de Quincy in criticism of the museum programs developed in revolutionary France (see Sherman, 1994) and has its most eloquent modern-day representative in Douglas Crimp's writings on the museum's ruins (Crimp, 1993). The tradition of argument is, however, a complex and multi-faceted one whose different strands have been weighted and accented in different ways. For Adorno, as Llewellyn Negrin has convincingly argued, the view of museums as mausoleums which Adorno traces to Valéry is counterbalanced by his discussion of Proust's understanding of the respects in which the museum confers on the artwork a new afterlife which has to be attended to in its positivity. In typical Adorno fashion, Negrin suggests, neither one of these positions is carried over against the other: each is allowed to stand, and each is allowed to serve as the partial correction and revision of the other, in a negative dialectic which sees the truth of the museum emerging from the unresolved tension between these contrary perspectives (see Negrin, 1993).

Crimp's arguments tend in a different direction. Taking his cue from Benjamin's remarks on collecting, he sees the art museum one-sidedly, as the very antithesis of a living art whose meaning and use depend on its immersion in a set of social relations and processes outside the museum. For Benjamin, collecting, in releasing the object from its original function in order that it can stand in a close relationship to its equilavents, is the diametric opposite of use. The object's validity as a part of a collection, however, depends on that collection retaining a personal connection to an owner: 'the phenomenon of collecting,' Benjamin argues, 'loses its meaning as it loses its personal owner' (Benjamin, 1970: 67). This leads him to suggest that public collections, precisely because of the usefulness to which they aspire, have to be assessed as a double failure, a double betrayal of the object: a betrayal of the meaning vouchsafed by its originating context from which it has been abstracted and a betrayal of the meaning guaranteed by the owner of the private collection. 'Even though public collections may be less objectionable socially and more useful academically than private collections,' he says, 'the objects get their due only in the latter' (1970: 203). Crimp incorporates this accusation of a double betrayal into his assessment of the museum. The objects in Benjamin's collection, he argues, are also 'wrested from history, but they are "given their due," re-collected in accordance with the political perception of the moment'. The museum, by contrast, 'constructs a cultural history by treating its objects independently both of the material conditions of their own epoch and of those of the present' (Crimp, 1993: 204).

Before advancing his critique of the public collection, Benjamin anticipates that his discussion of collecting may only have confirmed the reader's conviction that the collecting passion is behind the times as well as his or her distrust of the collector type. Yet nothing, he suggests, is further from his mind 'than to shake either your conviction or your distrust' (Benjamin, 1970: 66–67). Nor should we let him. Philip Fisher has given us the best reasons for not doing so when he remarks, apropos of Benjamin, that the argument concerning art's loss of aura fails to consider the ways in which, when art is placed in new contexts, 'new characteristics come into existence by the same process that earlier features are effaced' (Fisher, 1991: 17). In place of the metaphysic of origin which characterises Benjamin's approach in which the work of art is always haunted by the fading aura of the originating conditions of its production, the meaning of aesthetic objects for Fisher is always a matter of the ways in which they are socially scripted via the routines and practices of the institutions which regulate their display. 'When we think of an object as having a fixed set of traits,' he argues, 'we leave out the fact that only within social scripts are those traits, and not others visible or even real.' (1991: 18) The placing of art in the museum is not, from this perspective, a loss of history—it is not a double betrayal of the history it once had and of another ideal and imagined history it might have had—but, rather, the acquisition of another history, and of the history it *has* had.

There is, as I have tried to show, another way of writing the history of the art gallery, a history in which art gains rather than loses something. Fisher suggests how we might best think of this addition when he says, in a happy phrase, that the accomplishment of the modern art museum has been to bureaucratise art. Emphasising this aspect of the art gallery's history, moreover, will have practical consequences. For, in place of those avant-garde critiques which place the art gallery on one side of a divide and life on the other, and which seek to liberate art from the former for the latter, there is opened up the life of art's bureaucratisation as a distinctively modern, anti-auratic form of art's use and deployment which, since no amount of critique will conjure it away, needs to be assessed and engaged with on its own terms.

6 Regulated restlessness: Museums, liberal government and the historical sciences

In 1912, an anonymous reporter evoked the scene of the Australian Museum in Sydney in terms which suggested that a visit to the Museum might function as an exercise in evolutionary benchmarking. Here is how the reader is imaginarily placed—first before the Museum and then within it:

> On either side of the great stone steps that face you as you pass through the turnstile of the Australian Museum in College-street, stands in a glass cage a degenerate cousin of yours and mine. We, strolling round among the stuffed specimens, furred and finned and winged, stand on the top of the rung of the animal ladder. Elsewhere in the Museum are preserved the remains of representatives of creatures that swarm about the lowest rungs. So, thinking of these extremes, and all the queer forms in between, you have the principle of the ascending progress of life illustrated before you. But these poor great-chested, long-armed, bow-legged, furry apes, erect as if alive in their glass cases, with a frustrated half-humanity looking at you from beneath the great bony ridges that protect their eyes—they stand for retrogression, and the danger of slipping back towards the brute again; they show that progress is not everywhere.
>
> The broad-faced red-haired orang-outang from Burma or Sumatra, that waits for you at the right of the stone steps, the bigger grey-black gorilla to the left, and almost man-like chimpanzee amongst a crowd of monkeys not far off, were all on the road to something bigger; or at least their ancestors were. But for some reason they slipped off that road, kept to the tree-life, hid away, perhaps in isolated communities, and their brains shrank, while those of our own ancestors developed, until now we capture them in their native forests, and keep them in glass cases and zoological gardens, pointers toward a by-path in the history of development. (Anon, 1912)

The lesson to be learned in the Museum seems clear enough: stay on the main routes of progress or run the risk of becoming an exhibit. Much the same sort of lesson was available in the Ethnological Hall where Egyptian mummies and Aboriginal remains bore, in their different and complex ways, mute testimony to the perils of dallying by the wayside of the major thoroughfares of evolutionary advancement.[1] Of course, other representational strategies for the exhibition of ethnological materials were possible and these were especially in evidence where such materials were exhibited within an aesthetic frame.[2] By the time this anonymous report was written, however, evolutionary and degenerationist conceptions had long played a major role in organising the arrangements of both natural history and ethnological exhibits within museums just as, in forming a part of broadly circulated public discourses about museums, they had also helped to shape and mould the horizons of visitors' expectations.

The issues I want to explore here concern how we might best characterise and assess the manner in which such evolutionary discourses functioned when integrated into the museum environment. In doing so, I want to place these questions in a broader framework. This will involve considering the respects in which the use of evolutionary categories within museum displays formed part of a more general process through which, in the late nineteenth and early twentieth centuries, the historical sciences suggested themselves as resources that were useful for governing in new ways and on a scale that was quite unprecedented. By the historical sciences here I have in mind those disciplines which, through the use of inferential procedures, seek to reconstruct a past on the basis of the remnants it has left behind. Thus defined, the scope of the historical sciences is considerable. They encompass, as Donald Preziosi reminds us, the techniques of connoisseurship in art history, graphology, medicine and the forensic sciences, while also including modern linguistics whose founding methodological paradigms were basically historical (see Preziosi, 1989: 88–93, and Aarsleff, 1982).

The historical sciences I wish to focus on here, however, are those which Huxley identified in his famous essay 'On the method of Zadig: Retrospective prophecy as a function of science' (see Huxley, 1882). Huxley's concern in this essay was to extrapolate the implications of Darwin's methodological interest in the apparently insignificant details—the 'quirks and imperfections'—of evolutionary development. The sciences Huxley names are history, archaeology, geology, astronomy and palaeontology. All of these, as Carlo Ginzburg has subsequently elaborated the argument, are concerned to construct an account of past events and processes on the basis of the remnants of those events and processes which have survived into the present (Ginzburg, 1980). The only differences concern the nature of those remnants (written records, geological strata, fossil remains) and the nature of the past events and processes that are constructed on their basis (the history of human civilisations, the history of the earth, the history of life on earth). However, I shall also include anthropology among the historical sciences for the period I am concerned with in view of the role that was played by the doctrine of survivals in historicising presently existing peoples by interpreting their anatomies, customs and artefacts as the remnants of earlier stages of human evolution and civilisation.[3]

In what new and distinctive ways, then, did these sciences suggest themselves as useful for governing? In what new ways were they enlisted for and embroiled within governmental processes directed at forming and shaping the attributes of populations? And how can the new significance they were accorded within such governmental processes best be accounted for? I shall suggest that answers to these questions are best sought in the intersections between three discursive 'events': first, the importance of Darwin's work in fashioning a version of nature which could be harnessed for progressive purposes within liberal programs of social reform; second, the new disciplinary synthesis of geology, archaeology, palaeontology and anthropology which prevailed in the late nineteenth century and which, in opening up a new set of intersecting times, provided new temporal coordinates for governing and regulating the conduct of populations and individuals; and, third, the changing problematics of liberal government. I do not mean to suggest, however, that these three 'events' or the pattern of their interactions resulted in a single governmental deployment of the historical sciences or in their annexation to a singular social and political project. To the contrary, my purpose is to outline the respects in which new developments in the historical sciences lent themselves to a veritable swarming of governmental initiatives as a result of the new surfaces of person formation which these developments made available and the new ways of inscribing these into the operating practices of civic technologies which they suggested. In doing so, however, I shall give special attention to those new technologies and thematics of citizenship which, in aiming to form the citizen as a subject in time, deployed the historical sciences in a uniquely productive manner orientated to the production of a progressive self. I do so with a view to placing some limits on the applicability of those arguments which interpret the evolutionary paradigms that dominated the historical sciences over this period as bourgeois ideologies which served to legitimate existing class and racial hierarchies.

GOVERNMENTALISING THE PAST

A necessary first step in my argument is to establish that, in the last 20 to 30 years of the nineteenth century, the historical sciences acquired a new prominence within the practices of museums where their employment in new disciplinary and interdisciplinary configurations lent a significantly new aspect to the role it was thought museums might play in shaping citizens. This is not to deny that there had been geological, natural history and ethnological collections prior to this period. However, these had usually been housed in private or scholarly contexts to which access was restricted, while the historical sciences themselves were largely amateur pursuits enjoying little public esteem. In the late eighteenth century, for example, the scientific standing of natural history was insecure. Its status was considerably lower than that of the mathematical and physical sciences and, although the success of Linnaean principles of classification helped redress this balance, its credentials remained infirm, still those of the dilettante rather than those of the professional scientist (see Gascoigne, 1994: 62–66 and 86–87). Its public reputation was equally unstable: viewed as a part of the pre-scientific culture of curiosity, it was both feminised and infantilised—a suitable activity for amateurs, women and children (see Gascoigne, 1994: 80; Schiebinger, 1989; and Thomas, 1994). This is not to say that natural history was not popular before the late nineteenth century. To the contrary, its potential moral and pedagogic benefits were actively promoted by a range of voluntary and private associations over the mid-century period, prompting Lynn Barber, with the British context in mind, to refer to the decades between 1820 and 1870 as the 'heyday of natural history'. Its appeal, she argues, consisted in its ability to combine usefulness with moral uplift and healthy physical exercise:

> Natural history fitted the bill perfectly. It was scientific, and there was nothing more useful than science, as everyone knew. It was morally uplifting, because it enabled one to find 'sermons in stones, and good in everything'. It was healthy, since it involved going out of doors. For gentlemen it offered new pretexts to go out and shoot something, and for ladies it offered new subjects for water-colours, for albums, or for embroidery. It also tied in very conveniently with the contemporary mania for forming collections. (Barber, 1980: 16)

However, Barber is equally careful to note that there was little evidence of any extensive government support for, or involvement in, such activities. Natural history was not taught in schools and, except for its somewhat marginalised position in the British Museum, enjoyed little influence or prestige in Britain's major public cultural institutions. Moreover, in view of the influence of Paley's natural theology, according to which the purpose of studying natural history was to acquire a closer knowledge of and harmony with God, and the consequent close articulation between natural history and Tory Anglicanism, dissenting and reforming opinion often found nature's lessons unpalatable. There is, as a consequence, little evidence that liberal reformers viewed natural history collections as cultural resources which should be made more broadly available as parts of programs of civic education directed at the population as a whole.

The picture was similar in early colonial Australia, although for different reasons. Although natural history and scientific institutions played an important role in the cultural life of the major cities, their role in this regard was invariably restricted to the elites of colonial society. Even when established under the auspices of Mechanics' Institutes and with a commitment to the general cause of public education, such societies soon fell prey to the gentrification strategies of local government and business elites who manipulated the governance and management of the Institutes in ways that were expressly calculated to exclude the members of the lower social orders—the emancipists, for example (see Finney, 1980). Australia's early natural history collections thus existed initially largely as adjuncts to literary, philosophical and scientific societies which functioned mainly as semi-private meeting places for—in the main—ruling-class men. There was, equally, little promotion of natural history in the schooling system until the later part of the nineteenth century. Natural history, as Finney puts it, was considered 'to be a private pursuit of gentlemen rather than the concern of government' (Finney, 1993: 31).

The same was true of geological, archaeological, historical and ethnological collections. More often than not, such collections were merged with and into one another rather than having clearly separated disciplinary identities. They were, moreover, typically ahistorical in their organisation and structure and were most usually developed and maintained by amateur associations acting outside the formal structures of the state. In the British context, the Society of Antiquaries provided a context for the display and acquisition of status on the part of the gentry. Its ethos, accordingly, treated the past less as the field of an historical science than as a source of collectable objects. Antiquities, as Bowdein van Riper puts the point, were treated 'as art objects, to be valued for their beauty or uniqueness, rather than as relics of a vanished civilisation, to be valued for the light they could shed on the lives of those who made and used them' (van Riper, 1993: 18).

This was less true of archaeology where, under the combined influence of Georges Cuvier and Richard Owen on the one hand, and of Sir Walter Scott and Romanticism on the other, the project of reconstructing the lost totalities of the Medieval and Celtic pasts on the basis of their fragmentary remains was invested with a national significance. For the greater part of the 1840s and 1850s, however, this nationalised field of historical archaeology was disconnected from prehistoric archaeology and from ethnology. There were, as a consequence, no intermediating times of human development capable of connecting the new national times being excavated in the field of historical archaeology to the longer times of the earth's history opened up by early nineteenth century developments in geology and palaeontology.

More importantly, perhaps, although the early to mid-century period witnessed significant intellectual developments in the historical sciences, these had not yet challenged the social authority of traditional conceptions of time and history. Although their intellectual credence was under threat, the social influence of Biblical conceptions of time remained considerable. With some exceptions, which we shall come to later, there was therefore little sense of any pressing need for new approaches to managing the ways of being in time which characterised the historical horizons of the general population. There was also little sense of how the new horizons of time that were being progressively opened up by discoveries in geology and palaeontology might be adapted to produce new ways of being in time which, in providing new temporal grids for the regulation of human conduct, might suggest new discursive templates for governmental processes of citizen formation. The stress, rather, was on producing an accommodation between those discoveries and traditional forms for the social regulation of the population's being in time.

Yet if, at least in the European context, the historical sciences were thus not accorded any special significance when assessed in terms of their potential for governing, art and, more generally, the sphere of the aesthetic certainly was. Over the period from the mid-eighteenth to the mid-nineteenth century, when private collections were increasingly opened to the general public and invested with an educative task, it was typically artistic collections that were initially regarded as the most appropriate for this purpose. In the context of the French Revolution, it was the royal collection of art housed in the Louvre that was invested with the task of forming civic virtue in serving, as Pommier puts it, as a 'sanctuary of the example' (Pommier, 1989: 27). By contrast, although the *Musée d'histoire naturelle* was also opened to the public, it functioned more as a retreat from the historical fractures of the present into the still intact totality of eighteenth century classification than as a means for forming civic virtue (see Outram, 1984). Similarly, the South Kensington Museum, the nerve-centre of the public museum system developed in Britain in the 1840s and 1850s, was principally a museum of art and design and, within the governmental task of making the population self-civilising that was accorded this museum system, it was art that was accorded pride of place as the chief instrument for this task (see Purbrick, 1994). That this was so had principally to do with the coming together of two things: new conceptions of the population which, under the influence of Malthusian conceptions, placed a premium on the need for working-class men to develop new forms of self-restraint in their sexual and leisure activities; and Romantic conceptions of art which allowed the sphere of the aesthetic to be thought of as a resource for harmonising the person, bringing the conflicting aspects of (in this case) his personality under some form of direction and regulation (see chapter 5). In his Sheffield museum, Ruskin thus provided visitors with implements for drawing in order to encourage the subordination of the hand to the superior sense of the eye and thence to the controlling direction of the mind—a metaphorical subordination of manual to mental labour which, in enabling the individual labourer to bring himself under an interior form of central direction and control, would, ideally, achieve the same end with the position of the labouring classes within the body politic (see Helsinger, 1994: 13).

By contrast, it was only in the last 20 to 30 years of the nineteenth century that museums dedicated to the historical sciences—and especially natural history and ethnology museums—came into their own in being accorded a public prominence and pedagogic function which, in the main, supplanted the position earlier enjoyed by art in this respect. It was in this period that many of today's major metropolitan museums of natural history were initially established. In the United States where, in Charles Willson Peale's Philadelphia Museum, art and natural history were brought together in a distinctive and influential nationalist fusion which distinguished American museums from European ones (see Kulik, 1989), it was nonetheless not until the last quarter or so of the nineteenth century that the collections of most natural history societies and associations were translated into the holdings of public museums with an explicitly civic mission. The American Museum of Natural History in New York was incorporated in 1868 on terms which, although the development and maintenance of the collection were to be funded through private philanthropy, committed the Museum to a strong civic and public educational function to be regulated by the Commissioners of Central Park (see Rosenzweig and Blackmar, 1992: 349–57). Chicago's Field Museum of Natural History postdates the World's Columbian Exhibition of 1893 and was prompted by the considerable educational potential suggested by the success of both the ethnological and natural history displays at that exhibition (see Rydell, 1984). Similarly, it was not until 1881, when the new British Museum (Natural History) was opened at South Kensington, that London could boast of a dedicated natural history museum. Although the natural history collections of the British Museum had always proved popular with the public when they were housed at Bloomsbury—so much so for the proposal that they should be moved from the city centre to South Kensington to occasion concern that this might diminish their accessibility[4]—the policies of the British Museum restricted access to the collections in limiting opening hours to set periods of the week and actively discouraging women from attending.

Notwithstanding the greater distances involved in visiting it, the new museum proved a major success with the public, attracting up to 400 000 visitors a year in the 1880s and 1890s. This was in part attributable to the ways in which new conceptions of the public and civic functions of natural history museums began to inform the exhibition practices of those museums. In particular, the new public educational significance that was accorded natural history museums was institutionalised in the form of the division between their research and exhibition collections—the former classified scientifically for scholarly research and the latter arranged in a manner best calculated to educate the public. This division, first advocated by Edward Gray at the British Museum in 1858 and subsequently by Louis Agassiz at Harvard's Museum of Comparative Zoology, soon became a standard principle of collection arrangement. It was put into force at the British Museum (Natural History) in 1884 as a part of a commitment by Sir William Henry Flower, the Museum's Director, to a new form of didacticism which required museums to so arrange their materials as to make the principles underlying them and the message they were meant to display publicly legible (see Flower, 1898).

Ethnological collections were similarly separated from other collections and opened to the public in major institutions dedicated solely to such collections over much the same period. The *Musée d'Ethnographie du Trocadero*, for example, was opened to the public in 1879. Similar tendencies were evident in Germany where, by the 1890s, several cities—Berlin in particular—had major specialised collections devoted to ethnology. In Britain, by contrast, the ethnological collections at the British Museum remained a part of a larger composite Department of British and Medieval Antiquities and Ethnology. Established in 1866, this Department survived intact until 1921 (Caygill, 1981: 42–49)—a fact which occasioned considerable disquiet in the pages of the *Museums Journal*, the organ of the newly established Museums Association, where British ethnological collections were repeatedly compared unfavourably with German ones in the context of rising anxieties about the role ethnological museums should play in the colonial rivalries of Britain and Germany (see Coombes, 1994: 240–41; Lewis, 1989: 21–22). Nonetheless, ethnological collections did assume a greater public prominence as a result of a range of private initiatives through which significant ethnological collections were inscribed in new public contexts as parts of new programs of citizenship. The most influential of these consisted in Henry Pitt Rivers' educational experiment when he arranged for his ethnological collections to be exhibited in Bethnal Green in 1874 in an attempt to develop an instrument of public pedagogy that would help school the working classes in the civic lessons to be derived from Darwinian theories of progressive evolution. This served as a prelude to the collections being placed on more permanent display at, first, the South Kensington Museum and, subsequently, under Henry Balfour's direction, the University of Oxford. There were, however, other museums which, although not publicly funded, sought to make ethnological collections more widely available as parts of a public pedagogy—the Horniman Museum, for example, as well as the Hall of Primitive Medicine at the Wellcome Institute Historical Medical Museum (see Skinner, 1986).

The tendency in the United States was for ethnological and natural history collections to be developed together in composite institutions whose predominant signature was that of natural history. This was true of Chicago's Field Museum of Natural History, which included a significant ethnological component from the period of its initial establishment in the 1890s. However, it was not until nearly 30 years after it first opened that the American Museum of Natural History accorded a significant institutional priority to its ethnological collections in the announcement, in 1896, that the Museum planned to establish a new Department of Anthropology 'in order to illustrate the history of man in the same way as we are showing the history of animal life' (Annual Report, 1896: 17). Similarly, it was not until 1884 with the establishment of the Division of Ethnology in the U.S. National Museum at the Smithsonian Institution that the ethnological collections were singled out from the earlier '*omnium gatherum*' structure of the

Institution's collections both to receive special curatorial attention and to become a more prominent and clearly differentiated component of the Institution's public and pedagogic address (see Hinsley, 1981).

In Australia, there was a similar tendency towards composite museums of geology, natural history and ethnology, and for these to assume increasingly public forms by the closing decades of the nineteenth century. By the 1890s, the collections that had been gathered in association with the various philosophical, natural and scientific societies established earlier in the century had been translated into major publicly funded museums in each of the capital cities of the different states (see Kohlstedt, 1983). The same period also witnessed an increased stress on the educational functions of those museums in ways that were quite closely related to the vicissitudes of Darwinism in Australia. By and large, the major curatorial power-brokers in Australian museums were Owenites to a man and so remained openly hostile to Darwin until the 1880s: so much so, Finney records, that the major museums did not obtain copies of Darwin's *The Origin of Species* for their libraries until the late 1870s or late 1880s (Finney, 1993: 105–6).[5] At the National Museum of Victoria, initially housed in the University of Melbourne, Frederick McCoy retained Cuverian–Owenite principles of classification in his commitment to the conception of the Museum as a house of reason that should stand as an alternative—and thus remain aloof in relation to—the world of popular and public culture (see Goodman, 1990). It was not until 1900, when the Museum was moved into Melbourne's city centre, that its collections—consisting now, for the first time, of both natural history and ethnological components—were arranged in accordance with evolutionary principles and accorded a more clearly public educational function under the directorship of Baldwin Spencer.

In summary, then, while the precise timing might vary in accordance with specific local conditions and circumstances, the last 20 to 30 years of the nineteenth century and the opening decades of the twentieth saw markedly new kinds of attention and importance accorded to natural history and ethnological collections. As such, the processes involved in this transformation might usefully be seen as an instance of what Foucault has called 'the "governmentalisation of the state" ', through which tactics, objectives and instruments of governing formed, initially, outside the state are taken up by the state and subjected to more extensive and coordinated development (Foucault, 1978: 103). The techniques that had been developed in the earlier history of natural history societies and associations to use nature as a resource for cultivating selected attributes in elite social strata were now redeployed—and, in the process, transformed—in being connected to more general programs of social management. One of the more significant consequences of this was a change in the conception of the publics which it was thought such museums should aim to address and of the means they should employ to do so.

The development of the Boston Society of Natural History from its original conception as a learned society to, in 1867, a public museum provides a well-documented example of the kinds of changes I have in mind here. Established initially, in 1830, as a private association dedicated to the amateur scholarly pursuits of its exclusively male and middle-class membership, the opening, in 1867, of the Museum of the Boston Society of Natural History under the terms of a land grant soon gave rise to new principles for managing and displaying the collection. Under the influence of Samuel Scudder, the Society's librarian and custodian of its collections and a past pupil and disciple of Louis Agassiz, the collections were arranged with a public and didactic function, rather than research purposes, primarily in view. This was accompanied by a broadened conception of the sections of the population it was thought might benefit from the didactic influence of natural history displays. Women, who had previously been excluded from the association, were admitted into membership in the 1870s and, by the 1880s, the Museum had embarked on a program of active collaboration with the Women's Education Association. That children, too, were now regarded as in need of a natural history education was testified to by the establishment of the Teachers' School of Science, which aimed to train teachers in the moral lessons to be derived from the study of natural history in order that those lessons might then be carried into the classroom.

This latter development was a significant new departure for museums as a whole. Throughout the early to mid-nineteenth century, the child had either been a neglected or a wholly disparaged—and sometimes despised—object of museum attention. It was only rarely that museums made any specific effort to address or engage with the interests of children, or to encourage their attendance except insofar as they might visit as members of families. More to the point, their attendance was often actively discouraged. From the 1880s, by contrast, the child—cast, now, in the guise of child as future citizen—  becomes an increasing and, in some cases, obsessive object of attention within the policies and practices of museums, and especially natural history museums. Grace Fisher Ramsay, writing in the 1930s, traced the development, in the 1880s and 1890s, of a range of new programs initiated by a number of American natural history museums—the

Milwaukee Public Museum and the Park Museum of Natural History, Providence, Rhode Island, for example—which, either directly (as in the provision of public lectures for school parties) or indirectly (as in the provision of lectures for school teachers), had the child as their target (see Ramsay, 1938). However, the pride of place in her account—and with good reason—is accorded to the work of the Department of Public Instruction (subsequently the Department of Public Education) at the American Museum of Natural History, where she had herself worked for many years. Established in 1884, the Department of Public Instruction, from 1893, commenced a program of activities in conjunction with the education boards of, first, the government of New York State and, from 1895, of New York City also. By the early 1900s, this program could genuinely claim to be without parallel. Through every means possible—lectures for school children, the provision of a special Children's Room and, most distinctively, the provision of specimen boxes through which, via specially designed trucks, selections of the Museum's collections could be circulated to schools—the Museum strove relentlessly to deliver nature's message to the child. It claimed some success in doing so. In 1912, George Sherwood, the Curator of the Department of Public Education, was able to report that the course of children's lectures had been attended by 31 929 children—an increase of 9132 on the previous year—while 537 specimen collections had been circulated to 491 schools reaching 1 275 890 pupils (Annual Report, 1912: 41–42).

Quite apart from their own success in this matter, the school programs of the American Museum of Natural History became a model for international 'best practice'. In going to considerable lengths to publicise its educational activities through the journals it produced, the Museum became a beacon for museum administrators from around the world.[6] When, in 1913, Charles Hedley, an assistant curator at the Australian Museum, wrote a report of his visit in the previous year to a number of American museums, he dwelt in great detail on the activities of the American Museum of Natural History, portraying these as a shining example of how to extend the museum's sphere of usefulness 'beyond the galleries to the lecture hall and beyond the lecture hall to the suburban school' (Hedley, 1913: 7). As such, his report formed a part of an increasing emphasis on the Australian Museum's own public educational function—and especially its responsibilities to schools—that was evident, from 1889, in the Curators' Reports to the Board of Trustees as well as in the museum's correspondence with the New South Wales Department of Public Instruction, under whose auspices it was governed.[7] Even so, the American Museum of Natural History was not the only model cited in this regard. In the previous year, Charles Anderson, the Australian Museum's mineralogist, had written a report on his trip to a number of European museums. In doing so, he singled out the British Museum (Natural History) as especially instructive. Its education programs, its use of indexical principles of exhibition and its clarity of labelling, Anderson argued, established new standards regarding 'how a museum may best discharge its duty to the public'—even though he did think it prudent to warn that the Australian Museum should be careful not to become so attractive 'as to tempt the public to seek nature knowledge in the museum halls rather than in the bush and by the seashore' (Anderson, 1912: 85).[8]

The British Museum (Natural History) was also a point of reference for Albert Bickmore, the founding Curator of the Department of Public Instruction at the American Museum of Natural History. In his unpublished history of the Museum, Bickmore reported on the discussions he had had with Sir William Henry Flower when he had visited London in 1893–94, noting with pleasure the stress which the British Museum (Natural History) placed on its public educational function, especially in relation to children:

> I soon learned that the great minds which are moulding the destinies of the British nation were all agreed in our primary and fundamental belief, namely that that individual and that community and that nation, which is the best educated will be the one which will survive in the great contest of which the labour troubles in our country and in England during that summer were but the distant mutterings of a coming tempest which will sooner or later burst upon the civilised world.
>
> To prepare their people for this approaching storm they are bending all their energies to perfecting their system of education, not only for the city of London but for the whole United Kingdom, and one gratifying result has already been achieved, namely, that during the past year there has been a larger attendance of children of school age, particularly in Ireland, than there has ever been before in the history of the Empire. (Bickmore, n.d.: 121)

Bickmore is referring here to the changing conceptions of the museum's function associated with what can perhaps best be described as the 'second wave' of museum development in Britain. As Gaynor Kavanagh has noted, the number of museums established as a result of the enabling provision made in the *Museums Act 1845* was limited, especially as that provision was revoked by the *Public Libraries and Museums Act 1850* (Kavanagh, 1994: 10). As a consequence, except for a handful of cases, museum collections remained largely the preserve of voluntary local antiquarian, scientific and natural history societies. The second and more significant phase in the expansion of the public museum complex occurred in association with the shift from the *laissez-faire* liberalism of the Manchester school to the more interventionist and social-welfarist liberalism which prevailed from the 1870s to the Great War. This resulted in a spate of legislation enabling and encouraging local authorities to invest in the provision of public cultural resources, including museums, and this, in turn, led to a significant increase in the numbers of museums in the 1880s and 1890s.

This second phase of museum expansion was informed by a renewed and hitherto quite unparalleled stress on the museum's public educational functions and responsibilities. This change of emphasis was in turn closely related to the increasing professionalisation of museums and the growing connections between museums and the education system. The most important development regarding the first of these matters consisted in the establishment of the Museums Association in 1889. In the debates of the British Association for the Advancement of Science which had prepared the ground for the establishment of the Museums Association, the need for a greater stress on the museum's role as, in F.W. Rudler's terms, 'educational engines' (Lewis, 1989: 5) was a constantly recurring theme. The same was true of the debates conducted at the annual meetings of the Museums Association and reprinted in the pages of its organ, the *Museums Journal*, as well as in the parallel debates and inquiries of the British Association for the Advancement of Science, which retained a keen interest in museums through to the 1920s. The educational orientation advocated in these debates and inquiries had two clear points of address. First, as had been true of the earlier, mid-century phase of museum development, the workingman was still envisaged as a primary target of the museum's pedagogic mission—although, as we shall see, for different reasons. The initial list of the Museums Association's functions thus included that of the 'promotion of museum lectures to workingmen'. However, the list also included a commitment to encouraging the 'preparation of small educational loan collections for circulation among schools' (Lewis, 1989: 10) and it was this—the development of increasingly formalised connections with the schooling system and, as a part of this, an increasing concern with the child—that constituted the most distinctive addition to the ethos and orientation of British museums over this period. The Day School Code of 1894 was important here. In recognising that instruction in a museum might be regarded as school attendance, it stimulated the development of closer associations between teachers and curators. This tendency was strengthened by the *Education Act 1902*, which allowed for organised visits to museums to count as formal parts of the curriculum. It is only necessary to add, to complete the picture, that the collections of the majority of the museums actively involved in these debates and new practices centred on natural history, geological or ethnological materials.[9]

Wherever we look over this period, then, we find three developments occurring hand-in-hand. As museums were accorded a greater value as cultural resources to be harnessed to the tasks of forming a citizenry, so also an increased stress was placed on the potential of the historical sciences in this regard. Finally, women and, more especially, the child and future citizen were added alongside the workingman to the range of constituencies the museum was called on to address.

This is not to say that the civic value that had earlier been invested in the public display of art was of no continuing consequence in this period. Recent studies of the Whitechapel Picture Exhibitions organised in the 1880s and 1890s, as well as of the establishment, over the same period, of the Tate Gallery, have shown how art continued to be regarded as a resource that might be mobilised in projects aimed at inducting the poor into programs of self-governance and self-management (see Koven, 1994; Taylor, 1994). In both Australia and America where, for related nationalist reasons, art—as primarily European in its associations—had never suggested itself as quite so useful a civic resource as nature, the power for civic good that was attributed to art nonetheless remained a continuing influence: in the programs of the various Schools of Art and Mechanics' Institutes that had been established in most Australian towns of any size (see Candy and Laurent, 1994) as well as, in the American context, in the educational programs which institutions like the Metropolitan Museum of Art began to organise from the 1870s (see Ramsay, 1938: 4–14). What had clearly changed, however, was the pattern of stress and emphasis. By the late nineteenth century, art museums were tending increasingly to function as social marker institutions for the urban middle classes and, by and large, had vacated the field of popular instruction. The tendency of natural history and ethnology museums, by contrast, was in the opposite direction—from assemblages of objects of a scientific or curiosity value into instruments for a civically orientated public didacticism.

This change was evident, above all, in the changing conception of the function of the natural history collection and the principles of organisation it would need to adhere to in order to fulfil that function. I have already touched on these matters in my earlier comments concerning the emergence of a distinction between the research and the exhibition collections. What needs to be stressed here are the respects in which the museum object was quite radically reshaped. The rationalisation and streamlining of exhibits and the reprogramming of the museum environment to enhance its public educational functions brought about a transformation in the object's constitution and function. Emerging from these changes as a thoroughly governmentalised artefact, its role was now that of a bearer of programs of civic formation directed at the population as a whole.

It is in this light that we should view the debates, that were as novel as they were incessant, regarding the best way of arranging and labelling exhibits so as to render them auto-intelligible to an uneducated public. This principle was clearly enunciated by L.P. Gratacap, Curator of Mineralogy at the American Museum of Natural History, in the objection he lodged against the proposal that the Museum should adjust its priorities to become more of a centre for scientific research:

> It may be insisted, indeed, that the careful luminous exhibition and exposition of its collections, so that the public may fully understand them, and learn their lessons, is the chief purpose of the Museum. This work sedulously followed involves not simply a display of labelled objects, but a sequence and order that may teach a lesson. (Gratacap, n.d., Ch. 2: 88)

By the time it was published, Flaubert's depiction, in *Bouvard and Pecuchet*, of the museum as an institution dedicated to the fetishistic accumulation of objects as ends in themselves was already out of date as, by then, the museum object was already being lined up and made to march to the tune of its governmental deployment.

NEW TIMES, NEW SUBJECTS

It seems clear, then, that the historical sciences, in being accorded a particular prominence in the public educational programs of museums as well as functioning as crucial mediators between museums and the education system, played an increasingly crucial role in governmental processes aimed at forming and shaping the attributes of citizens. In some contexts, moreover, the role of the historical sciences in this regard clearly supplanted the importance that had earlier been attributed to aesthetics as a resource judged capable of equipping populations with a capacity for self-management. Why should this have been so? What kinds of attributes were the historical sciences judged likely to help cultivate?

Some of the considerations bearing on how we might want to answer such questions are relatively close to hand. If the historical sciences were increasingly regarded as useful for governing, this was partly because their prestige had been carefully nurtured over the intervening period. In extending time beyond the conventional Biblical chronology of 6000 years and, additionally, developing ways of making these newly discovered pasts—the pasts of human prehistory, of extinct forms of life and past states of the earth's existence—visible and so capable of assuming a material form within the present, nineteenth century natural history, archaeology and geology had, by the mid-century, both opened up new horizons of time and devised means for making these a palpable and widely disseminated component of the contemporary public culture.[10] This brought with it increased prestige which the leading practitioners of these sciences were not slow to exploit. Nicolaas Rupke's biography of Richard Owen, for example, shows how carefully Owen fashioned the reconstructions of dinosaurs made possible by new techniques and discoveries in palaeontology so that they might serve as public icons of museums and their contribution to public knowledge (see Rupke, 1994).

Then again, it seems clear that, at least in some contexts, changing patterns of gender relations played a role in these developments. Kathleen McCarthy has observed the strong anti-aesthetic orientation which characterised post-bellum American culture. The feminisation of culture—which had hitherto been interpreted positively as a beneficent aspect of the civilising process (see Douglas, 1978; Bushman, 1992)—came to be regarded as a problem. Viewed now as effete and emasculating, the sphere of the aesthetic—of art and intellectual culture—was to be abandoned for nature which was itself being increasingly recodified as a masculinised domain. An article in an 1897 issue of *Atlantic Monthly* advised men to:

> leave the closed air of the office, the library or the club, and go out into the streets and the highway. Consult the teamster, the farmer, the woodchopper, the shepherd or the drover. You will find him as healthy in mind . . . [and] strong in natural impulses, as he was in Shakespeare's time. From his loins, and not those of the dilettante, will spring the man of the future. (cit. in McCarthy, 1991: 152)

Donna Haraway's discussion of the masculinist culture of nature which dominated the programs of the American Museum of Natural History through the late nineteenth and early twentieth centuries can leave us in no doubt regarding the influence which such conceptions had on the ways in which, in at least one part of its public discourse, the Museum interpreted its civic duties and obligations over the period I am concerned with (see Haraway, 1992).[11] For Henry Fairfield Osborn, the Museum's Director, the task of the Museum was to restore 'the compelling force of the struggle for existence in education', and this meant that it had to turn its face against that 'final step in the emasculation' of education which had 'substituted the woman for the man teacher' (cit. in Rainger, 1991: 115).

Be this as it may, the more general reasons for this newly found museological prominence of the historical sciences have to do with the new disciplinary synthesis that was forged, after 1860, between prehistoric archaeology, natural history, geology and anthropology. The publication of Darwin's *Origin* in 1859, together with the discovery of human remains at Brixham Cave in 1860 in a strata which incontrovertibly established the antiquity of human life on earth, served to insert human life into the recently excavated deep histories of geology and natural history while also, in the theory of natural selection, providing a mechanism which seemed capable of connecting the two. This was an accomplishment which, in the fields of archaeology and anthropology respectively, was carried through by John Lubbock in his 1865 text *Pre-Historic Times* and by Tylor in *Primitive Culture* (first published in 1871).[12] As a consequence of these developments, questions concerning the social management of time—or, more accurately, the social management of populations *in* time and *by means* of time—assumed a new importance. On the one hand, the unprecedented duration of these new times posed new and distinctive problems regarding how to reorganise and regulate the discursive horizons of a population which found itself precipitated into new depths of time. At the same time, however, these new temporal coordinates and the evolutionary mechanisms connecting them furnished a means of enhancing the resources and tactics of liberal government in providing for the insertion of individuals in time in ways which allowed them to become auto-developing or self-progressing subjects.

This, at any rate, is the case I want to argue with regard to the late nineteenth and early twentieth century functioning of the historical sciences within the 'exhibitionary complex' (see Bennett, 1988). To do so, however, it will be necessary to take issue with the prevailing interpretation of the relations between the exhibitionary deployment of the new evolutionary paradigms governing this disciplinary ensemble and the related projects of liberalism, colonialism and imperialism. In most recent accounts of the role of the historical sciences in exhibitionary contexts over this period, the accent has fallen on their legitimation or hegemonic functions. The construction of evolutionary series running continuously from natural through to human life, most accounts suggest, served to legitimate and naturalise the hegemony of Europeans over colonised peoples while, at the same time, also legitimating and naturalising forms of class and gender hegemony within the boundaries of nation states.[13] As an aspect of this argument, finally, such displays are said to have promoted self-confident forms of white supremacism—a view we find in recent accounts by both Annie Coombes and Elizabeth Edwards (see Coombes, 1994: 64; Edwards, 1992: 6).

It is far from my purpose to suggest that this tradition of analysis is wholly off the mark. To the contrary, the body of evidence that has been marshalled in its support is, in some senses, overwhelming. Be this as it may, the mechanism of effects which the argument posits does strike me as deficient. For it assumes that the historical sciences, once placed in an exhibitionary context, function like ideologies. As such, the argument envisages, as the imaginary addressee of such ideologies, persons who will accept the legitimacy of the places they occupy as both the superordinates of some and the subordinates of others. This further implies, to borrow a term from Stuart Hall, that the 'ideological effect' of the historical sciences is that of legitimating the existing social order by convincing all social agents—and, in this case, especially dominant ones—of the inherent rightness of the social places they occupy (see Hall, 1977). In contradistinction to such accounts, and to the largely psychological mechanism on which they rest, I want to propose another way in which we might account for the field of effects established by the historical sciences, and for their *modus operandi* once they were installed in exhibitionary apparatuses. I shall do so by outlining the respects in which the horizons of time opened up by these sciences established new discursive coordinates which, in allowing for the person to be historicised in new ways, opened up the prospect for new kinds of 'progressive' work on the self. This is to suggest that the exhibitionary institutions in which the historical sciences were deployed should be viewed not as the containers for ideologies performing a legitimation function, but as cultural technologies which inducted their visitors into new ways of acting on and shaping the self that allowed the person to be inserted into the new progressive ordering of time offered by the disciplinary syntheses I have referred to. They functioned, that is to say, in a manner calculated to produce what I shall call a 'regulated restlessness' on the part of their addressees, locating these, always, at a point of tension within a dialectic between perfection and imperfection, rather than inscribing them into an historically complacent acceptance of given positions.

Or at least, to place appropriate limits round my account, I shall suggest that this was true of *some* of the forms in which the historical sciences were deployed in museums. For the logic of Nicholas Thomas' compelling criticisms of attempts, like those of Homi Bahba and Gyatri Spivak, to develop a general account of the relations between culture and colonialism rather than differentiated accounts of the role of cultural practices in different colonialisms, suggests that, if we set out in search of a general set of relations between museums, the historical sciences, the civilising programs of modern forms of government and colonial relations and practices, we shall not find it (Thomas, 1994). Thomas' examination of the variable collecting contexts in which colonised objects became entangled point in a similar direction, suggesting that what we find, instead, is a massive variability of practices and relations with the same objects taking on significantly different meanings and functions according to the contexts in which they were exhibited. The depiction, in London's Missionary Museum, of the religious artefacts of Pacific peoples as rejected idols, given up by their owners in rejection of the sin and folly of idolatry, offered an evangelical construction of such peoples which saw them as already on the road to full and equal membership of a Christian community. This was, Thomas argues, a political and semiotic project of an entirely different kind from private collections of curiosities assembled in colonial contexts by wealthy settlers. Far from suggesting a common humanity between coloniser and colonised, such displays more typically rendered up the colonised population in the form of an unreformed and unreformable savagery in ways that allowed them to provide artefactual props for local practices of racial extermination (see Thomas, 1991: 152–58, 163–67).

My purpose, then, is limited to the role of the major public museums of natural history and ethnology located in the main cities of the major metropolitan powers and their colonial outposts. It is also limited to the relations between such museums and their addressees. For, although women and children were now included among these, black and colonised peoples were not. Their role within the 'exhibitionary complex' was limited to the object domain, supplying exemplary artefacts, human remains and living specimens. They had no place within the implied address of museums: they did not figure among its potential subjects or beneficiaries. Literally, they did not count: as late as 1932, when the Museums Association conducted a survey of Empire Museums, its report on the museums and art galleries of South Africa discounted the black population as irrelevant to its calculations regarding the ratio between the number of museums in South Africa and its population (see Miers and Markham, 1932).

I shall place a final limitation on myself, for I shall be particularly concerned to outline the respects in which, in late nineteenth and early twentieth century Britain, the new disciplinary synthesis forged between the historical sciences was articulated to the new liberalism and its reformist social agendas. In doing so I shall try to make intelligible why and how Darwinian theory could be appropriated by liberal and reforming currents of social thought in ways that were quite distinct from those suggested by more familiar accounts of social Darwinism. This will, in turn, involve recovering the respects in which the role of the historical sciences over this period has to be considered in new contexts—pushed out from the field of representational practices to which most recent discussion has largely been confined to consider the ways in which evolutionary thought came to play a key role in attempts to formulate a new liberal ethics of citizenship.

SHAPING THE PROGRESSIVE SELF

A theoretical basis for such an account is most clearly available in Adrian Desmond's revisionist interpretation of Darwin's place in the history of evolutionary thought (see Desmond, 1989). A part of Desmond's concern is to restore and make sense of Darwin's appeal to liberal and reforming opinion in the mid- to late nineteenth century period. To this end, he makes two main points. First, to the degree that social life was plotted analogically on the model of natural life, Darwin's theory of evolution lent itself to liberal and reforming programs in opening up the possibility that simple and primitive forms of life might evolve into more complex and developed ones. Whereas Cuvier's doctrine of the fixity of species condemned each form of natural life to its preordained ecological niche and, by analogical extension, implied that existing human hierarchies of race and gender were immutable, Darwinian theory allowed that natural (and, by extension, human) life might ascend through the ranks.

Second, however, Darwin detached this expectation from the radical and even revolutionary associations it had earlier enjoyed in the 1830s and 1840s when, in close association with the Chartist movement, the Lamarckian school of evolutionary theory had allowed and encouraged the expectation that, just as lower forms of life might evolve into higher ones without let or restriction, so the lower social orders might legitimately aspire to lift themselves into the highest social ranks and, in the process, level out the distinctions between themselves and their 'betters'. The 'social Lamarckian science of progressivism, materialism and environmental determinism,' as Desmond puts it, was harnessed to the cause of working-class emancipation 'to underwrite the change to a democratic, cooperative society' (Desmond, 1989: 329). Darwin, by contrast, while allowing for a mechanism of transformism through which lower forms of life might evolve into higher ones, simultaneously placed a constraining, conservative force at the heart of that mechanism to the degree that, far from guaranteeing a free and unconstrained capacity for forms of life to evolve into progressively higher forms, he placed the barrier of natural selection between, so to speak, those which made it and those which did not.

It is in the light of these two considerations that we can begin to understand why the historical sciences suggested themselves as readily adaptable to the reforming programs of liberal and reforming opinion in the closing decades of the nineteenth century. Before that they had offered an unpalatable range of choices. They were either, through their associations with radicalism, too hot to handle, or, as with Richard Owen's revival of Cuvier's theory of archetypes, which aimed to stem the evolutionary slide of Lamarckianism, too conservative in their demonstration of the inviolability of existing social divisions to be of much appeal to liberal, middle-class reforming opinion. As a consequence, although the natural history collections in the British Museum were massively popular, liberal and reforming opinion was cautious regarding their pedagogic value to the degree that their arrangement in accordance with Owen's principles suggested an implicit (although ambivalent) support for aristocratic authority and old England (see Rupke, 1994: Chs 1 and 2). The principles of Darwinism, by contrast, allowed rhetorics of progress to be detached from their earlier radical associations and to be connected to reformist and civilising programs which aimed to lift the population 'through the ranks', but in a regulated manner, gradually and in a piecemeal fashion rather than through sudden ruptural transformations, and in ways which, while retaining distinctions of rank intact, sought merely to distribute the population through them differently.

Darwin's nature, then, was, as Adrian Desmond and James Moore put it in their biography of Darwin, a reforming nature (Desmond and Moore, 1992). It was, however, a reforming nature of a very distinctive kind. Earlier in the century, the nature fashioned in association with the projects of radical Unitarianism—which had been an important aspect of Darwin's childhood milieu—had clasped evolution and reform into an essential unity. The progressive reform of society was viewed as the automatic result of a self-developing nature whose auto-progressive mechanisms were translated to society through a natural propensity to self-reform and improvement inscribed in the constitution of the human subject. Between such conceptions and later

Darwinian formulations there intervened what James Paradis and George Williams describe as 'the normative perspective of populations' derived from Malthus (Paradis and Williams, 1989: 9). This established a new methodological naturalism, one with consequences that were ambivalent. For, although this naturalism inscribed an evolutionary mechanism at the centre of nature, that mechanism was by no means benign and its outcomes by no means guaranteed. 'The face of nature,' as Desmond and Moore put it, 'was no longer smiling; it scowled at a gladiatorial arena, strewn with the corpses of the losers' (1989: 265). Similarly, if the 'grand crush of population' gave an impetus to evolution, initiating a struggle for existence through which human as well as natural life might ascend to higher forms of perfection, there was no guarantee that such struggles would result in progressive outcomes. For Darwin, Desmond and Moore argue, the belief in 'inexorable ascent and guaranteed progress', as applied to both nature and human society, had to be abandoned as a 'radical myth' (1989: 275).

This takes us to the political ambiguity inherent in Darwin's work. On the one hand, in fashioning a nature which was neither radical nor Anglican, which was anti-Tory in opposing meritocratic principles of social organisation to those based on inherited privilege and which, in demonstrating that evolution resulted from the cumulative effects of a multitude of tiny variations in a manner that lent support to gradual and ameliorative programs of social change (evolution, Darwin wrote, 'baffles the idea of revolution'—cit. in Desmond and Moore: 294), Darwin cast nature in an image that could be harmonised with, and adapted to, liberal programs of social reform. On the other hand, this nature did not guarantee any particular set of outcomes and its mechanisms, when translated to society, could not be counted on to start or to carry on functioning automatically. It is in this light that we can best understand the anxiety about progress that Darwin's work helped to generate. This anxiety was most clearly manifested, in the British context, in the debates of the Ethnological Society and the British Association for the Advancement of Science, both of which played an important role in fashioning a new set of scientific coordinates for liberalism in parallel with the new philosophical coordinates supplied by T.H. Greene and the new political coordinates of Gladstonian liberalism. For there is evident in these debates a nervousness about the nature–society interface, an uncertainty about the crossover of evolutionary mechanisms from the one to the other, an anxiety—very clear in Tylor's *Primitive Culture*, for example—about how, when and where the mechanisms of social evolution first get started and how they can be kept on the go. However much nature provided a new model and template for reform, it was clear it could not be counted on. It stood, so to speak, in need of a cultural supplement, a supplement that was to be provided mainly through the stress the new liberalism placed on public education.

Melvin Richter attributes this emphasis on education to the way in which the new liberalism, while retaining a commitment to the earlier principles of economic liberalism which limited the role of state action to the removal of obstacles which might impede the self-regulating mechanisms of the market, interpreted those principles in a manner which justified an extended conception of the role of state action in the moral sphere. Although state action could not play a direct role in the cultivation of moral attributes, since these could only emerge from the self-activity of individuals, it could play an indirect role in freeing citizens from hindrances or disabilities so as to enable them to develop their moral potentialities themselves (see Richter, 1964: 283–89). Richter also suggests that this tendency toward a more state-interventionist liberalism has to be seen in conjunction with the changing meaning and currency of the concept of reform. In the early nineteenth century, to reform a person or institution had carried connotations of restoring an original condition of excellence by removing the abuse and distortions that had come to corrupt its character or functioning. By the later decades of the century, by contrast, the concept of reform had come to stand for 'improvement, not by return to any previous state of affairs, but rather by progress to some new and higher form of the original ideal' (1964: 317). It was in this clasping of reform and improvement, Richter suggests, that a new ethics of the person was formed around the responsibility of the individual to develop and cultivate an incessantly progressive relationship to the self.

It is in this light that we should view the relations between the new developments in the historical sciences and the burgeoning literature—with texts by Huxley, Toynbee, Spencer and L.T. Hobhouse—which sought to connect those developments to the field of ethics in its bearing on the duties and obligations of citizenship. For what we see in this literature, or at least some of its strands, is a concern with the respects in which the new orderings of the past produced by these sciences could be fashioned into a discursive template for the formation of a progressive ethics. In allowing the self to be historically stratified, to be archaeologically layered so that a tension might be established between its undeveloped and 'primitive' components on the one hand, and its more dynamic and progressive aspects on the other, this ethics placed the self in an historicised zone where the processes of person formation were able to be temporalised in new ways.

We can also see in these debates a concern to defend liberal techniques of governance—the techniques of governing at a distance—as the only possible means of producing persons who would be so situated in the new evolutionary orders of time that contributing to the ongoing progress of society through the cultivation of an historicised and progressive relation to the self would stand as a duty, an ethical imperative. This is clear in Huxley's 1893 essay *Evolution and Ethics* in which, in an argument which clearly links eugenicist conceptions of evolutionary cultivation to a Benthamite version of panoptic government, he argues that 'the pigeon fancier's polity' (Huxley in Paradis and Williams, 1989: 81) of eugenics revives the fantasy of a totally administered society that would be dependent on an administrator's ability to distinguish the fit from the unfit in the cultivation of a despotically selected evolutionary ideal:

> And this ideal polity would have been brought about not by gradually adjusting the men to the conditions around them, but by creating artificial conditions for them; not by allowing the free play of the struggle for existence, but by excluding that struggle; and by substituting selection directed towards the administrator's ideal for the selection it exercises. (1989: 78)

Huxley's concern here is not to defend 'the free play of the struggle for existence'. To the contrary, what he calls the 'ethical process' consists, essentially, in placing limits on the degree to which this struggle influences the organisation of human society. His objection, rather, is that the eugenicist 'logical ideal of evolutionary regimentation' assumes forms of administrative omniscience (the ability to distinguish the ethically or civically fit from the unfit) that are unattainable, while also substituting a despotically imposed ethical regime for one arising out of the self-directing activities of individuals.

A similar orientation is evident in Walter Bagehot's contention, in *Physics and Politics* (1873), that despotism is unfavourable to the principle of variability which, in society as in nature, he argues, provides the essential mechanism of progress. He thus objects that 'the most rigid Comtists teaching that we ought to be governed by a hierarchy' just as much as the 'secular Comtists who want to Frenchify the English institutions' by introducing 'an imitation of the Napoleonic system, a dictatorship founded on the proletariat' suppress the sources of social variability in subjecting society to the rigid ordering of a despotic plan. Instead, Bagehot finds a political analogue for Darwin's principle of natural selection in what he characterises as the main principle of democratic government: that government be subjected to, and be regulated by, discussion. The introduction of the principle of discussion into a polity, he argues, breaks down the yoke of fixed custom and so releases potentially progressive sources of variability.

For Bagehot, it is only liberal and democratic forms of government that can produce individuals who might become self-progressing and he sees their insertion in the new orders of time opened up by the historical sciences of geology, archaeology and anthropology as being crucial in this respect. Yet, if he sees these as supplying the coordinates within which individuals might become freely self-progressing, he is also anxious that such a capacity for progress should be regulated, should be held in check unless it might be tempted to go too far and too fast. Having identified a progressive mechanism in the sources of variability provided for by democratic government, Bagehot looks for a restraining mechanism, which he finds in the principle of 'animated moderation'. Unable to precisely define this principle, Bagehot instead exemplifies it by discussing the distinguishing qualities of the Englishman:

> And if you ask for a description of a great practical Englishman, you will be sure to have this, or something like it, 'Oh, he has plenty of go in him; but he knows when to pull up.' He may have all other defects in him; he may be coarse, he may be illiterate, he may be stupid to talk to; still this great union of spur and bridle, of energy and moderation, will remain to him. (Bagehot, 1873: 201–2).

I shall return to this last aspect of Bagehot's argument shortly. Meanwhile, my more general purpose has been to suggest that the late nineteenth century synthesis of the historical sciences furnished a new discursive template of person-formation, one which allowed white Europeans to be envisaged and fashioned as self-progressing subjects inserted in new orders of evolutionary time. As such, the historical sciences played an important role in defending liberal principles of government against the statist conceptions of eugenics in making progress depend on the self-activity of individuals rather than on administratively imposed programs of social selection. It is also possible, when viewed in this light, to see why the historical sciences came to occupy a position of prominence within the problematics of liberal government that had previously been reserved for art. The earlier concerns which had informed the deployment of aesthetics in museums in order to initiate processes of person-formation through which, by aspiring to the forms of completeness represented by works of art, individuals would become self-civilising remained important. The concern to transform the workingman into a self-reforming 'prudential subject' who would eschew drink and bestial sexuality for a life of providence and self-restraint remained a continuing concern of late nineteenth century liberal government. However, the governmental deployment of aesthetics in museums in this way did not provide a means of fashioning persons who could take up the progressive places and roles accorded them within the new concerns of liberal government.

Jonathan Hutchinson put the point I am after here nicely in his 1908 Presidential Address to the Museums Association:

> The old-day conception of humanity which taught that except for a highly favoured few it was enough that a man should be of sober and quiet habits, a faithful husband, a kind father, and a docile parishioner, and that at the age of 65, earlier or later, he should thankfully migrate to a place of reward and rest is rapidly being pushed aside by a wider appreciation of individual duty and responsibility. We now view the passing generations as links in an almost interminable chain of life, and every individual as a constituent element in such chains. We know with absolute certainty that the progressive development of humanity and with it the happiness of the coming ages will be influenced for good or evil by our conduct. Whilst we desire to enable all whom we can interest to attain a state of happy contentment with things as they are we wish that it may not be incompatible with an incessant desire to make them yet better. (Hutchinson, 1908: 15)

Like Bagehot, Hutchinson is here calling for a kind of 'animated moderation' in which a wish to progress is simultaneously stimulated and held in check. A similar orientation is embodied in what was perhaps the most influential museum application of the post-Darwinian synthesis of the historical sciences: the typological method. The application of Darwinian categories to the discursive program of museums was, of course, a halting, hesitant and inconsistent affair giving rise to a number of different display practices. For the most part, however, the incorporation of Darwinian principles into the organisation of natural history exhibits resulted in the depiction of long and slow lines of evolutionary development achieved as a consequence of progressive adaptations to changing conditions of existence. This resulted in a high degree of correspondence or 'fit' between the principles governing natural history displays and those governing archaeological museums which, since its initial use in a mid-century display at the National Museum of Copenhagen, were increasingly dominated by the three-age (stone, iron, bronze) system. The typological method developed by Henry Pitt Rivers provided an ethnological complement to these display techniques, and one that was to prove widely influential internationally, in part because of its popularisation at world fairs by American ethnological curators like Otis Mason and Henry Putnam.

The key to the typological method consisted in the doctrine of survivals according to which the artefacts, customs and ways of life of presently existing colonised black peoples were treated as the remnants of forms of social life in periods prior to those for which material evidence had survived in the archaeological record. Such customs and artefacts, it was argued, provided a means of making human prehistory visible; they provided a geographically displaced record of what human life, society and technology might have been like in European prehistory. They represented a time of the past which, having conveniently stood still, could illuminate those 'primitive' phases of human development whose marks had been erased elsewhere. In the typological method, accordingly, the artefacts of colonised peoples were extracted entirely from their originating cultural contexts to be placed at the beginning of evolutionary sequences which told the history of human technical and cultural development in the form of long and universal tendencies of development leading from the simple to the progressively more complex—from, in the case of Pitt Rivers' display of weaponry, the Aboriginal throwing stick to the medieval musket.

Or, more accurately: from a bewildering variety of Aboriginal throwing sticks, each arranged in an order of evolutionary succession, to an equally bewildering range of medieval muskets, also ordered in evolutionary terms, with each intervening stage of the development of weaponry illustrated in equally painstaking evolutionary detail. In subscribing to Darwin's contention that 'evolution baffles revolution', Pitt Rivers' purpose was to embody this message in the form of ethnological displays. He accordingly arranged these to show how, in society and technology just as much as in nature, the course of progress consisted of a multitude of accumulating but minor adaptations with a view to teaching, as he put it, 'the law that Nature makes no jumps' (Pitt Rivers, 1891: 116). It is, then, perhaps not surprising that most interpretations of Pitt Rivers' typological method have emphasised the respects in which it was envisaged as a display technique which, in incorporating Darwinian principles into ethnological displays, might serve as an exhibitionary antidote to the socialist agitation that was proving increasingly influential with the poor of 'outcast London' in the 1860s and 1870s.[14] While there can be no doubt that this was so, it does not, I believe, take us to the full complexity and ambiguity of the typological method or explain why it should have proved so portable to other national contexts and situations. For, as I have suggested elsewhere (see Bennett, 1995: 195–201), the typological method, in making progress visible and performable in the form of a succession of evolutionary stages which could not be skipped or bypassed, explicitly sought both to stimulate progress while at the same time regulating it. It aimed, that is to say, to historicise the person by placing him (primarily) in the midst of an evolutionary series which, although calculated to teach the lesson that progress could only come one step at a time, did nonetheless encourage the visitor to see himself as in transit, as on a road from and to somewhere. The visitor, in short, was placed in a particular form of being in time which, to the degree that that time was endowed with an inherent—albeit retarded—progressive momentum, required that its participants engage in an unremitting labour of progressive self-development if that momentum were not to give way to inertia. Its aim, we might say, was to produce a moderated animation—a provocation to progress that sought also to limit and direct the forms that progress might take.

Looked at in this light, we can see how the typological method—as well as the natural history displays on which it was modelled[15]—functioned as progressive technologies aiming to produce new historical subjects with new and carefully regulated developmental capacities. But what mechanism is at work here? Stephen Jay Gould suggests how we might answer this question in his discussion of the role that imperfection plays in the organisation of historical narrative in Darwin's work. 'Evolved perfection,' Gould suggests, 'covers the tracks of its own formation.' (Gould, 1987: 43) This being so, since perfection must stand in a condition of 'timeless balance', history—narrative—can only be revealed through 'quirks and imperfections'. It is, for Darwin, these 'oddities and imperfections' that record the pathways of historical evolution and which motivate the narrative of evolutionary development. When placed in museum displays, those same imperfections established new coordinates for an historicising of the self in the organisation of evolutionary narratives governed by a dialectic of perfection and imperfection, of completion and incompletion, in which progress was made visible and—in the form of the visitor's itinerary—performable as the visitor was installed in the space of restlessness between the two: between less and more evolved human types, races, technologies and forms of civilisation. Rather than functioning like an ideology which works to secure social relations by inscribing social agents into an historically complacent acceptance of their given positions, typological displays were calculated to produce a regulated restlessness, a worrisome insertion of the self into a developmental time which generated a requirement for a progressive movement through time while simultaneously restraining that movement.

Peter Brown's comments on the functioning, in the early Christian period, of the single-sex model in which women were regarded as failed or imperfect men offers an analogous dialectic of perfection and imperfection which might help to make this point. My concern here is with the respects in which, according to Brown, this system was 'exploited to subject men themselves to an unremitting process of fine-tuning' (Brown, 1988: 10). Precisely because their superiority to women was not based on a 'physiology of incommensurability' but on their bodily capacity to generate and retain heat more effectively, then so, unless both body and self were maintained in an appropriately virile manner and condition, each man might relapse into femininity:

> No normal man might actually become a woman; but each man trembled forever on the brink of becoming 'womanish.' His flickering heat was an uncertain force. If it was to remain effective, its momentum had to be consciously maintained. It was never enough to be male: a man had to strive to remain 'virile.' He had to learn to exclude from his character and from the poise and temper of his body all telltale traces of 'softness' that might betray, in him, the half-formed state of a woman. (1988: 11)

The deployment of the historical sciences in museums promoted a similar restlessness on the part of those who constituted the museum's primary addressees: the white male populations of colonial powers. The sliding scale of humanity allowed by evolutionary thought, the possibility of progression through the ranks which was also a possibility of falling back through the ranks, served—when installed in the exhibitionary regimes and performative routines of the museum—as an apparatus which helped to keep those who were at the head of progress' advance, or just a few steps behind, forever on their toes while, at the same time, always in their place.

At the start of the century, nature, in its most influential British appropriations, had been polarised between, on the one hand, a Tory and Anglican Paleyism—later intermixed with elements of Owen's peculiar brand of Cuvierism—which consecrated existing social hierarchies and the distribution of social agents within those hierarchies, and, on the other, a red Lamarckianism which would have torn down those hierarchies in promoting the untrammelled mobility of social agents, encouraging the lower social orders to ascend through the ranks without let or restriction. By the end of the century, both of these appropriations of nature had been displaced by a reformer's nature which—consistent with the liberal principle of 'governing at a distance'—provided a new ethical technology of person-formation through which individuals were to be inducted into and led to practise a new progressive relation to a self whose interior constitution had been historicised.

PART III

Practice

7 Culture, power, resistance

Culture, power, resistance: wherever and whenever cultural studies is discussed, these three terms are in play. How is culture tangled up with the exercise of power? What forms of resistance arise from, and are provoked by, these entanglements of culture and power? How can these resistances be translated into, or connected to, something else—organised movements of political opposition, for example? Questions of this kind have been at the centre of debate in cultural studies from the outset. They are clearly implicated in the very title of *Resistance through Rituals*, for example, a book which can deservedly claim to have first placed the trio of culture, power and resistance squarely on the intellectual map of Anglophone cultural studies. Yet, curiously enough, none of the essays brought together in this collection offers a sustained discussion of the concept of resistance. There is an index of key terms with entries relating to culture, class, hegemony and ideology, but none relating to resistance except as a sub-category of the entry relating to 'working class', where it functions as a synonym for industrial struggle.

This is symptomatic of the concept's career within the vocabularies of cultural studies. Although used extensively, the concept of resistance has received relatively little sustained theoretical attention, but has rather been taken on trust as 'a good thing' and certainly 'to be encouraged'. Where a theoretical lineage has been called for, this has usually been supplied by reference to Michel de Certeau's accounts, in *The Practice of Everyday Life*, of the different ways in which apparently quite distinct forms of cultural power—from the organisation of urban space to systems of textual meaning—are creatively adapted at the level of everyday popular cultural practices. There is much to value in these accounts which have enriched our understanding of the processes through which subordinate groups are able to use the resources of dominant cultures to fashion their own enclaves within them, to render the space of 'the other' habitable in affording a means of escaping it without leaving it. Equally, though, de Certeau's approach to resistance has real limits which need to be respected. This has not always been the case. To the contrary, while astringent criticisms have not been lacking, de Certeau's text has, in the main, been indulgently received in a manner that has also legitimated an indulgent critical practice which, claiming the authority of both de Certeau and the early work of the Birmingham school, has resulted in a kind of ABC of cultural studies, a rote litany in which, yes, culture is always on the side of power, and yes, of course, the subordinate always resist socially dominant forms of cultural power—and do so, moreover, seemingly everywhere and all of the time—from positions of relative cultural powerlessness. It has also legitimated a rote politics in which it is assumed that it is the duty of the intellectual to empathise with and nurture practices of resistance wherever they might be found. To be sure, this has also entailed, in some formulations, a commitment to taking issue with the existing forms that resistance takes in order to channel it in new directions. Nonetheless, the basic assumption has been, and remains, that cultural studies should concern itself with tracking down resistances and that, when it has found them, it should take their side. This is an automatic theory generating an automatic politics, both of which, according to Meaghan Morris, had become, by the late 1980s, the banal by-products of a minor industry sustained 'somewhere in some English publisher's vault' by 'a master-disk from which thousands of versions of the same article about pleasure, resistance, and the politics of consumption are being run off under different names with minor variations' (Morris, 1988: 15).

In all of this, the concept of resistance has fared rather badly. Yet it is a concept we need to retain. Resistance undoubtedly takes place, and it is important that we should be able to offer both a description of resistances as practices of a particular kind and an account of the conditions on which those practices rest. We shall only be able to do so, however, provided that we are clear from the outset regarding the necessary limits of any such account. It is especially important (so to speak) to resist the temptation of assuming that resistance should be theorised in the form of a general account of the ways in which relations of culture and power are reacted to by those whom they subordinate. Relations of culture and power, that is to say, should not be thought of as necessarily generating resistance or resistances just as it should be allowed that they might generate other forms of critical reaction or interaction that are not intelligibly described as resistive. We need a fuller and richer cartography of the spaces between total compliance and resistance, one which, in preventing these from functioning as bipolar opposites, will allow, in Geertz's terms, a 'thicker' description of the complex flows of culture which result from its inscription in differentiated and uneven relations of power (see Geertz, 1973). This entails, as a second condition, accepting that resistances need not all be of the same kind but, depending on the particular circumstances that generate them and the particular disposition of the cultural flows in which they are inscribed, may assume different forms with quite different political implications. Respecting these conditions will entail a third as their consequence: namely, the recognition that questions concerning the roles and responsibilities of intellectuals in connection with the relations of culture and power they analyse are not reducible to the positions that they take up in relation to practices of resistance, just as those positions may well need to be differently assessed depending on the precise kinds of resistance that are at issue.

CIRCUMSCRIBING RESISTANCE

Resistance is not among the terms Raymond Williams discusses in his *Keywords*, which is a pity, as some attention to the history and characteristics of its usage might have helped in defining more clearly the assumptions the term brings with it when it is translated from the other contexts of its usage to the cultural field. For, whether in physics, industry or political theory, resistance is usually described as a defensive reaction of one force or body against another in conditions where the force or body that resists is regarded as existing separately from the force or body that it resists. In the physical sciences, for example, resistance means, according to the *Oxford English Dictionary* (OED), the 'opposition of one material thing to another material thing, force, etc.,' or 'the opposition offered by one body to the pressure or movement of another' as in Thomas Hobbes' definition of resistance as 'the endeavour of one moved body . . . contrary to the endeavour of another moved body'. The connection here between resistance and physical repulsion is carried over into industrial uses of the term. Here 'resist' functions as a noun referring to preparations that are applied to a surface in order to protect it from the effects of some agent that is to be applied to that surface in an industrial process. In such cases—the use of a resist in pottery, for example, to prevent glaze attaching to certain parts of the pot—resists have a defensive or protective function. Similar connotations attach to the more general usage of 'resist' as a transitive verb which, when applied to things, means to 'stop or hinder (a moving body); to succeed in standing against; to prevent (a weapon, etc.) from piercing or penetrating'. The uses here are often military (as in the *Encyclopaedia Britannica* 1797 entry on the merits of circular versus square towers in resisting the attacks of battering engines) or analogues thereof (Milton's reference to 'Spiritual Armour, able to resist Satan's assaults').

This same sense of opposing a force which stems from outside the resisting agency also characterises the general uses of the term when applied to human agents. Defined as 'the act, on the part of persons, of resisting, opposing, or withstanding', the OED's illustrations of resistance refer to military situations in which one force opposes or withstands the threat of a source of power that is external to it (as in war between sovereign territories) or of a source of power that is imposed on it from above in ways that are perceived as alien and oppressive. 'To putt therewith a greate fortification about the same for resistance of the say'd enimies' (1417) exemplifies the first of these usages; 'There is yet a spirit of resistance in this country, which will not submit to be oppressed' (1769) exemplifies the second. Similarly, the verb 'to resist' is defined as an action taken by an agent against a force which arises outside of that agent as an alien and coercive, or corrupting, force. To resist is to 'withstand, strive against, oppose' what might be 'a person, his will', 'an attack, invasion, blow, or hostile action of any kind', 'a moral or mental influence or suggestion', 'something proposed to be done or likely to happen, a law or command', or 'a natural force, weakness or disease'. In all of these cases, that which is to be resisted derives from some sphere outside the immediate influence of the resisting agent and the purpose of resistance is to limit the degree to which that invasive force is able to encroach upon the conditions of life of those who resist. In the case of resisting 'a moral or mental influence or suggestion', however, this struggle against an external moral force (early usage most typically describes this as a struggle against temptation) is also translated into an inner struggle of an internally divided self whose component parts are at war with one another. This is also true of contemporary uses within psychoanalysis.

Of course, these brief notes are neither as comprehensive nor as rigorous as Williams' *Keywords* entries. Nonetheless, the lexicographical characteristics of the concept emerge clearly enough to allow a rough and ready synopsis of the implicit meanings that have accompanied its importation into the concerns of cultural studies. Resistance is an essentially defensive relationship to cultural power that is adapted by subordinate social forces in circumstances where the forms of cultural power in question arise from a source that is clearly experienced as both external and other. As such, it arises in relationships of cultural superordination/subordination which have an impositional logic—that is, where a dominating culture is imposed on a subordinate culture from without and, in extreme cases, aims at eradicating the latter and substituting itself in its place. Resistance is, accordingly, always—at least in part—a conservative practice that is orientated to the defence or strategic adaptation of the subordinate culture in question in a hostile and threatening environment in which the continuing viability of that culture is placed in question. To the degree that resistance is orientated to repulsing, to warding off, the influence of the dominating culture to which it opposes itself, it follows that the resources of resistance must be located, at least in some measure, in a source located outside of that dominating culture. In some accounts, these resources are derived from the subordinate culture in question as well as from the dynamic patterns of its interactions with the dominating culture. In others, resistance is grounded in a space that is located outside the particular pattern of interactions which characterises the relations between particular dominant and subordinate cultures. This might be the space of a generalised romantic construction of 'the people' or that of 'the body' as a source of somatic resistances that are somehow beyond history.

As we shall see, precisely how the resources of resistance are accounted for and where they are located makes a good deal of difference politically. First, though, a brief discussion of the account of resistance offered in *Resistance through Rituals* will facilitate a fuller description of this logic of resistance, as well as illustrating its clearly circumscribed nature as a characterisation of the reactions to cultural power that might be adapted on the part of those whom such power subordinates. The perspective of *Resistance through Rituals* depends on a bipolar construction of the field of power in which the hegemony of the ruling class hems in the culture of the working class, limiting it to a restricted sphere of influence which is, by its very nature, defensive and reactive:

> In relation to the hegemony of a ruling class, the working-class is, by definition, a *subordinate* social and cultural formation . . . Of course, at times, hegemony is strong and cohesive, and the subordinate class is weak, vulnerable and exposed. But it cannot, by definition, disappear. It remains, as a subordinate structure, often separate and impermeable, yet still contained by the overall rule and domination of the ruling class. The

> subordinate class has developed its own corporate culture, its own forms of social relationship, its characteristic institutions, values, modes of life. Class conflict never disappears. English working-class culture is a peculiarly strong, densely-impacted, cohesive and defensive structure of this corporate kind. (Hall and Jefferson, 1976: 41)

Working-class culture, then, is inherently resistive: it stands opposed to, and seeks to limit the incursions of, ruling-class culture and it does so from a space, rooted in the conditions of working-class life, that is located both outside of and in opposition to ruling-class culture. Nonetheless, there are times when this resistive aspect of working-class culture is less noticeable than others. This is especially true of those periods when working-class culture has entered into a more or less balanced accommodation with ruling-class culture; periods in which there is, again, a more or less settled cultural equilibrium between the two classes in which the working class has warrened out a space for its own distinctive values and forms of life within the dominant culture. It is, however, in periods when such equilibria are disturbed that the resistive aspects of working-class culture come once again to the fore. It is from this perspective that the studies collected in *Resistance through Rituals* account for the emergence of working-class male youth subcultures in the postwar period. These are construed as essentially defensive reactions to a situation in which the accommodation between the working-class and ruling-class cultures which had characterised the 1930s and 1940s was profoundly disturbed by the intrusive invasion of the postwar ideologies of consumerism, affluence and growth into the traditional forms of working-class culture. This sense of a traditional working-class cultural formation whose defensive ramparts have been breached by a new and aggressive phase of capitalist expansion, thus occasioning more overt and innovative forms of resistance to repel or limit the invasive effects of a new form of the dominant culture, runs throughout *Resistance through Rituals*. For Tony Jefferson, for example, teddy-boy culture was:

> an attempt to defend, symbolically, a constantly threatened space and a declining status . . . a reaffirmation of traditional slum working-class values and the 'strong sense of territory', as an attempt to retain, if only imaginatively, a hold on the territory which was being expropriated from them, by developers, on two levels: (1) the actual expropriation of land; (2) the less tangible expropriation of the culture attached to the land, i.e. the kinship networks and the 'articulations of communal space' mentioned by Cohen. (Hall and Jefferson, 1976: 81)

A similar perspective informs John Clarke's assessment of skinhead culture as an attempt to mobilise the resources of working-class culture, particularly its collectivism, in a kind of desperate, last-ditch attempt to defend a way of life that was being rapidly dismantled:

> The underlying social dynamic for the style, in this light, is the relative worsening of the situation of the working class, through the second half of the sixties, and especially the more rapidly worsening situation of the lower working class (and of the young within that). This, allied to the young's sense of exclusion from the existing 'youth sub-culture' (dominated in the public arena by the music and styles derived from the 'underground') produced a return to an intensified and 'Us–Them' consciousness among the lower working class young, a sense of being excluded and under attack from a variety of points. The resources to deal with this sense of exclusion were not to be found within either the emergent or incorporated elements of youth sub-cultures, but only in those images and behaviours which stressed a more traditional form of collective solidarity. (1976: 99)

In this account, working-class subcultures are essentially defensive cultural formations which, at one and the same time, both draw on and seek to reconfigure those traditional elements of working-class culture which have been prised apart to render it vulnerable to the incursions of a new form of the dominant culture. Indeed, it is because of this, its primarily defensive and so reactive qualities, that the authors of *Resistance through Rituals* stress the inherently limited political value of the symbolic forms of resistance they are concerned with. Such resistances may be—indeed, certainly should be—factors which a politics should take into account, but they do not amount to a politics or provide an adequate basis for the development of one. They fall short at the individual level ('There is no "sub-cultural career" for the working-class lad, no "solution" in the sub-cultural milieu, for problems posed by the key structuring experiences of the class.'—1976: 47) just as they do at the collective level ('There is no "sub-cultural solution" to working-class youth unemployment, educational disadvantage, compulsory miseducation, dead-end jobs, the routinisation and specialisation of labour, low pay and the loss of skills.'—1976: 47).

Michel de Certeau's work lacks—quite self-consciously so—any equivalent point of appraisal located outside the tactics of resistance it has been concerned to chart and, in so doing, to restore to the field of legibility. This is, I think, one of the reasons that its influence has proved more widespread than that of *Resistance through Rituals* in providing a vocabulary of resistance while, at the same time, not seeming to offer a political meta-discourse with aspirations to assess either the limits or the virtues of everyday practices of resistance. There are, however, two other reasons for the more enduring influence de Certeau's work has enjoyed. The first is that de Certeau provides a more nuanced account of the varied and pliable ways in which the practices of everyday life play in the space of 'the other' to warren out a space for the oppressed in which, if nothing else, they are able to 'make do', to preserve a distinctive way of doing and living that does not sacrifice their alterity to the overwhelming presence of the dominating culture in question. Second, of course, the language of 'the other' has proved far more mobile than the language of ruling-class and subordinate-class cultures in being transportable across different fields of power (those of class, gender and colonisation) to net the practices of everyday life in a common problematic irrespective of their social locations.

Yet, while these have proved advantages in terms of extending the sphere of influence of de Certeau's arguments, the plasticity of his concepts has proved a liability in terms of de Certeau's capacity to adequately differentiate between, and account for, specific forms of resistance. What de Certeau's account of everyday practices most lacks, that is to say, is anything approaching an adequate sociological or historical description of those practices that would be capable of locating them within, and accounting for them in terms of, specific social milieux. Instead, what is offered is a poetics of the oppressed, an essentially aestheticising strategy in which the prospect of understanding the specific social logics informing specific forms of resistance is traded in, far too easily, for a generalised account of transgression which, as Morris puts it, depends on 'a unifying myth of a *common* otherness' in which the qualities of 'Black, Primitive, Woman, Child, People, "Voice", Banality' derive an identical value from their function as negation (Morris, 1990: 36).

Jeremy Ahearne, in arriving at a similar assessment, also notes de Certeau's tendency to deliberately sharpen the imaginary divisions between the discourses of politico-administrative reform and the residue of popular practices which those discourses are unable to master. He does so, Ahearne suggests, by insinuating 'into the exposition of his analyses his own poetic figures (voices from woods and valleys, sirens and witches . . .)' which, while imbuing his texts with 'a peculiarly seductive resonance', effectively results in documentary evidence being subjected to 'a form of poeticisation' (Ahearne, 1995: 141). The result, Ahearne argues, is that de Certeau, in sacrificing 'interpretative sobriety' (1995: 141) for aesthetic effect, also runs 'the risk of lapsing intermittently into an unqualified apologetics for ordinary practices' (1995: 151). There is, however, another aspect to de Certeau's discussion which is arguably more consequential. In his account of 'the historiographical operation', de Certeau offers a subtle and probing account of the ways in which 'historians make *something different*' (de Certeau, 1988: 71) by translating a set of raw materials into a fashioned product: history. De Certeau's accomplishment in *The Practice of Everyday Life* runs in the opposite direction. For, in opting for a poetic as a disguised form of meta-discourse, de Certeau is, in effect, able to make nothing out of something by dissolving socially differentiated forms of resistance into a single rhetorical figure with no clear connection to actually existing social relations.

It will be instructive, in developing this argument, to look first at de Certeau's concept of tactics in view of the role this performs in underpinning his account of the nature and function of popular practices. De Certeau develops his account of tactics by means of a contrast with strategy, the term he proposes for the administrative projects arising from political, economic and scientific rationality. As such, the main defining features of strategy are, first, the fact that it proceeds from a definite place which can secure its own existence as distinct from its environs and, second, that it is thereby able to construct the things, activities and persons to which it is applied in the form of exterior objects to be acted on. In de Certeau's words:

> I call a 'strategy' the calculus of force-relationships which becomes possible when a subject of will and power (a proprietor, an enterprise, a city, a scientific institution) can be isolated from an 'environment.' A strategy assumes a place that can be circumscribed as *proper (propre)* and thus serve as the basis for generating relations with an exterior distinct from it (competitors, adversaries, 'clienteles,' 'targets,' or 'objects' of research). (de Certeau, 1984: xix)

If the ability to conduct strategy thus presupposes a certain degree and kind of power, a tactic is 'an art of the weak'—that is, of those who, lacking the power to secure a definite place for their own actions, are obliged to act constantly in the space of the other, undermining that space and making it habitable through the ruses and deceptions which characterise tactics as a set of maneouvres that have always to be conducted in the heart of enemy territory. The military analogies are explicit in de Certeau's most extended discussion of the concept:

> a *tactic* is a calculated action determined by the absence of a proper locus. No delimitation of an exteriority, then, provides it with the condition necessary for autonomy. The space of a tactic is the space of the other. Thus it must play on and within a terrain imposed on it and organised by the law of a foreign power . . . It does not, therefore, have the options of planning a general strategy and viewing the adversary as a whole within a district, visible, and objectifiable space. It operates in isolated actions, blow by blow. It takes advantages of 'opportunities' and depends on them,

> being without any base where it could stockpile its winnings, build up its own positions, and plan raids. (1984: 36–37)

At first sight, this account seems to rest on a different logic from the one which I have suggested characterises resistance in its denial of a space outside the effects of power from which resistance can be conducted and, equally, to whose defence it is committed. It is here that the difference between *The Practice of Everyday Life* and *Resistance through Rituals* is clearest: resistive practices, in de Certeau's account, are involved less in the defence of a subordinate culture against the incursions of a dominant one than in effecting a creative, adaptive play in the space of the other. Two further consequences follow from this. First, such practices emerge, in the case of de Certeau, as being considerably less constrained than are the Birmingham school's subcultural resistances which, in the stress placed on their ritual aspects, are clearly conceived as highly traditional and regulated forms of social activity. It is this relative neglect of the traditional, sometimes conservative and often highly constraining and ritualised aspects of resistance that facilitates de Certeau's poeticised and transgressive interpretation of this concept. I shall return to this point later. For now, though, the second consequence of the lack of a defensive element in de Certeau's account of tactics concerns the way he excludes spatial considerations from their analysis. Spatial metaphors abound in *Resistance through Rituals*, where the subordinate culture which serves as the originating source of resistance is usually conceived as a distinctive space threatened from without (witness Jefferson's use of the imagery of invaded territory in his discussion of teddy-boy culture). For de Certeau, by contrast, the fact that 'a tactic is determined by the *absence of power*' (1984: 38) and that there is therefore no secure place from which it can be conducted, no culture outside the dominant one in which it can be anchored, defines it as a practice that is cohered essentially by its relationship to time. Strategies, since they rest on 'a place of power', seek to 'privilege spatial relationships' by reducing temporal relations to spatial ones in allocating all practices to a place in which they can be targeted as the objects of strategy. Tactics, by contrast, place their bets on time:

> Tactics are procedures that gain validity in relation to the pertinence they lend to time—to the circumstances which the precise instant of an intervention transforms into a favourable situation, to the rapidity of the movements that change the organisation of a space, to the relations among successive movements in an action, to the possible intersections of durations and heterogeneous rhythms, etc. (1984: 38)

An adequate discussion of the role that relations of space and time play in de Certeau's account of the relations between strategy and tactics would—as Morris shows—need to take account of his distinction between polemological and utopian space (see Morris, 1990: 27). My interests here, however, are more limited. For it becomes clear, on closer inspection, that de Certeau's account of tactics constitutes less an exception to the bipolar logic of resistance than the extreme case of that logic, one in which it is carried to excess in the magnification of one pole of power to the point where it becomes all-encompassing and the diminution of the other to the point where it disappears entirely, becomes a zero power. This results from the extreme literalism which characterises de Certeau's interpretation of Foucault's panopticon vision of the disciplinary society. As Ahearne notes, for Foucault there often seems to be no outside to power, nothing outside itself from which it can be resisted, and nothing to repress any longer since all individuals have been folded into the disciplinary mechanisms of panoptic power as necessary elements of their functioning (see Ahearne, 1995: 146). What thus emerges as a problem in Foucault's work—in essence, a problem generated by the rhetorical excesses which characterise Foucault's account of the disciplinary society—is accomplished by definitional fiat in *The Practice of Everyday Life*. John Frow has commented on this aspect of de Certeau's work. Noting that, for de Certeau, 'power is held absolutely or not held at all', Frow continues:

> Nowhere in his work is there anything other than a polar model of domination, according to which sovereign power is exercised by a ruling class (or, more often, by an 'elite'; or else by a technocracy or a technocratic rationality defined without reference to a class) over a mass of oppressed popular subjects who lack all power. (Frow, 1991: 57–58)

Panoptic power, then, is ubiquitous and all-triumphant: there are no longer any spaces outside it capable of nurturing the cultural resources through which it might be resisted or counter-attacked. All of the fortifications and barriers behind which the subordinate might have developed cultural spaces of their own are down; all of the ditches and banks of civil society within which autonomous forms of life once flourished have been razed. All that exists is absolute power faced with the ultimately atomistic sources of resistance, monadic individuals who, however, have been stripped of all weapons and fortifications except for guile, ruse and deception.

It is worth interposing here that similar problems do not characterise Foucault's later writings on governmentality. Indeed, contrary to his account of discipline, the mechanisms of modern forms of liberal government, as Foucault construes them, are themselves partly responsible for generating counter-demands on government owing to their inability to entirely satisfy the demands they generate. It is, Graham Burchell contends in summarising this line of argument, 'in the name of forms of existence which have been shaped by political technologies of *government* that we, as individuals and groups, make claims on or against the *state*' (Burchell, 1991: 145). The advantage of this perspective from the point of view of my concerns here is the scope it offers for accounting for the emergence of relations of culture and power which have a generative effect in relation to the subordinate, giving rise to an active and disputatious and, above all, demanding relationship to cultural power that takes place in relation to the processes of government. Here, then, is the basis for an account of a productive set of relations of culture and power that is not dependent on the bipolar problematic of power associated with accounts of resistance.

Options of this kind are not available to de Certeau, who is only able to posit an overwhelming power on the one hand, and the resistive resources of guile, deception and cunning on the other. But whence come these attributes? How are they transmitted? These are questions de Certeau is unable to answer because he has deprived himself in advance of the means of doing so. It is no accident that his discussion is thin at the level of historical and sociological description, for there are, simply, no spaces, except the spaces of power, to be described. It is in the vacuum this creates that de Certeau inserts his poetic figures. Since he has himself, by definitional declaration, erased all spaces outside the spaces of power, he has no alternative but to poetically evoke a series of outsides—the woods and valleys Ahearne comments on, or the 'cellars and garrets' (1984: 106) which supply his imaginative outside to the urban text—which can stand in the place of the sociological spaces he has obliterated. By the same token, since these are fantasy spaces, they do not provide any specific cultural resources which might account for the specific direction, form and tenor of particular kinds of resistance. Where do the ruses of tactics come from? What accounts for their guile and deception? No one can say, and certainly not de Certeau, whose only account of these is to recast them in a series of images which convert any particular resistances on the part of particular actors into the mere contingent stand-ins for, variously, the opacity of popular culture, 'a dark rock that resists all assimilation' (1984: 18), 'the enigma of the consumer-sphinx', or for an operational logic which stems from outside culture and history entirely and 'whose models may go back as far as the age-old ruses of fishes and insects that disguise or transform themselves in order to survive' (1984: xi).

A similarly extreme form of bipolarity characterises de Certeau's construction of the relations between the city text as envisaged in panoptic schemes of urban administration and those 'ordinary practitioners of the city', walkers, who, living below the thresholds of visibility constituted by the administrative systems in which the city is constructed as an ordered plan, evade that order by substituting in its place a '*migrational*, or metaphorical city' that arises out of the unplanned and uncoordinated myriad surreptitious acts of resistance that city-dwellers perform, quite unconsciously, every day. This is quite clear from the way in which de Certeau develops his argument as a riposte to Foucault's perspective of discipline in his concern to identify the 'multiform, resistance, tricky and stubborn procedures that elude discipline without being outside the field in which it is exercised' (de Certeau, 1984: 96). Proceeding in this way, de Certeau seeks to undo the perspective of discipline from within, to leave the totalising projects of urban administration in shreds and tatters, ruptured by the countless millions of daily practices which elude their reach. De Certeau's city seethes from within:

> one can follow the swarming activity of these procedures that, far from being regulated or eliminated by panoptic administration, have reinforced themselves in a proliferating illegitimacy, developed and insinuated themselves into the networks of surveillance, and combined in accord with unreadable but stable tactics to the point of constituting everyday regulations and surreptitious creativities that are merely concealed by the frantic mechanisms and discourses of the observational organisation. (de Certeau, 1984: 96)

Of course, de Certeau is quite right to argue that the panoptic script of city planners does not entirely determine the practices of those who live in or use city spaces. This is not in question. Rather, it is the manner in which de Certeau construes and accounts for those practices that is the problem. This is partly a matter of his tendency to, once again, locate such practices in the domain of the ineffable: he constantly speaks of those practices which rustle beneath the visible text of the city's surface as being beyond the sphere of legibility and so also beyond the reach of analytical description. Walkers 'make use of spaces that cannot be seen'; the paths they cut through the city's undersides 'elude legibility'; the sum total of these practices amounts to 'an *opaque and blind* mobility of the bustling city' (1984: 93) that escapes the reach of representation; '*forests of gestures*' whose movements 'cannot be captured in a picture' or be 'circumscribed in a text'

(1984: 102). Jeremy Ahearne rightly argues that these passages are motivated by a rhetorical opposition 'between a "visual" knowledge fissured by the very distanciation which constitutes it and a "tactile" knowledge all the more authentic or "immediate" for its lack of vision' (Ahearne, 1995: 178). This opposition has obvious implications for the writing strategies that are available to de Certeau in obliging him to forgo the possibility of describing practices in terms of an external analytical vocabulary since this would, *eo ipso*, place him on the side of knowledge and power. He writes, therefore, as if he were listening to the city, conveying an audio-tactile sense of its subterranean rumblings. Unsurprisingly, de Certeau finds it necessary to abandon this stance from time to time in resorting to formal theoretical vocabularies as a way of explicating his position. This is true, in his discussion of the city, of his use of speech–act theory to account for the 'walking rhetorics' of 'ordinary practitioners of the city'. In his account of these 'pedestrian speech acts', however, de Certeau can only allow that the walker actualises the possibilities contained in the ideal spatial order of the city or disrupts that order by inventing new possibilities, or some combination of the two. This results in a view of walking as a space of enunciation which 'affirms, suspects, tries out, transgresses, respects, etc., the trajectories it "speaks"' adding up to a set of 'enunciatory operations . . . of an unlimited diversity' that are irreducible to 'their graphic trail' (de Certeau, 1984: 99).

We can see here how the extreme bipolar construction of the organisation of the field of power that de Certeau starts out from is attached to a structuralist opposition between the system of language rules and individual speech acts in a way which entails that the creativity of speakers can only be accounted for in terms of a poetics operative at the level of individual style. Yet it is clear that, in their daily lives, city users are not simply confronted with the ideal text of the planned city as something they must follow or not. This by no means forms the only way in which city space is mapped for potential users. Its spaces are opened up and mapped out differently by the ways in which individuals' itineraries are plotted and organised through and by their affiliations to a myriad of organisations whose operations are conducted at a sub-panoptic level: sporting clubs and associations, firms, charities, cultural societies and organisations, religious institutions, neighbourhoods. If we are to understand how cities are used by ordinary people in their everyday lives, we need to pay attention to the differentiated ways in which their relations to urban space are organised by the urban trajectories, maps and itineraries that arise from their differential relations to a range of economic, social and cultural associations and forms of life. It is in the intersections between these varied trajectories, maps and itineraries, and the ideal text of the city, that the real, only too plainly visible and describable differences in the ways in which cities are used can be fathomed—and fathomed in ways that would make a difference to their political assessment. From de Certeau's perspective, the walker who deviates from the ideal city text of panoptic administration is eluding the regulation of an order imposed from above in the name of an individual creativity and inventiveness whose rules cannot be specified. In truth, however, such a walker may merely be following another order or, indeed, instituting such an order.

HUNTERS, POACHERS AND GAMEKEEPERS

Perhaps, then, where de Certeau sees poachers there are only gamekeepers. The prospect is worth entertaining for the light it might throw on de Certeau's approach to the politics of reading. This, too, is characterised by the same antinomies which organise his accounts of tactics and city walking. On the one hand, reading has traditionally been conceptualised as part of 'a "scriptural" system' which, although its particular institutional forms have varied historically, has always operated in accordance with the conviction that the public is moulded by writing, 'that it becomes similar to what it receives, and that it is *imprinted* by and like the text which is imposed on it' (de Certeau, 1984: 167). On the other hand, 'the silent, transgressive, ironic or poetic activity of readers' always eludes this putatively totalitarian system through its construction of an elsewhere—to read is 'to constitute a secret scene . . . ; to create dark corners into which no one can see within an existence subjected to technocratic transparency' (1984: 173)—which, like de Certeau's other outsides, defies any properly analytical location or description and so can only be endlessly evoked. All the same, de Certeau's account of reading is unusual in the explicit role he accords identifiable agents in organising the scriptural regimes which seek to regulate the activity of reading through the interposition of relationships of authority which overdetermine the reader's practice:

> The fiction of the 'treasury' hidden in the work, a sort of strong-box full of meaning, is obviously not based on the productivity of the reader, but on the *social institution* that overdetermines his relation with the text. Reading is as it were overprinted by a relationship of forces (between teachers and pupils, or between producers and consumers) whose instrument it becomes. The use made of the book by privileged readers

> constitutes it as a secret of which they are the 'true' interpreters. It interposes a frontier between the text and its readers that can be crossed only if one has a passport delivered by these official interpreters, who transform their own reading (which is *also* a legitimate one) into an orthodox 'literality' that makes other (equally legitimate) readings either heretical (not 'in conformity' with the meaning of the text) or insignificant (to be forgotten). (de Certeau, 1984: 171)

There are few problems here, at least not from my perspective. The contention that reading is always in some way institutionally and discursively superintended does, however, become a problem for de Certeau. For how is he then to situate his own accounts of reading without taking the position of those who profess 'the knowledge of the "masters" ' (1984: 172) in such matters? And how, then, could he present himself as merely the silent witness of the swarming, multitudinous transgressions of everyday life he wants us to hear in a manner consistent with his wariness, best expressed in his essay 'The beauty of the dead' (1986), of those romantic discourses of 'the people' and 'the popular' which have served as the complement to ruling-class projects aimed at eradicating or restructuring the subaltern strata in question? The concerns this prompts are evident in the following passage:

> The autonomy of the reader depends on a transformation of the social relationships that overdetermine his relation to texts. This transformation is a necessary task. This revolution would be no more than another totalitarianism on the part of an elite claiming for itself the right to conceal different modes of conduct and substituting a new normative education for the previous one, were it not that we can count on the *fact* that there *already* exists, though it is surreptitious or even repressed, an experience other than that of passivity. A politics of reading must thus be articulated on an analysis that, describing practices that have long been in effect, makes them politicisable. (1984: 173)

The difficulty, of course, is that the politics to which de Certeau gestures here can only be a nameless one. For were it to name itself, to define itself in positive terms, it would then be committed to substituting a new normative paradigm for an earlier one—and de Certeau's attempts to side-step the imbrication of relations of knowledge and power would be punctured to reveal, instead, a pedestrian reformer whose practice was complicit and tangled up with the exercise of power. De Certeau faces the prospect only to shun it, resorting instead to the evocation of the dark, silent, secret and unfathomable nature of reading outlined above.

Reactions to this aspect of de Certeau's work have varied. For writers like Henry Jenkins, it is clearly something to be avoided.

Indeed, although making good use of de Certeau's fertile concept of 'textual poaching' and the insightful way de Certeau uses this in his phenomenological accounts of how reading can operate creatively in the space of 'the other', Jenkins' work is, in other respects, the very antithesis of de Certeau's in the richness which characterises his sociological descriptions of the creative and adaptive readings which characterise the use of science fiction texts by particular groups of readers whose social place and location is described in painstaking detail (see Jenkins, 1992; Jenkins and Tulloch, 1995). As we have seen, however, this option is not open to de Certeau, owing to his erasure of any spaces to which such sociological and historical descriptions might be attached. Although a 'generous free spirit himself', Robert Darnton has argued, de Certeau's protest against 'the idea that ordinary people were simpletons who could be moulded like wax by the media' was not developed into 'a sustained and substantiated theory of how people actually did read' (Darnton, 1996: 185). That this is so, however—that de Certeau ends up merely gesturing to the place of reading as one characterised by a poetic unfathomability—is, in the final analysis, a matter of theoretical and practical necessity: there is, quite simply, nothing else he can do given the ground he has staked out for himself.

However, it would be misleading to believe that, in being such a generous free spirit, de Certeau succeeds in escaping the orbit of those institutional and discursive forms through which reading is socially superintended in various ways. For haven't we heard all this before? The reading that eludes explicit knowledge; that constitutes itself in a secret place; that remains unfathomable, out of analytical reach: what else is this but to attribute to the reader precisely those properties which the literary reading attributes to the literary text in rendering its meaning indecipherable and undecidable? De Certeau imagines he sidesteps the effect of all apparatuses on his own practice. In fact, he merely extends the reach of the apparatus of literary education in producing, in the figure of what I have elsewhere called 'the indicipherably active reader', a reader 'whose activity, while subject to an endless theoretical affirmation, is simultaneously unfathomable since neither the place of the reader that reads nor that of the text that is read is susceptible, even in principle, to a definite determination' (Bennett, 1996: 153). The career of the indecipherable literary text has a long and, now, well-chronicled history as a device which serves to induct the reader into a program of self-reform in which the reader confronts and overcomes his or her own incompleteness and imperfections in a process of self-inspection and self-revision which, since there are no definite meanings that can put a stop to it, extends indefinitely into the infinitely receding space of the text's indecipherability (see Hunter, 1988). The translation of this indecipherabilty to the reader in the manner that de Certeau proposes, and especially its application to the sphere of popular readings, has merely opened up the latter to a refurbished version of the literary apparatus. For the fathomless depths of the indecipherable reader allow the popular text to be pedagogically organised as a vehicle for inducting students into resistive readings which, with the assistance of the cultural studies teacher, can be corrected, revised and even assessed. It is, however, difficult to see how this amounts to anything but a form of licensed poaching performed under the watchful, tutelary eye of gamekeepers still in the employ of the literary apparatus. Here, then, in spite of himself, de Certeau operates with a meta-discourse that is constructed by means of the very poetical figures he uses in his endeavours to evade such an enunciative position.

There is, however, a different perspective from which to approach the metaphors of hunting which pervade de Certeau's text. For de Certeau, these references serve as a means of establishing a continuity between the everyday practices of contemporary popular culture and the wit and cunning of a pre-industrial folk. The individual within contemporary technical systems of cultural production, he suggests, must struggle to outwit those systems, to pull tricks on them, by rediscovering 'within an electronicised and computerised megalopolis, the "art" of the hunters and rural folk of earlier days' (1984: xxiv). Hunters, poachers, gamekeepers: the images abound in an elaborate metaphorics of power and its transgression. Yet that metaphorics can easily, in different contexts, be turned on its head. Tom Griffiths provides a convenient example in the way he uses the terms to explore the complex and ambiguous role that images of hunting played in the relations between Australia's early European occupants and its indigenous inhabitants. On the one hand, precisely because it was a shared practice, hunting served only to mark the distance between European civilisation and indigenous culture:

> Europeans had happened upon a continent of hunters; and they brought with them a hunting culture. But, for the colonists, these two forms of hunting symbolised the distance between their society and that of the Aborigines. Europeans perceived the indigenous culture as preoccupied with subsistence hunting, an activity that was seen as desperate and dependent. In the imperial culture, hunting was an elite sporting and intellectual pursuit, class-conscious and recreational: it was a quest for sport, science and trophies, a 'refined' hunting and gathering. (Griffiths, 1996: 12)

On the other hand, although really as an accentuation of this difference rather than as its antithesis, Aborigines were also translated from hunters into hunted in the early collecting practices of Australian natural history and ethnology. 'The gathering of objects for study and display,' Griffiths argues, 'was seen as a refined and educated form of hunting, but it was no less imperial' (1996: 19). In the process, the society and culture, the artefacts and the remains, of Australia's hunter-gatherers made the transition to the other side of the hunting equation in becoming, precisely, the hunted and the gathered to be displayed, alongside Australia's flora and fauna, as the trophies of a conquering and dispossessing power.

In this history of invasion and dispossession, then, images of hunting cleave to the pole of the powerful rather than the powerless just as the techniques of hunting formed a part of the arsenal of power rather than of the tactics of resistance. Killing, classifying and gathering: these, and not guile and cunning, are the attributes of hunting as a practice of the dominant which, far from 'making do' in the space of 'the other', plunders and, in extreme cases, annihilates that space. Why should this matter? Is this because all things have always been 'queer and opposite' in this 'bright and savage land'? Clearly not. My interest in Griffiths' account consists in the way it relativises de Certeau's metaphorics of hunting and, in so doing, calls attention to a significant limitation inherent in his account of resistance. For there is surely no disparity in power relations more extreme than that which has characterised the relations between Australia's European colonisers and its indigenous inhabitants. Given this, the means through which indigenous Australians have resisted the invasive effects of western culture, retaining traditional practices intact while at the same time adapting and actively reshaping them in the context of the overwhelming preponderance of a dominating culture that sought to assimilate them out of existence, ought to be a textbook case of de Certeau's account of tactics of resistance. Indeed, de Certeau invites such an interpretation in directly applying his perspectives to colonial situations in his account of the way in which the indigenous Indians of the Americas made use of the rituals and representations of Spanish culture to fashion a set of habitable practices for themselves within a culture that they had no choice but to accept. 'They were other within the very colonisation that outwardly assimilated them;' de Certeau argues, 'their use of the dominant social order deflected its power, which they lacked the means to challenge; they escaped it without leaving it' (de Certeau, 1984: xiii).

Yet recall what de Certeau has to say about the way in which resistive tactics articulate the relations between space and time. Tactics, he argues, abandon space for time, for a clever, tricky, essentially opportunistic use of time which exploits the transformative possibilities of particular moments. There is no doubt that practices of this sort have formed a part of the story of Aboriginal resistance to European culture, but it is not the whole of that story, or even its centre. To the contrary, the centrality accorded to the land within Aboriginal culture and the positioning of the land as a source of cultural renewal located outside of European culture has meant that Aboriginal cultural resistance has been, above all else, connected to a strategy of place. Fred Myers makes a similar point. Commenting on the role that is accorded Aboriginal culture within the postmodernist project of a '"nomadology" as a way of finding a path through this placeless rhyzomic world', he argues that such views subject Aboriginal identities to a double colonisation in appropriating them for western usage while at the same time denying them their own histories in the failure to realise that 'Aboriginal Australians are precisely those who insist on not being *displaced*' (Myers, 1995: 82). This strategy of place, moreover, has been connected to a tactics of time in quite a different manner from that which de Certeau envisages. For indigenous perspectives of resistance are not founded on the fleeting, opportunistic, passing moment of time that de Certeau celebrates. Nor are the strategies based on the land committed to 'the erosion of time' (de Certeau, 1984: 38). To the contrary, they are committed to the *extension* of time, to stretching indigenous time as deep and as far back into the past as possible, anchored always in the land, in order to project an equivalently lengthy future into which a distinctive indigenous culture will survive.

Contrary to de Certeau, then, here is a logic of practice in which we find a tactics of time as a tactics of *la long durée* arising out of a strategy of space which provides an anchoring point for a time that is not assimilated into the dominant one. Chris Healy has offered a telling example of these interacting aspects of indigenous resistance in his discussion of the forms of social memory embedded in the accounts of Captain Cook that have been produced and circulated within Aboriginal culture. He is particularly concerned with the role of space in organising narrative, and especially the way in which time is organised in terms of the 'histories of places which are deeply historical' (Healy, 1996: 57). The following passage from a Yarralin history of Cook as told by Hobbles Danaiyair indicates the role of the land in sustaining a narrative in which European invasion is represented as a crisis, yes, but, in the long term, as a mere interruption in a story of continuing Aboriginal presence founded in Aborigines' relationship to the land, a relationship that is presented here, finally, in a post-*Mabo* telling, as one of ownership:

> Alright. When him start to building Sydney Harbour, that means he get all the books from London, Big England. Bring a lot of man coming back again . . . Captain Cook sendem over here shooting lotta people . . . That's why these Aboriginal people make an army . . . We been ready for whitefellows all right . . . And they been really, really cranky [angry], my people. Hitem with spear, killem . . . Because they been have spear and whitefellow been have a rifle. That been beat him . . .
>
> Right. And my people been start to work around . . . Anybody sick, anybody sick in the guts or in the head, Captain Cook orders: Don't give him medicine. When they getting crook, old people, you killem first. When they on the job, that's right, you can have them on the job. But don't payem him. Let him work for free . . .
>
> You Captain Cook, you kill my people. And right up to Gurinji now we remember . . . Why didn't you look after London and Big England? You bring that Law . . . Same book . . . And he still got it today. My Law only one. Your law keep changing. You been coverem up me gotem big swag [concealing from the people the truth]. We remember. We thinking. Because we got all the culture. We know your mob now. You'll have to agree with us, agree with people on the land. You gonna agree because Aboriginal owning. (cit. Healy, 1996: 60)

Here, then, is a particular, circumscribed, precisely located practice of resistance that de Certeau's categories simply slide past. I am, however, as interested in the manner in which Healy discusses this and similar black histories of Cook as I am in the content and organisation of those histories. Two issues stand to the fore here. First, while Healy stresses the importance of these black histories in organising a distinctive form of indigenous memory that has played a crucial role in sustaining Aboriginal resistance to European historical narratives, he does not see these histories playing in a single resistive register. To the contrary, he argues that their passage into non-Aboriginal culture—a passage managed through carefully-calculated tellings—has formed part of a pedagogic strategy orientated to educating non-Aboriginal Australians in the cultural and political possibilities of indigenous perspectives. Second, while seeking to identify the political registers of a distinctively Aboriginal historical practice, he is careful to make it clear that these are not the only historical resources that indigenous Australians are able to access and use in support of their struggles. The ability of indigenous Australians to make, and to make use of, these distinctive forms of social memory should not, he argues, be taken to imply that they are unable to also make effective use of other, non-Aboriginal forms of social memory in pursuit of their social and cultural claims. He has in mind here 'the range of ways that Aboriginal people make expert use of positivist histories; from judicial proceedings to land claims and "stolen children" reclaiming their genealogy through the scriptural record of state institutions' (Healy, 1996: 70): a way of using the resources of 'the other' that is about far more than simply 'making do'.

Examples of this kind could be multiplied, but let me give just one more. In 1996, the National Indigenous Media Association of Australia hosted a launch for a research report on the audience for Brisbane's indigenous community radio station 4AAA. The report showed that 4AAA was being tuned into by 100 000 people a week—about 8 per cent of the available audience, including a large non-indigenous listenership.[1] In explaining the significance of this, Ross Watson, 4AAA's manager, placed the findings in the context of the reconciliation process in terms which envisaged the station as working *both* to maintain Aboriginal culture and identity *and* to bring a 'black footprint' into white homes, thereby helping to disarm and break down the barriers of white fear. In this conception, 4AAA was seen as a new space—an audio-space—from which to act on the space of the other by developing a long-term strategy of education designed to promote greater cross-cultural understanding.

The point of these examples, however, is not, yet again, to make indigenous culture the 'graveyard' for the generalisations of European social theory. Rather, it is that any form of resistance, when looked at in detail, in its particular contexts and conditions, will reveal itself to be a similarly intricate and complex part of a multi-faceted set of practices through which the subordinate resist and take issue with, while also seeking both to understand and to educate, the cultures that subordinate them. De Certeau's account of resistance should be resisted because, ultimately, in spite of its poetic commitment to the common man, it diminishes the effective agency of real historical actors and the rich variety of the means they develop to take issue with those forms of power which oppose and oppress them.

8 Culture and policy

In the first issue of *Text*, the newsletter of the Centre for Cultural and Media Studies at the University of Natal, Keyan Tomaselli describes the most important change of emphasis in the recent work of that Centre as being 'the dramatic shift from theories and strategies of resistance to policy research'. 'Where policy research prior to February 1990 was seen by some academics, as negatively "idealist" or pejoratively "utopian",' Tomaselli continues, 'policy research has now assumed major significance as the country desperately attempts to address vital problems.' (Tomaselli, 1992: 2) It is easy to see, given the changing political context of South Africa, why this shift 'from resistance to policy' should have taken place. It is also easy to see why, internationally, few intellectuals would object to the adoption of such a position in the contemporary South African context or, if they did, that they would be prepared to say so. To do so would be to place oneself on the wrong side in relation to the democratic process that has delivered the South African state into the new and, for the moment, benign form of an ANC government.

The response to similar suggestions in the Australian context—where the political conditions which make them intelligible can claim a longer history—has, by contrast, been a quite vexatious one. John Frow and Meaghan Morris have argued that the so-called 'policy debate' conducted in a range of fora—conferences, journals, the media—in the late 1980s and early 1990s, mainly in Australia but occasionally spilling over into the international circuits of cultural studies debate, 'produced much heat and less light' (Frow and Morris, 1993: xxix). Perhaps so. My own assessment, though, is that the debate was both a necessary one and that it has proved productive.

It was necessary in the sense that it was not possible, in the mid-1980s, to connect policy work to the concerns of cultural studies except, more or less apologetically, as an aside from 'the real' theoretical and political issues which, it was assumed, lay elsewhere. This is not to say that policy concerns had not figured in earlier stages in the development of cultural studies. To the contrary, as I argued in the first chapter, they were and remained central to the concerns of Raymond Williams. This was largely a personal commitment, however, and one which had relatively little impact on debates within cultural studies.[1] The most significant exception to this was comprised by the interest that was shown in the cultural policies of the Greater London Council as an important bulwark against the early phases of Thatcherism until, of course, the GLC was itself dismantled. In Australia, similarly, the only synthesising engagement with cultural policy was Tim Rowse's *Arguing the Arts* (Rowse, 1985), although there had been important work done in the field of media policy from at least the late 1970s. Policy issues, however, were not effectively knitted into the fabric of debate within Australian cultural studies during these early years of its emergence as a discipline. They did not figure prominently within conferences and were seldom aired in the pages of the *Australian Journal of Cultural Studies* or its successor, *Cultural Studies*, when it went international. In these circumstances, as Tom O'Regan describes them, those who wanted to engage with policy issues had found it necessary to 'set up shop somewhere else' by describing their work in other terms—as, in his case, variously that of 'cultural historian, film critic, sociologist, and political scientist' (O'Regan, 1992: 415–416). Policy issues, in short, had not been given, in either the Australian or British contexts, any principled rationale or justification that defined a clearly articulated role for them within cultural studies. The same was true in the United States, where the disconnection of cultural studies from any effective socialist traditions has minimised the significance it accords the relations between culture and government. As a consequence, policy work could be, and too often clearly was, seen in all of those national contexts as a narrowly pragmatic activity lacking any broader theoretical or political interest. It also reeked of a politically unpalatable compromise with 'the state'. Against this background, the development of an argument which insisted on the need to locate a policy horizon within cultural studies as a necessary part of its theorisation of, and effective practical engagement with, relations of culture and power was a necessary step if such concerns were to be placed effectively on the agendas of cultural studies.

I suggest that the debate has proved productive for two reasons.

The first is that, at least in the Australian context, it has played a role in facilitating the development of new forms of collaboration between intellectuals working in the field of cultural studies as teachers and researchers and other cultural workers and intellectuals working within specific cultural institutions or in the branches of government responsible for the management of those institutions. Of course, more systemic tendencies have driven these developments which are best viewed as local manifestations of a more general response within the humanities academy to the requirement for greater relevance to contemporary practical needs and circumstances that governments now typically press for in return for the taxpayers' dollar. To recognise these new realities is not, of course, to idealise them as if every response for greater relevance were clearly formulated. Nor does it entail an overestimation of the kinds of contributions intellectuals can be expected to make to policy, as if these could—or, indeed, should—override the imperfect and compromised nature of any policy-making or political process. However, being sensibly cautious on these matters is a far cry from the kinds of wholesale regret with which some sections of the cultural left have responded to demands for the greater 'practicalisation' of the academy unless those demands can meet the measure of some ideal critical calculus of their own making. While such views still have their advocates, it can now confidently be expected that such advocacy will prove increasingly inconsequential, just as it can be expected that the locus of productively critical work will shift to the interface between pragmatically orientated theoretical tendencies and actually existing policy agendas.

This brings me to my second point, for while the propositions I have just advanced would not recruit the support of the majority of those who locate their work within cultural studies, they would recruit *some* support and, if my antennae are reading the changing environment correctly, are likely to prove more successful in this regard. However, this is less to say that the advocates of cultural policy studies have proved successful in winning new converts to their case than it is to suggest that the 'policy debate' was itself a symptom of what was already a clearly emerging division between revisionist tendencies within cultural studies—tendencies, that is, wishing to embrace reformist rhetorics and programs—and tendencies still committed to the earlier rhetorics of revolution or resistance. The 'policy debate', viewed in this light, served a catalysing function in serving as a means of clarifying options which were already evident as emerging tensions within cultural studies. Be this as it may, policy-related arguments now occupy a recognisable position within the landscape of cultural studies debates, a position in which it is clear that the references to policy serve to flag a more general set of issues concerning the kinds of political stances, programs, styles of intellectual work and relations of intellectual production that can now cogently be claimed for cultural studies work.

These are the issues with which I want to engage here. However much heat or light it may once have generated, the 'policy debate' has been 'off the boil' for some time now and I have no wish to heat the topic up again by reviving the controversies which characterised it. There is some value, however, in looking beneath the surface of those controversies to identify some of the discursive antagonisms which the debate activated. For these have a longer history and, if we can identify the historical provenance of the discursive grid which places culture on one side of a discursive divide and policy on the other, we shall have gone a good way towards undermining the logic of this antagonism and the related oppositions which are frequently articulated to it.

This is not, I should stress, a matter of pointing an accusing finger at those who criticised the proponents of the 'policy case'. To the contrary, I want to take my initial bearings from two such critics—Meaghan Morris and, although he had earlier seen himself as a proponent of the 'cultural-policy push' (O'Regan, 1992: 415), Tom O'Regan—both of whom, while supporting the view that cultural studies should concern itself with policy issues, registered their main concern (with some justice) as being with the polarised options which policy advocates seemed to be posing. Morris thus objected that 'the big dichotomy of "Criticism and Policy" ' had proved unable to focus debate in a fruitful and realistic way and saw 'policy polemic' as 'haunted by phantom *tendencies* that never quite settle into a mundane human shape' (Morris, 1992: 548). Tom O'Regan's nuanced and challenging discussion of the 'policy moment' led in a similar direction. Objecting to the over-polarised option of 'criticism or policy', O'Regan rightly points out that the relations between these are both permeable and variable:

> As far as intervention and self-conduct are concerned, the very issue of choosing between policy and cultural criticism—which to write for, which to inhabit—must turn out to be a question admitting no general answer. There are no *a priori* principles for choosing policy over cultural criticism. Nor can any presumption be made about social utility and effectiveness as necessarily belonging to one or the other. Cultural policy and criticism are not hermetically sealed but are porous systems; open enough to permit transformation, incorporation and translation, fluid enough to permit a great range of practices and priorities. To put this crudely: words like

> 'social class' and 'oppression' (and their attendant rhetorics) may not enter the vocabulary of government policy, but without their social presence in credible explanatory systems, any policy directed towards securing equality and equal opportunity would be diminished in scope and power. The recognition of oppression informs the policy goal of access, the persistence of social class underwrites the goal of social equality. Cultural policy and criticism are different forms of life, but they often need each other, they use each other's discourses, borrowing them shamelessly and redisposing them. (O'Regan, 1992: 418)

Given this, O'Regan argues, the call to change cultural critics into cultural bureaucrats reflects a failure to correctly identify the often indirect, but nonetheless real and consequential, contribution which cultural criticism makes to the policy process in, through time, shifting the discursive grounds on which policy options are posed and resolved.

I can find little to quarrel with here except to suggest the need for more clearly stressing the two-way nature of this traffic if we are also to understand how the discursive terms in which some forms of cultural criticism are themselves conducted—those which speak in terms of cultural rights, for example—are often a by-product of specific forms of governmental involvement in the sphere of culture. Where I think O'Regan is mistaken is when, in the light of considerations of this kind, he suggests that those who have argued that cultural studies should reorient its concerns so as to accord policy issues a greater centrality have been 'attacking phantom targets' in supposing that such concerns could not simply be accommodated within existing traditions of work within cultural studies. Notwithstanding his own good sense in stressing the permeability of the relations between cultural policy and cultural criticism, there are versions of cultural criticism which *do* rest on a principled rejection of any engagement with the mundane calculations of bureaucratic procedures and policy processes. As we saw in Chapter 1, Frederic Jameson offered one version of this position in his unqualified rejection of policy questions as of no possible relevance to the critical intellectual. Nor was this an isolated instance: indeed, a veritable cacophony of voices was raised in principled condemnation of the policy option as such.[2]

The difficulty which O'Regan's arguments tend to gloss over, then, is that there have been influential traditions within cultural studies which have sought to render criticism and policy constitutively impermeable to one another. The grounds invoked for this have been variable, ranging from the anti-reformist heritage of some traditions of Marxist thought to radical-feminist perceptions of the state as essentially patriarchal and, therefore, beyond the reach of useful engagement. These are, however, variants of more general positions which have been applied to justify the adoption of a position of critical exteriority in relation to other policy fields—those of economic or social policy, for example. Objections of this kind have usually been based on the grounds that any policies emerging from the state are bound to reflect the interests of a ruling class or of patriarchy rather than because of any intrinsic properties that are attributed to the economy or to the field of the social as such. The more distinctive reasons that have been advanced in opposition to an engagement with cultural policy, by contrast, have rested on a view of culture which is in some way intrinsically at odds with, and essentially beyond the reach of, the mundane processes of policy formation.

This, then, is one of the issues I want to look at: the respects in which the shape of the criticism–policy polarity has been configured by a unique constellation of issues, pertaining solely to the field of culture, which are the legacy, broadly speaking, of Romanticism. I shall broach these issues by reviewing what Theodor Adorno had to say about cultural policy in the context of his broader discussion of the relationships between culture and administration. The discussion in question has been referred to by a number of contributors to 'the cultural policy debate', mainly to suggest that we should view Adorno's account as exemplary in its refusal to dissolve the contradictory tensions between culture and administration (see, for example, Jones, 1994: 410). I shall suggest, to the contrary, that the historical limitations of Adorno's account are now only too apparent and that it is, accordingly, now possible to see beyond the rims of the polarities which sustained it.

I shall take my bearings for the second issue I want to discuss from a related polarity, and one O'Regan introduces in contrasting a 'bottom-up' concern with policy, which he argues has always characterised cultural studies, with the 'top-down' approach which he attributes to advocates of the 'cultural-policy push'. In the 'bottom-up' approach, policy is 'understood in terms of its consequences and outcomes, and in terms of the actions of those affected by it, as they exert some measure of influence upon the process' (O'Regan, 1992: 409). The 'top-down' approach, by contrast, recommends that cultural studies 'should reorient its concerns so as to coincide with top-down programs and public procedures, become bureaucratically and administratively minded in the process' (1992: 412). In the course of his discussion, O'Regan draws on a term I had proposed in suggesting that intellectuals working in the cultural field should think of themselves as 'cultural technicians'—a concept which O'Regan interprets as being about 'securing policy resources, consultancies and engagements'

(1992: 413). This is an unfortunate representation of the concept, since the context in which I had introduced it was as part of an argument that was intended to call into question the very construction of the kind of bottom-up–top-down polarity O'Regan proposes. For such polarities lose their coherence if the relations between the kinds of politics cultural studies has supported and modern forms of government can be seen as relations of mutual dependency to the degree that the former ('bottom-up' politics) often depend on, and are generated by, the latter ('top-down' forms of government).

'How cultural forms and activities are politicised and the manner in which their politicisation is expressed and pursued: these,' I argued, 'are matters which emerge from, and have their conditions of existence within, the ways in which those forms and activities have been instrumentally fashioned as a consequence of their governmental deployment for specific social, cultural or political ends.' (Bennett, 1992: 405) It was in this context that I proposed the term 'cultural technicians' as a description of the political role of intellectuals which, rather than seeing government and cultural politics as the *vis-à-vis* of one another, would locate the work of intellectuals within the field of government in seeing it as being committed 'to modifying the functioning of culture by means of technical adjustments to its governmental deployment' (1992: 406).

This is not, of course, a matter of 'working for the government' (although it may include that) or of formulating policy in a 'top-down' fashion. To the contrary, my concern was with the ways in which the practice of intellectual workers both is, and is usefully thought of, as a matter of 'tinkering with practical arrangements' within the sphere of government—that is, the vast array of cultural institutions, public and private, that are involved in the cultural shaping and regulation of the population—in ways that reflect the genesis of cultural politics from within the processes of government, rather than viewing these in the form of a 'bottom-up' opposition to policy imposed from the top down. By way of making this argument clearer, I shall review a contemporary example of radical political engagement represented by those who argue that museums should be transformed into instruments of community empowerment and dialogue. I shall do so with a view to illustrating how this politics involves, precisely, a series of adjustments to the functioning of museums which, far from changing their nature fundamentally, reconnects them to a new form of governmental program and does so—as any effective engagement with the sphere of culture must—precisely by tinkering with the routines and practices through which they operate.

THE AESTHETIC PERSONALITY AND ADMINISTRATION OF CULTURE

It is useful to recall that recent debates regarding the relations between culture and policy are not without historical precedent. Their closest analogue, perhaps, was the debate between the Frankfurt school and the American traditions of applied social research represented by Paul Lazarsfeld during the period when Lazarsfeld was seeking to involve the Frankfurt theorists, particularly Adorno, more closely in the work of the Office for Radio Research which he directed. The tensions this engendered were perhaps best summarised by Adorno's testy remark, recalling his rebuttal of a request from Lazarsfeld that he (Adorno) should aspire to greater empirical precision, that 'culture might be precisely that condition that excludes a mentality capable of measuring it' (cit. in Jay, 1973: 222). This tension between the aesthetic realm and the requirements of bureaucratic calculation and measurement was one to which Adorno returned in a later essay on the relations between culture and administration which, if its limitation is that its diagnosis is ultimately caught and defined by the terms of this antinomy, identifies its historical basis with unparalleled acuity. Adorno characteristically insists on retaining both aspects of this antinomy, refusing both an easy resolution that would side, unequivocally, with the one against the other as well as the temptation to project their overcoming through the historical production of a higher point of dialectical synthesis. For Adorno, culture and administration, however much they might be opposites, are also systemically tangled up with one another in historically specific patterns of interaction from which there can be no escape.

The terms in which the tensions between the two are to be described are made clear in the opening moves of the essay:

> Whoever speaks of culture speaks of administration as well, whether this is his intention or not. The combination of so many things lacking a common denominator—such as philosophy and religion, science and art, forms of conduct and mores—and finally the inclusion of the objective spirit of an age in the single word 'culture' betrays from the outset the administrative view, the task of which, looking down from on high, is to assemble, distribute, evaluate and organise . . .
>
> At the same time, however—according to German concepts—culture is opposed to administration. Culture would like to be higher and more pure, something untouchable which cannot be tailored according to any tactical or technical considerations. In educated language, this line of thought makes reference to the autonomy of culture. Popular opinion even takes pleasure in associating the concept of personality with it. Culture

> is viewed as the manifestation of pure humanity without regard for its functional relationships within society . . . (Adorno, 1991: 93)

This sense of a constitutive and inescapable tension ('culture suffers damage when it is planned and administered' but equally, culture, 'when it is left to itself . . . threatens to not only lose its possibility of effect, but its very existence as well'—1991: 94) suffuses the essay, gaining in layers of complexity as the analysis develops. The two realms, Adorno argues, rest on antithetical norms:

> The demand made by administration upon culture is essentially heteronomous: culture—no matter what form it takes—is to be measured by norms not inherent to it and which have nothing to do with the quality of the object, but rather with some type of abstract standards imposed from without, while at the same time the administrative instance—according to its own prescriptions and nature—must for the most part refuse to become involved in questions of immanent quality which regard the truth of the thing itself or its objective bases in general. Such expansion of administrative competence into a region, the idea of which contradicts every kind of average generality inherent to the concept of administrative norms, is itself irrational, alien to the immanent ratio of the object—for example, to the quality of a work of art—and a matter of coincidence as far as culture is concerned. (1991: 98)

In a situation in which 'the usefulness of the useful is so dubious a matter', a line drawn 'strictly in ideology', the 'enthronement of culture as an entity unto itself' mirrors and mocks 'the faith in the pure usefulness of the useful' in being looked on 'as thoroughly useless and for that reason as something beyond the planning and administrative methods of material production' (1991: 99). At the same time, there can be no withdrawal from administration which, in the past as in the present, persists as a condition of art's possibility:

> The appeal to the creators of culture to withdraw from the process of administration and keep distant from it has a hollow ring. Not only would this deprive them of the possibility of earning a living, but also of every effect, every contact between work of art and society, something which the work of greatest integrity cannot do without, if it is not to perish. (1991: 103)

At the same time that art 'denounces everything institutional and official' (1991: 102), it is dependent on official and institutional support, just as administration invades the inner life as with the 'UNESCO poets' who 'inscribe the international slogans of high administration with their very hearts' blood' (1991: 107).

While thoroughly aware that the system he describes is historically specific, Adorno can see no way beyond it, no set of relations in which culture will not be, at the same time, critical of, while dependent on, an administrative and bureaucratic rationality, no way in which culture can escape the gravitational pull of the everyday forms of usefulness to which it presents itself as an alternative. The best that can be hoped for, Adorno argues, is the development, in the cultural sphere, of 'an administrative praxis' which, in being 'mature and enlightened in the Kantian sense', will exhibit a 'self-consciousness of this antinomy and the consequences thereof' (1991: 98). What Adorno has in mind here becomes clearer towards the end of his essay when he articulates his vision for a cultural policy. A cultural policy that is worthy of the name, that would respect the specific content of the activities it would administer, Adorno argues, must be based on a self-conscious recognition of the contradictions inherent in applying planning to a field of practices which stand opposed to planning in their innermost substance, and it must develop this awareness into a critical acknowledgement of its own limits. Practically speaking, this means that such a policy must recognise the points at which administration 'must renounce itself' in recognising its need for 'the ignominious figure of the expert' (1991: 111). Adorno is, of course, fully aware of the objections this position might court and he rehearses them fully, particularly the 'notorious accusation . . . that . . . the judgement of an expert remains a judgement for experts and as such ignores the community from which, according to popular phraseology, public institutions receive their mandate' (1991: 111). Even so, the expert is the only person who can represent the objective discipline of culture in the world of administration where his (for such experts, Adorno assures us (1991: 113), are 'men of insight'), expertise serves as the only force capable of protecting cultural matters from the market ('which today unhesitatingly mutilates culture' (1991:112)) and democracy (in upholding 'the interest of the public against the public itself' (1991: 112)). It is from this perspective that Adorno concludes his account of the relations between culture and administration in suggesting that there is still room for individuals in liberal-democratic societies to unfreeze the existing historical relations between the two. 'Whoever makes critically and unflinchingly conscious use of the means of administration and its institutions,' he suggests, in the slim ray of hope he allows himself, 'is still in a position to realise something which would be different from merely administered culture.' (1991: 113) 'Whoever', in this context, however, is not quite so open a category as it seems, for Adorno has in fact already closed this down to the expert, the aesthetic personality who alone is able to act in the sphere of administration in the name of values which exceed it, a lonely historical actor destined to be lacerated by the contradictions he seeks to quell in culture's favour.

It is easy to see why, in terms of both his intellectual formation and historical experience, Adorno would be driven to a conclusion of this kind. It is equally clear, however, that the position is no longer—if ever it was—tenable. For, in its practical effects, it amounts to an advocacy of precisely those forms of arts administration that have been, in varying degrees, successfully challenged over the postwar period because of the aesthetic, and therefore social, bias they entail. The criticisms that have been made of the rhetorics of 'excellence', as interpreted by expert forms of peer evaluation, within the evaluative criteria and processes of the Australia Council are a case in point (see Rowse, 1985; Hawkins, 1993). The grounds for such criticisms, moreover, have typically been provided by a commitment to those democratic principles of access, distribution and cultural entitlement whose force, in Adorno's perspective, the enlightened administrator was to mute and qualify in a cultural policy worthy of the name. What has happened over the intervening period to make Adorno's position pretty well uninhabitable, except for a few retro-aesthetes, has been that culture has since been relativised—in policy procedures and discourses just as much as in academic debate—and, except in the perspective of cultural conservatives, relativised without any of the dire consequences Adorno predicted coming true.

In the course of his essay, Adorno signals his awareness that the ground of culture on which he takes his stand is giving way beneath him. 'The negation of the concept of the cultural,' he writes, 'is itself under preparation.' (Adorno, 1991: 106) He suggests that this entails the death of criticism as well as the loss of culture's autonomy:

> And finally, criticism is dying out because the critical spirit is as disturbing as sand in a machine to that smoothly-running operation which is becoming more and more the model of the cultural. The critical spirit now seems antiquated, irresponsible and unworthy, much like 'armchair' thinking. (1991: 107)

The truth is the opposite. It is precisely because we can now, without regret, treat culture as an industry and, in so doing, recognise that the aesthetic disposition forms merely a particular market segment within that industry, that it is a particular form of life like any other, that it is possible for questions of cultural policy to be posed, and pursued, in ways which allow competing patterns of expenditure, forms of administration and support to be debated and assessed in terms of their consequences for different publics, their relations to competing political values, and their implications for particular policy objectives—and all without lacerating ourselves as lonely subjects caught in the grip of the contradictory pincers of culture and administration. There are no signs, either, that this has entailed the death of criticism if by this is meant taking particular policy and administrative arrangements to task because—from a stated perspective—they fail to meet specified political or cultural objectives, or because they are contradictory or technically flawed. If, by contrast, it means the death of criticism as an activity that proceeds from a position—Adorno's culture—that is located in a position of transcendence in relation to its object, we should not mourn its passing. That critics have had to forsake such high ground in recognising 'the professional conditions they share, for the most part, with millions of other knowledge workers', Andrew Ross has argued (Ross, 1990), is no cause for lament. To the contrary, the less academic intellectuals working in the cultural sphere are able to take refuge in antinomies of this kind, the less likely it is that their analyses will be eviscerated by a stance which, in their own minds, gives them a special licence never to engage with other intellectuals except on their own terms.

COMMUNITY, CULTURE AND GOVERNMENT

Let me go back to O'Regan and the role that he accords the concept of community in illustrating the differences between the 'bottom-up' and 'top-down' approaches to policy. From the former perspective, 'cultural studies engaged with the policy development of the state, from the point of view of disadvantaged recipients or those who are excluded from such policies altogether, and it sought to defend or to restore community' (O'Regan, 1992: 410). For the latter, by contrast, the goal 'is no longer to celebrate and help restore the community which survives and resists manipulative social and cultural programs; it is rather to accept the necessary lot of intervention and to recognise that such communities are themselves the by-product of policy' (1992: 412). What this polarised construction misses, I think, are the more interesting issues, which O'Regan glimpses in his concluding formulations, concerning the respects in which what, at first sight, appear to be autochthonous forms of 'bottom-up' advocacy of community so often turn out to be generated from within, and as a part of, particular governmental constructions of community. Yet the antinomy is not, of course, of O'Regan's making. To the contrary, it is inscribed within the history of the concept of community which, as Raymond

Williams has noted, is such a 'warmly persuasive' word that whatever is cast in the role of 'not community' is thereby, so to speak, linguistically hung, drawn and quartered by the simple force of the comparison. The state, in being portrayed as the realm of formal, abstract and instrumental relationships in contrast to 'the more direct, more total and therefore more significant relationships of community' (Williams, 1976: 66) has fared particularly badly in this respect.

Whenever 'community' is drawn into the debate, then, we need to be alert to the fact that it brings with it layers of historical meaning that have become sedimented in contemporary usage—the common people as opposed to people of rank or station; the quality of holding something in common; a sense of shared identity emerging from common conditions of life—which imply a condemnation of whatever has been constructed as its opposite. A few examples drawn from contemporary debates regarding the relations between museums and communities will show how this, the rhetorical force of the term, operates. Advocates of the community perspective within these debates typically speak of museums as means of empowering communities by encouraging their participation in, and control over, museum programs. This perspective of museums as vehicles for discovering and shaping a sense of community, of a shared identity and purpose, has been developed as a criticism of earlier views of museums which saw their roles primarily in didactic terms. The ideals of the ecomuseum thus constitute an explicit break with, and critique of, the 'top-down' model of museums which sees museums as having a responsibility to instruct their publics in favour of a more interactive model through which the public, transformed into an active community, becomes the co-author of the museum in a collaborative enterprise 'designed to ensure "mutual learning" and the participation of all', whose ultimate goal is 'the development of the community' (Hubert, cit. in Poulot, 1994: 66). From this perspective, the administrative vocabulary which speaks of museums in terms of their relations to audiences, citizens or publics appears abstract and alienated, just as the realms of government or of the state stand condemned as external and impositional forms which are either indifferent or antagonistic to the creative cultural life of communities.

Yet it is also the case that it is precisely from within the practices of government that 'community' acquires this paradoxical value of something that is both to be nurtured into existence by government while at the same time standing opposed to it as its antithesis. The points Poulot makes in his discussion of the ecomuseum movement provide a telling example of this paradox.[3] The distinguishing feature of the ecomuseum movement, Poulot argues, consists in the way it connects the concern with the preservation and exhibition of marginalised cultures which had characterised the earlier folk-museum and outdoor-museum movements to notions of community development, community empowerment and community control. The ecomuseum, as Poulot puts it, is 'concerned with promoting the self-discovery and development of the community' (Poulot, 1994: 75); 'it aims not to attain knowledge but to achieve communication' (1994: 76); it is concerned less with representation than with involvement—'the ecomuseum searches, above all, to engage *(voir faire)* its audience in the social process' (1994: 78); and its focus is on everyday rather than on extraordinary culture. And yet, Poulot argues, no matter how radically different the program of the ecomuseum may seem from that of more traditional museum forms, it is one which, at bottom, is motivated by similar civic aspirations, albeit ones that are applied not universally to a general public but in a more focused way related to the needs of a particularly regionally defined community. The ecomuseum, he argues, embodies a form of 'civic pedagogy' which aims to foster self-knowledge on the part of a community by providing it with the resources through which it can come to know and participate in its culture in a more organised and self-conscious way. Viewed in this light, Poulot suggests, the ecomuseum is best seen as a 'kind of state-sponsored public works project' which seeks to offer 'a program of "cultural development" of the citizen' (1994: 79).

This identifies precisely why equations which place museums and communities on one side of a divide as parts of creative, 'bottom-up' processes of cultural development and the state or government on another as the agents of external and imposed forms of 'top-down' cultural policy formation are misleading. However much the language of community might imply a critique of the more abstract relationships of government or of a state, what stands behind the ecomuseum are the activities of government which, in establishing such museums and training their staff, developing new principles for the exhibition of cultural materials and a host of related tinkerings with practical arrangements, organise and constitute the community of a region in a form that equips it to be able to develop itself as a community through acquiring a greater knowledge and say in the management of its shared culture. This is not to deny the reality of the existence of regions or, more generally, particular social groups outside and independently of particular governmental programs—whether these are those of museums, programs of community development or community arts programs. Nor is it to suggest that the ways in which communities might be constructed and envisaged are restricted to such governmental practices—far from it. What it is to suggest, though, is that community can no more function as an outside to government than government can be construed as community's hostile 'other'. When, in the language of contemporary cultural debates, 'community' is at issue, then so also is government as parts of complex fields in which the perspectives of social movements, and of intellectuals allied to those movements, and shifts in the institutional and discursive fields of policy, interact in ways that elude entirely those theorisations which construct the relations between the fields of culture and politics and culture and policy in terms of a 'bottom-up'–'top-down' polarity. An adequate analytical perspective on cultural policy needs, then, to be alert to the patterns of these interactions. But then so, too, does an adequate practical engagement with cultural policy need to be alert to the fact that being 'for community' may also mean working through and by governmental means.

A consideration of James Clifford's qualified advocacy of a community perspective in contemporary museum practice will help in exploring the implications of this argument further. While this has been a long-standing feature of Clifford's work, I am particularly interested in the role that arguments about community play in Clifford's essay, 'Museums as contact zones', in view of the historical coordinates which organise his discussion. Clifford's central concern in this essay is to relativise and pluralise museums. Drawing on the distinction Mary Louise Pratt (1992) proposes between territories and contact zones to distinguish between museums of the past and museums of the present and the future, he suggests that the nineteenth century museum-as-collection functioned as a frontier, structuring the itineraries of objects—and especially of ethnological objects—as a passage from colonial periphery to metropolitan centre where, alongside the other institutions of colonial science, the museum constituted a site of authoritative knowledge and interpretation. In this way, the museum object served as the vehicle for a form of inter-cultural communication characterised by relations of 'uneven reciprocity' (Clifford, 1997: 193). The contemporary museum-as-contact zone, by contrast, relocates the object as the site for a process—often bitterly contested—of the negotiation of meanings and values between different cultures. Detached from the monologic universalism of the museum-as-collection, the object is now the site, instrument and occasion for dialogic exchanges structured, ideally, as non-hierarchical relations of reciprocity, between different cultures and communities. No longer the accredited agent of a privileged knowledge, the curator is now called on to orchestrate a polyphonic dialogue between the different voices and values emerging from the multiple constituencies that comprise the culturally complex structure of contemporary civil society.

Having posited an historical distinction between the nineteenth century museum-as-collection and the contemporary museum-as-contact zone, however, Clifford qualifies the force of that distinction. He does so by showing how, in spite of their aspirations to a monologic universalism, nineteenth century collecting and exhibition practices also functioned as contact zones which, albeit in the context of radically uneven power relations, encompassed different kinds of cultural exchange whose variety and complexity can only be fully understood if the intentionality of the colonised—who were often active and willing participants in the exchanges upon which such practices depended—are given their proper place. Clifford's arguments here are similar to those of Nicholas Thomas in his study of the radically different kinds of relationships—of representation, exhibition and exchange—that the material cultures of both colonisers and colonised became entangled in during the still ongoing history of colonialism in the Pacific. For Thomas, a de-fetishisation of the objects of material culture is necessary if we are to understand the radically polysemic nature of the exchanges in which those objects came to be involved in the contexts of colonial histories. What is given in such relationships, he argues, cannot tell us what was received any more than what was received can tell us what was given; the identity of the objects given and received disguises the variability of the meanings invested in shared relationships of exchange (see Thomas, 1991: 108). Clifford's construction of museums as contact zones is similarly alert to the complexity, variability and two-way structure of the relations of use and meaning in which the history of colonialism has inscribed the objects which have been exchanged across its boundaries. This leads him to place a similar stress on the radical mutability of objects and their meanings. It is from this perspective that Clifford concludes his discussion in speaking of museums as institutions which, in managing 'the travel of art objects between different places . . . as a result of political, economic, and intercultural relations that are not permanent' (Clifford, 1997: 221), inscribe those objects in relations of use and meaning that are forever changing and forever unfinished.

The concept of community enters into Clifford's discussion in the further move he makes in extending the perspective of contact zones from the trans-national relationships of colonialism to the relationships between museums and 'groups within the same state, region, or city—in the centres rather than the frontiers of nations and empires'

(1997: 204). Historically, Clifford argues, such relationships have typically been characterised by patterns of exclusion, owing to the ways in which museums, in their representational regimes and forms of address, have privileged the perspectives of particular classes, races and genders over others. The contact perspective he recommends is called on to restructure such relationships into ones of greater discursive reciprocity. 'To the extent that museums . . . understand themselves to be interacting with specific communities across such borders, rather than just educating or edifying a public,' Clifford argues, 'they begin to operate—consciously and at times self-critically—in contact histories' (1997: 204). When 'community' enters the discussion, then, it brings in its tow the familiar opposition between, in this case, the lateral forms of cross-cultural mediation which characterise the museum-as-contact zone and the vertical 'top-down' forms of communication implied by the notion of educating or edifying a public. It is here—not in the program that he proposes for the museum-as-contact zone but in the manner in which he represents that program—that Clifford is led somewhat astray by the rhetorical force of the terms he uses. For that program is just as dependent on vertical forms of communication as those it seeks to displace, just as the 'top-down' activities of government are equally necessary to the process of involving communities in the forms of dialogue he envisages.

It will be necessary, in pursuing these points, to complicate slightly the historical perspective which informs Clifford's discussion. Clifford's historical concerns, in his comments on 'the museum-as-collection', focus on the passage of objects and meanings from the colonial periphery ('site of discovery') to the metropolitan centre ('a site of gathering'). This perspective on the historical itineraries of objects needs to be complemented by a consideration of the respects in which museum practices were simultaneously inscribed in another set of frontier relations, in which the museum additionally functioned as 'a site of dispatch' in the strenuous efforts it made to bridge the chasms of (depending on the context) class or ethnicity which threatened the body politic with internal division. The objects acquired from the sites of discovery—and these included geological, archaeological and natural history objects as well as ethnological ones—did not simply sit in metropolitan museums as sites of gathering; they were also—in a number of ways—repackaged for export across the varied internal frontiers which marked the social landscape of, depending on the museum concerned, a particular city, region or nation. These were frontiers which, in the very process of constructing them, museums also strove to breach in their endeavours to reach new publics—not, to be sure, to involve them in 'contact zones' in the manner proposed by Clifford, but rather to establish points of connection that would serve to incorporate the outer zones of the body politic into programs of civic education.

These remarks relate principally to the last quarter of the nineteenth century and the opening decades of the twentieth. It was during this period that the history of the museum became most effectively and deeply—and, as it turned out, enduringly—tangled up in the histories of colonialism and imperialism. It was also during this period that the view was first clearly articulated that the museum's civic and public educational functions should be directed at the population as a whole, a view which achieved institutional expression in the development of increasingly close and formal relationships—in Australia, the United States and Britain—between museums and the newly forming systems of mass education. These two aspects of museum practice were closely intertwined to the degree that the museum's civic and public educational functions came to be increasingly bound up with the ways in which the artefacts—natural and ethnological—that were gathered from the outer frontiers of colonialism were then dispatched across the internal frontiers marking the domestic social spaces of the metropolitan powers. The relations between these two aspects of the museum's history and of the different frontiers they implied is graphically evident in the annual reports of the American Museum of Natural History. These regularly interlaced two sets of statistics and two different ways of representing the Museum's activities cartographically that were organised around the relations between these two different frontiers and the quite different artefactual itineraries that were plotted across them. One set of figures and maps told the story of the Museum's acquisitions, dotting the Americas with the sites from which—as a result of the expeditions it funded—its collections were accumulated. Here, then, the relationship between the Museum's 'sites of discovery' and its function as a 'site of gathering' was graphically realised. But the same was true of the Museum's role as a 'site of dispatch'. This was made statistically and cartographically visible in the figures describing how many specimen boxes—selections of nature placed in special cabinets and dispatched to public schools via a fleet of lorries specially designed for the purpose—had been sent out each year as well as in the maps showing how far into New York's slums and outlying areas those boxes of carefully packaged nature had penetrated as part of a civic program that was designed to integrate the city child, and especially the migrant child, into the body politic.

A civilising agent planted in the midst of a city whose inner frontiers it desperately needed to cross if it were to live up to the expectations placed on it: the image is a common one for new museum initiatives of this period. It characterised the first public exhibition of the Pitt Rivers collection in Bethnal Green and was a part of the reason—soon jettisoned—for situating the Tate Gallery at Millbank (see Taylor, 1994). And if the American Museum of Natural History sent natural history collections to New York's city schools, the Liverpool County Museum pioneered—so far as I can tell—the use of miniature ethnological collections for the same purpose (see Coombes, 1994: 174). Similar imperatives attended the development of art museums in Britain's industrial cities. For T.C. Horsfall, the Committee of the Manchester Art Museum was an 'apparatus devised by a society of analytical and synthetical social chemists . . . for the purpose of bringing these elements of civilisation into effective contact in the lives of as many as possible of the inhabitants of Manchester' (Horsfall, 1982: 52).

Four aspects of museum debate and practice over this period are worth noting if we are to understand how museums set about fulfilling their roles as sites of dispatch. The first concerns the respects in which the constitution of the museum object was altered, and lastingly so, in being governmentalised: that is, in being enlisted to serve as a component of civilising and educative programs directed, ideally, towards the population as a whole rather than functioning aesthetically as ends in themselves or as cultic objects intended to support elite forms of sociability. The militaristic associations of the notion of enlistment emerge from the ways in which these matters were debated at the time. They are evident, for example, in the terms Professor Boyd Dawkins used, in an address to the Museums Association, to chastise local museums. As mere collections of 'miscellaneous objects, huddled together with more or less care, and more or less—generally less—named', he argued that they had 'no more right to the name of a museum than a mob has to be called an army' (Dawkins, 1892: 17). The classification of objects, their clear and neat labelling, their separation into clearly differentiated disciplinary frameworks (anthropology, natural history, archaeology), their organisation into developmental series: in all of these ways, museum objects were made to march to a different tune in being redesigned and recontextualised, through a whole series of technical adjustments to practical arrangements, to serve as the props for programs of cultural and civic management.

Museums were just as concerned, to come to my second point, to introduce discipline and order into the regimes of the visitor as they were into the arrangement of objects. These concerns centred on the conduct of the working classes, as they had for the greater part of the mid-century period. Although, by the 1880s and 1890s, significant sections of the working classes had been tutored in the forms of comportment appropriate for museum visiting, those new museum initiatives that were explicitly designed as beachheads into the working-class heartlands of Britain's major industrial cities still conjured with the prospect of a population whose bodily conduct needed to be regulated. For Horsfall, struggling to bring civilisation to the 'semi-barbarism' of Ancoats, it was not just the 'horrible filthiness of the air' but also the foul behaviour of the visitors that presented a problem to be combated—so much so, he advises, that the Committee had 'found it unsafe to encourage visitors to stay long in the museum by providing chairs in all the rooms' (Horsfall, 1892: 62). For James Paton, reporting, in 1898, on the opening of the People's Palace in Glasgow Green, the cultural and political heartland of working-class Glasgow, things seemed to go more smoothly—but only after appropriate steps had been taken:

> At first, the spitting habit, so characteristic of an east-end multitude, gave us a good deal of trouble; but the posting of a few bills and a little firmness on the part of the attendants soon produced a good effect, and it is now, as far as we are concerned, almost completely eradicated. A tendency to shouting among the younger part of the visitors had also to be put down, but, with very few exceptions, the admonitions of the attendants were taken in good part, and we have found that the stretching of a piece of string across any portion of the room is quite sufficient to keep the people out of the part marked off. (Mr G.W. Ord, Curator in Charge, cit. in Paton, 1898: 58)

My third point concerns the inordinate stress that was placed, in the period I am concerned with, on the eye as virtually the only, and certainly the privileged, means of the visitor's instruction. The principles underlying the museum practices of the time are, in this sense, perhaps best described as ocularcentric owing to the emphasis they placed on clear and distinct techniques of visual instruction as the principal means of communicating to visitors what it was they had to come to learn and understand. If the museum saw itself as operating on and across a divide between classes, it relied on a tactics of visibility as the primary means of beaming its message across that frontier. 'Correct classification, good labelling, isolation of each object from its neighbours, the provision of a suitable background, and above all of a position in which it can be readily and distinctly seen' (Flower, 1893: 24): these were the principles enunciated by Sir William Flower,

Director of the British Museum (Natural History), in proposing a scopic regime that would be clearly pedagogical. However, we find a similar stress on the priority of the visible recurring throughout the literature of this period. A few examples from the contributions to the annual proceedings of the Museums Association will help make the point. For F.E. Weiss, the museum was 'an important and valuable instrument of instruction—instruction which is directed to and assimilated by the eye' (Weiss, 1892: 25). Jonathan Hutchinson complained, when collections were incorrectly arranged, of 'the vacant gaze of the uninstructed as they wander through galleries in which on every side are accumulated objects which would enchain their interest if only they could understand them' (Hutchinson, 1893: 49). For John Chard, the purpose of taking natural history exhibits to 'the crowded districts of the lower parts of Liverpool' was to '*open the eyes, and through them the ears and hearts* of boys and girls' (Chard, 1890: 63). Even when museum demonstrators and guides were introduced in the 1890s, the need to align sight and sound was compelling. F.W. Rudler was clear on this:

> In order that a demonstration be successful, it is essential that everyone present should *hear* what the demonstrator says, and *see* the objects which he is describing. The speaker should face his party, be in a slightly elevated position, and while he is referring to a given specimen, all the audience should be able to see the specimen *at the same time*, so as to follow the words of the demonstrator. But, how rarely can these conditions be fulfilled! (Rudler, 1891: 71)

Were this condition not fulfilled, the museum visit would degenerate into a series of uncoordinated conversations and undirected looking as 'many of those on the outskirts of the party lose interest in the demonstration, and are led to chat together or straggle away from the demonstrator, each looking at the specimens which attract his own fancy' (1891: 73).

I shall take my bearings for my fourth point from Michel de Certeau's discussion of the way in which ethnography translates speech into writing and, in doing so, produces history. For de Certeau, ethnography is a practice which, in transcribing the speech of the other, necessarily passes that speech on in such a way that it is 'destined to be heard otherwise than in the ways in which it is spoken' (de Certeau, 1988: 210). Whereas 'speech neither travels very far nor preserves much of anything' (1988: 216), ethnography, in placing the speech of the other into writing, detaches it, as a signifier, from the presence of the individual or collective body. This inscription of the speech of the other into writing, de Certeau goes on, is central to the discursive mechanisms through which writing produces history in locating, in the construction of the other as nature or as primitive, a point of anteriority on which a history can be founded and from which that history can be set into motion. 'Ethnology,' he writes, 'will become a form of exegesis that has not ceased providing the modern West with what it needs in order to articulate its identity through a relation with the past or the future, with foreigners or with nature' (1988: 221). If we apply this perspective to museums, it is clear that, as institutions for managing the travel of objects, more is involved in the museum itineraries of ethnological objects than their simple transition from 'over there' to 'over here', from site of discovery to site of gathering. The route travelled by ethnological objects on entering into museum collections has also paralleled that of quoted speech in ethnographic discourse; it, too, has been a journey into the realms of writing where, as we have seen, sight has priority over sound and where, accordingly, meaning is constructed independently of presence and voice just as it has also involved a journey into *histoire* as the objects of others have typically been cast in the role of modernity's artefactual prehistory.

What, then, pulling these points together, do museums look like when considered from the perspective of the internal frontiers which have conditioned how they have defined their place, role and function in relation to their cultural hinterlands? It is clear that the relationships that were fashioned across these frontiers could no more be described as relations of equal exchange than could those relations associated with the external frontiers of colonialism through which objects, peoples and customs were transported from peripheral 'sites of discovery' to metropolitan 'sites of gathering'. Indeed—and it is on this point that I think it necessary to part company with Clifford—they were not relations of exchange at all, but relations of government in which objects were enlisted for reforming programs which, in varying ways, aimed to imbue target populations with specific civic attributes. In their functioning as centres of dispatch, museums repackaged the objects collected from remote sites of discovery in order that they might serve as highly condensed and codified chunks of government, the artefactual props for civic programs directed at specific sections of the population and through which, ideally, individuals would become self-civilising in taking over the ideals represented by the museum's artefactual regime and fashioning these into models for conduct that would serve as self-acting imperatives. As such, the museum object was to perform its work of government in a custom-built environment in which the architectural organisation of relations of space and vision and the arrangement of exhibits in the form of an ordered itinerary combined to regulate the conduct of visitors in a manner calculated to cultivate appropriate forms of comportment for public and civic spaces. This work of government, finally, was to take place within the scene of writing through mechanisms of meaning and effect that were dependent on the mediation of objects through systems of visualisation which transformed the travelling objects of colonialism into pieces of historical discourse.

The perspective of museums-as-contact zones is at odds with these earlier understandings of the museum's function in virtually all respects. The view that museums might have an educative role and responsibility in relation to a public or a citizenry is seen as one that needs to be displaced in favour of museums involving themselves in relations of reciprocal interaction with the different communities which comprise their cultural hinterlands. In place of the language of education, instruction and civic reform, Clifford envisages the museum as a place in which diverse communities might enter into exchange with one another, with the museum playing the role of mediator, a facilitator of multiple dialogic exchanges governed by relations of uneven reciprocity, rather than acting as an agent in its own right in pursuit of its own civic or educative programs. The museum-as-contact zone is less a centre of dispatch than a clearing house in which, called on to 'work the borderlands between different worlds, histories, and cosmologies', museums must decentre themselves, accepting that their objects and displays are entangled in 'unfinished historical processes of travel' just as they themselves are 'traversed by cultural and political negotiations that are out of any imagined community's control' (Clifford, 1997: 213). If museums are to function effectively as clearing houses, as transit centres managing the intersecting semiotic projects of different communities, Clifford argues, curators will have to 'reckon with the fact that the objects and interpretations they display "belong" to others as well as to the museum' (1997: 209) in ways that entail a radical relativisation of knowledges. This involves not just a shift from monologue to dialogue. It also implies a shift in what Marshall McLuhan would have called the 'ratio of the senses' addressed by the museum, a shift away from a didactic regime based on a privileging of ocularcentric forms of vision to a conception of the museum as a place where objects can serve as a prompt for conversations through which meanings and perspectives can be shared. In this respect, Clifford's vision for the museum calls to mind the emphasis that was placed on sound and conversability in natural history museums in the early Italian Renaissance. In a context in which curiosity functioned as a civic practice, museums were places for civic talk, for ritualised conversations in which a common civic status was both stated and affirmed. 'Displaying nature,' as Paula Findlen puts it, 'was a prelude to conversing about natural history.' (Findlen, 1994: 100) True, the voices Clifford is concerned with are sometimes clashing and discordant ones rather than the gentle and refined exchanges of a civic *politesse*. A further difference is that, for Clifford, museums are now to be places for a global conversability, for cross-cultural dialogues in what, at times, seems like a realisation of the ethnographer's dream of allowing others to speak, and be heard, in their own voice in relations of discursive reciprocity which also aspire to be ones of full presence in which what is given and what is received might be more fully harmonised.

There can be little doubt, then, that the program Clifford maps out for museums is significantly different from the nineteenth century conceptions of the museum's function I have briefly reviewed. Yet it is still a program of the same type—a move, ultimately, in the same space as a part of the same set of relations of government and culture in which, in and through the very restiveness of his criticisms, Clifford's work is located without in any way implying a complacent acceptance of existing institutions and practices. For what is the perspective of museums-as-contact zones if not a proposal that, by tinkering with a range of practical arrangements, the inherited form of the museum might be refunctioned in a manner calculated to bring about a redirection—indeed, reversal—of its reforming potential in accordance with a multicultural civics premised on a need for greater cross-cultural understanding and tolerance? What does this view of museums amount to if not a new discursive strategy for enlisting objects in the service of government as parts of programs of civic management aimed at promoting respect for, and tolerance of, cultural diversity? And, although the curator's role may be different, is this still not one performed in the service of government through the deployment of specific forms of expertise? Are these not also, and inevitably, relations of knowledge and power? And is it not also true that the communities that the museum is to involve in dialogue are often the artefacts of its own activities rather than autochthonous entities which come knocking at the museum's door seeking rights of equal expression and representation? And is not the museum-as-contact zone, in organising polyphonic dialogues between the communities it constructs, doing so still with a view to functioning as a centre of dispatch? Are the relationships that museums are able to fashion with and between such communities enough? Does this—can this—account for even a significant proportion of their actual cultural reach and influence? Are museums not still concerned to beam their improving messages of cultural tolerance and diversity as deeply into civil society as they can reach in order to carry that message to those whom the museum can only hope to address as citizens, publics and audiences? And do we not, through a battery of access policies, wish—indeed require—that they do so?

My argument, then, is that it is through the creation of the contact zones that they organise and manage that museums are now refashioning their civic role in accordance with changing political circumstances and the new knowledges which provide them with their primary intellectual tools. If this is so, however, we shall have to see these contact zones as both the sites and artefacts of government and, as such, tethered to the civic programs which put them—and the intellectuals who work within and criticise them—at work in the world. And the opposition between a 'bottom-up' community policy perspective and a 'top-down' policy perspective of government and the state is nowhere to be found.

9 Out in the open: Reflections on the history and practice of cultural studies

In his recent essay, '"A moment of profound danger": British cultural studies away from the Centre', Richard Miller assesses both the virtues and the shortcomings of the Open University *Popular Culture* course (Miller, 1994). This course, produced for first presentation to students in 1982, was an interdisciplinary course using all of the Open University's teaching vehicles—printed study guides, radio and television programs, a summer school and specially produced textbooks—to offer a broad-ranging introduction to popular culture in all its diverse forms: film, television, youth subcultures, the lived cultures of everyday life, popular literature. As such, the course was also very much a creature of its times to the extent that its theoretical approaches to the study of popular culture were considerably influenced by the debates which characterised British cultural studies in the late 1970s. It has, indeed, since come to be seen as an important 'moment' in the development of cultural studies pedagogy in view of the role that the teaching materials prepared for the course—which were widely circulated in Britain, Australia and America—played in facilitating the development of cultural studies curricula in other contexts.

It is from this perspective that Miller approaches the course. He does so, however, with a broader purpose in view: to contribute to a history of cultural studies that will pay closer attention to the institutional conditions which regulate its practices and which, in so doing, may also sometimes constrain and limit its possibilities. His attention thus focuses on the respects in which a careful examination of the *Popular Culture* course—or, as it is now widely known, U203—can direct our attention to 'the tensions between the theoretical positions that have been staked out by cultural studies and the pedagogical practices it has called on in specific institutional settings to bring others into its field of study' (Miller, 1994: 419).

As the person who convened the production of U203, I do not want to take specific issue with any of the particular failings Miller attributes to the course. It is worth saying, though, that his criticisms are advanced in a productive and helpful spirit precisely because of his concern to relate the pedagogical theory and practice of the course to the institutional conditions of its production. This means that Miller pays close attention to the history and organisational structure of the Open University and this, in turn, allows him to assess what he sees as the course's principal shortcomings as being, at least in part, attributable to the fact that the course team was obliged to fashion 'pedagogical solutions out of materials that were not of the team's own making' (1994: 434). This does not prevent him—and rightly so—from suggesting that other decisions might have been made which would have led to better teaching outcomes. Nonetheless, his overall purpose is to understand the course as the outcome of—to coin a phrase—particular 'relations of pedagogical production', rather than to attribute its failings to the shortcomings of individuals.

Inevitably, while I agree with some of Miller's criticisms, I think others miss their mark. But then the same is true of the various reviews of, and commentaries on, the course that have been published in what is now an extensive literature of public debate regarding its contributions—warts and all—to cultural studies. It has, naturally enough, been pleasing that the course has been taken so seriously and, at least until now, it has seemed to me that the proper response to this debate has been simply to let it happen rather than be tempted to 'set the record straight' or to defend the course against its critics. This has seemed especially appropriate given that the team which produced the course has not met since 1982 and so has not been in a position to formulate a collective response to the debates its work has occasioned. Certainly, I have not been in a position, and have had no wish, to respond proprietorially on behalf of the course. It is simply not that kind of thing: too many people played major roles in developing and teaching it for an individualised response of that kind to be appropriate.

If, on this occasion, I am inclined to put cursor to screen in reply this is because of the more general issues Miller's discussion raises. It is not, then, what Miller says about *Popular Culture* that I want to dispute. Rather, my concern is to take issue with the more general theoretical and political perspectives which inform his history and criticisms of the course. Towards the end of his article, Miller advises that he sees his discussion of U203 as being consistent with a suggestion I had made, in a more recent article, that any adequate understanding of the history of cultural studies will depend on a move away from purely theoreticist accounts of its moves (or stumblings?) from one theoretical position to another and towards an appreciation of its institutional underpinnings in educational contexts and relations (Bennett, 1992). But that then raises questions about how such institutional conditions and relations are appropriately taken account of and incorporated into a history of cultural studies. It is, then, with matters of this kind that I shall concern myself, for I think that Miller's approach to such questions—and his related views regarding what should be the proper aims and methods of cultural studies teaching—are, although conventional enough, beset with difficulties. My purpose is therefore to use Miller's assessment of 'what went wrong' in trying to implement a cultural studies project at the Open University to get 'out in the open' a set of stances and orientations which, I suspect, are widely shared, but which I think stand in the way of developing an adequate approach to both the history of cultural studies and the further development of its present practices.

I shall organise my discussion around three issues. The first arises out of Miller's assessment of U203 as 'a potentially instructive lost opportunity' (Miller, 1994: 432). This is based on his view that it failed in its attempt to put into effect the suspension of the normal pedagogical relations between teachers and students which, he argues, had characterised the formative period of cultural studies at the Birmingham Centre for Contemporary Cultural Studies (CCCS). I shall argue that U203 did not 'fail' to emulate the CCCS in suspending the normal relations between teacher and taught simply because it never sought to do so. I also suggest that there are good reasons why such an enterprise would have been unintelligible.

The second set of issues I want to comment on concerns the perspective from which Miller broaches the task of writing a history of cultural studies that will take account of the institutional circumstances and conditions of its existence. As his title suggests, he takes his bearings here from Stuart Hall's contention that the institutionalisation of cultural studies constitutes a 'moment of profound danger' (Hall, 1992: 285). As I have already argued, the difficulty with this account is that it attributes to cultural studies an initial set of conditions which are viewed as a-institutional, anti-institutional or (more usually) institutionally marginal and then tells its subsequent history as one in which, whether it succumbs to it or not, it is forever faced by the prospect that the radical potential inherent in its originating conditions will be curtailed (see Chapter 2).

Miller, alert to the difficulties which such a perspective can occasion, is careful not to idealise Birmingham as some pure moment of origin for cultural studies which then results in its subsequent institutionalisation having to be told as a story of inevitable decline and co-option. His focus is more particularising and differentiating than that in its concern with the different shapes which the pedagogical projects of cultural studies assume when implemented in different institutional contexts. However, what he fails to do is to think beyond the conditions specific to particular institutions to ask what might be the broader factors responsible for the rapid institutional take-up and development of cultural studies. He also fails to consider how these developments might be accounted for by processes which are operating at a more structural level than the intentions, schemes and desires of cultural studies teachers and theorists.

To raise issues of this kind, I shall suggest, entails seeing cultural studies as having been a wholly institutionalised set of practices from the very outset to the degree that the activities of the CCCS and other related developments had their underlying conditions in the changing dynamics of tertiary education over the postwar period. Unless we begin to pitch our histories of cultural studies at this level and so begin also to trace the high degree of 'fit' or congruence between its trajectories and those which have driven the expansion of higher education, there is little prospect that we shall prove able to account for the past of cultural studies in ways that will prove of much service in understanding the educational contexts in which, for better or worse, most of its future work will be located.

This, then, is to question once again the 'myth of the margins' through which cultural studies has typically accounted for its own development. It is a myth, however, which well merits a dry-eyed farewell in view of the respects in which it incapacitates us from thinking about what the purposes of cultural studies teaching can and should be in the concretely available institutional contexts in which it now takes place. This leads me to the final point on which I wish to take issue with Miller: the norm of what an ideal cultural studies pedagogy might look like which informs his criticisms of U203. For Miller, a pedagogic 'turn to cultural studies' must be committed to nurturing student resistance. It is, he suggests, in those moments 'when students resist, refuse, mock, transform, re-invent and question the various ways the educational mission of cultural studies is being realised in their classrooms, that it becomes clear that the work left to be done involves inventing a pedagogical practice that acknowledges and responds to student resistance' (Miller, 1994: 433). I shall suggest that, to the contrary, we have every reason for 'resisting resistance' as an intelligible generalised goal for cultural studies pedagogy. For it is when it seems to be most transgressive and radical by flaunting its resistive credentials as a theory of pedagogy that cultural studies reveals itself to be in the grip of the most conservative and normalising of pedagogic machineries.

THE INSTITUTIONAL CONDITIONS OF CULTURAL STUDIES

As I have already noted, Miller is wary of the pitfalls of writing the history of cultural studies as the story of a fall from a moment of pure origin. Yet he fully endorses Hall's argument that the moment of cultural studies' institutionalisation constitutes 'a moment of profound danger', and then goes on to take a step which Hall does not take in equating this moment of institutionalisation with the move of cultural studies 'away from the Centre'. The issue Miller poses is whether the new pedagogic and intellectual practices nurtured at Birmingham could survive this move 'away from the Centre'. What were these practices? Miller follows Hall in describing the early years at Birmingham as ones in which the teachers and students collectively 'made up' cultural studies through collaborative practices. For Miller, these practices define a set of 'intellectual and pedagogical possibilities' that are 'now no longer available', as cultural studies has ceased to be a field 'committed to challenging disciplinary boundaries' and has begun 'to be stabilised as an area of study within the academy' (1994: 420). Viewed in this light, the move 'from Birmingham to Milton Keynes' (where the Open University is located) is presented as a reinstatement of the 'normal pedagogic relations' between teachers and taught in the form of a highly didactic course which, in delivering cultural studies as a form of packaged and administered knowledge, constructed its students as passive learners in limiting itself to assessing their understanding of what the course had taught them.

There is a good deal of truth in this characterisation of U203, although whether this should be regarded as a limitation or as a significant accomplishment is a moot point to which I shall return. But what is most conspicuously absent from Miller's account is any mention of the fact that the move 'from Birmingham to Milton Keynes'—if such it was—was also a move of cultural studies out from a postgraduate setting into a mass undergraduate context. This is by far and away the most important difference between the two contexts. The CCCS was, at the time, an exclusively postgraduate and research centre and, even though it was an extraordinarily productive and inventive one which really did succeed in involving teachers and taught in collaborative projects, this is not an altogether exceptional accomplishment. Indeed, it is a part of the conventional concept of graduate education that the divisions between teachers and taught are *supposed* to weaken, and that collaborative endeavours across this divide resulting in joint working papers, publications, seminars and the like are *supposed* to happen. The move 'from Birmingham to Milton Keynes' has absolutely no bearing on such intellectual and pedagogic possibilities being brought to an end. For these are possibilities which have nothing to do with a particular discipline, but are rather generated by particular kinds of graduate contexts where staff and graduate activities are able to nucleate around shared intellectual projects. This kind of collaborative work has happened before in contexts which have nothing to do with cultural studies and it has happened since. This is not to underestimate the CCCS achievement. Rather, the point is to dispute the notion that the accomplishment was a unique one made possible solely by virtue of the disciplinary characteristics of cultural studies or that it can be taken to characterise a distinctive phase of the development of cultural studies that can no longer be emulated.[1] The central issue, however, and it is one which cannot be faced squarely unless it is posed clearly, is whether the kinds of trainings that are appropriate to and possible at the postgraduate level can constitute a meaningful model for undergraduate curricula. U203 is, from this point of view, a bad case for Miller's argument. More relevant comparisons with the CCCS's work in the 1970s might be provided by undergraduate cultural studies curricula developed over the same period—as at Portsmouth Polytechnic, for example—or, perhaps even more tellingly, by the CCCS's subsequent involvement, from the early 1980s, in planning and teaching an undergraduate program in cultural studies. I do not know the details of these histories. It would, however, be surprising if the constraints associated with undergraduate teaching—especially at first-year levels—had not resulted in the use of more conventional and clearly delineated roles for teachers and taught, including quite straightforwardly didactic lectures and wholly conventional forms of examination and assessment. This is partly a matter of the pressure of numbers which, especially at commencing undergraduate level, typically restricts the scope for the highly labour-intensive and expensive forms of interactive teaching which Miller views as ideal. However, it also reflects the need, which obtains just as much in cultural studies as elsewhere, for students to receive a certain amount of schooling in the debates and methods of any area of intellectual inquiry before they are able to become the kinds of partners in the learning and research process which, in its heyday, the CCCS accomplished.

It might be suggested that these considerations apply with particular force in the Open University context, where the normal constraints of undergraduate teaching are compounded by those associated with the highly mediated forms of distance education which characterise open learning systems. Indeed, this is the tack Miller takes in attributing the shortcomings of U203, and especially its failure to provide 'an oppositional educational experience', to the 'structural limitations of distance education'. In this assessment, the Open University is seen as having 'provided the educators with access to technology that enabled them to disseminate the insights of work in cultural studies to large numbers of previously excluded peoples at very low cost' while, at the same time, constraining 'both the formal presentation of cultural studies' work and the pedagogical encounter between the educators and students' (1994: 424). In doing so, he aligns his assessment of the Open University with that of Raymond Williams. Although he always lent the University as much practical support as he could, Williams argued that, compared with the relations of democratic mutuality which he attributed to the relations between teachers and taught in traditional extra-mural or adult education classes, the Open University imposed a centralised curriculum and a bureaucratisation of the teacher–student relationship. In the postwar extra-mural class, Williams argues, the students 'retained as a crucial principle the right to decide their own syllabus' (Williams, 1989: 156). By contrast, the Open University, in 'inserting a technology over and above the movement of the culture . . . lacks to this day that crucial process of interchange and encounter between the people offering the intellectual disciplines and those using them, who have far more than a right to be tested to see if they are following them or if they are being put in a form which is convenient—when in fact they have this more basic right to define the questions' (1994: 157).

The line of argument is a tempting one, especially as, in this particular case, it would result in a generous assessment of U203 in—as Miller proposes—attributing what he sees as the shortcomings of its didacticism to 'the system'. However, it suffers from three major flaws. First, such criticisms of open learning systems and of the communications technologies on which they depend are too easily liable to Derrida's critique of phonocentrism in that they depend absolutely on a privileging of speech over writing, of the face-to-face encounter over a technologically mediated relationship of teacher and student.[2] This is surely a case of the 'rearviewmirrorism' that McLuhan argues characterises initial encounters with new technologies. Neither the actual nature of open learning teaching systems nor their potential to be developed to allow for greater flexibility in the relations between teachers and taught are helped by viewing them as simply failed tutorials or imperfect seminars. This is to overlook the fact that the tutorial and the seminar are themselves not natural encounters, not simply face-to-face conversations based on principles of communicative reciprocity, but highly formalised teaching technologies which have a history and, indeed, so far as the future development of higher education is concerned, are themselves likely to become increasingly historical as they account for a diminishing proportion of the teaching methods used in higher education. Rather than lapsarian accounts of open learning technologies, then, we need ones which are not *a priori* prejudiced against them because of their difference from some normative ideal (the seminar or tutorial) whose virtues are taken as unquestioned. For example, surveys of students taking part in the new Open Learning Initiative in Australia have found that, for a good many of those for whom this has been their first contact with higher education, the anonymity of 'the system'—the fact that they do *not* have to meet other students or staff or declare to the world that they are giving university study a go—has been crucial to their preparedness to enrol and submit their work for assessment.

This leads me to my second point, for—and it really is an astonishing lapse—Williams' comments on the differences between the Open University and earlier forms of extramural or adult education omit all mention of what is arguably the most crucial difference between them. For what was wholly new and radically progressive about the Open University in the British context was that it provided open access to degree qualifications whereas earlier forms of university extramural or adult education did not usually offer or typically lead to any qualifications. Indeed, it was this, their utter failure to make any significant progress in credentialling the work of their students, that was primarily responsible for creating the vacuum that the Open University was meant to fill.

This difference was and remains absolutely crucial. Most of the extramural classes offered by British universities from the 1950s to the 1970s in the arts and social sciences were typically taken by students who enrolled on a general interest basis. Very little, if any, work was required of students on a week-by-week basis; no work was submitted for assessment; no formal qualifications resulted. This is not said in criticism. I cut my own professional teeth working for four years as a staff tutor in an extramural department, an experience from which I learned tremendously and which I have always valued. And I spent my next four years working as a staff tutor in one of the Open University's regions where I had regular, direct and extensive contact with students. It was wholly clear, however, that the two contexts were quite different regarding the kinds of political and pedagogic questions they raised. For the Open University context raised questions regarding the politics of credentialism of a kind that were virtually absent from the extramural sector. What might have been counted sufficient as an index of progressive pedagogy in the one case—the democratic mutuality of exchange in Williams' idealised extramural class—had, and still has, very little to contribute to the challenge of providing an unscreened, 'mass' population with open access to programs of study leading to degree qualifications. In such a context, ensuring that those degree qualifications will stand up, that they will be acceptable to other universities and employers, was, and is, both a political act and the primary responsibility of teachers to students.

I will return to this issue in the next section. Meanwhile, the third reason for scepticism regarding Williams' account of the differences between extramural education and the Open University has to do with the role which this construction of the extramural sector has played in accounts of the origins of cultural studies. For one of the overriding disadvantages of constructing the history of cultural studies in the form of a narrative of institutionalisation, a move from the margins to the centre, is that, as Derrida predicted it always will, the question of the location of the centre and the margins proves to be a constantly moveable feast. For the Hall of 1992, the moment of cultural studies' trans-Atlantic passage stands as the key moment of its institutionalisation. For Miller, the move from Birmingham to Milton Keynes is another such moment. In an earlier assessment, however, Hall sees extramural departments as the initial incubators for cultural studies—places marginal to the centres of English academic life where cultural studies could thrive on the nourishment provided by direct contact with working-class students—and its move to the Centre as no more than a refuge, a place to which the politics of the New Left retreated when its engagements with the dirty outside world were no longer possible (see Hall, 1990).

I have already indicated, in Chapter 2, why I think this construction of the extramural sector as an originating radical locale for cultural studies is unconvincing. The root of the difficulty does not lie in the view that cultural studies has often gained its first institutional toeholds in contexts outside the mainstream academic departments of established universities. For it is clearly true that it has flourished and, indeed, continues to flourish more in such contexts: more in new universities than older ones, for example, and more in ex-polytechnics and institutes of technology than in the established university sector. It is also true that there is still a good way to go before cultural studies can claim to seriously rival the institutional power of more established humanities disciplines. But this is a fairly routine story in the emergence and establishment of new areas of inquiry and teaching, and we shall make more concrete progress if we think of it in these terms. The problem with the role accorded the marginality of cultural studies consists rather in the extra political and theoretical freight this marginality has had to carry in additionally being called on to furnish cultural studies with its distinctive epistemological protocols. For its resistive origins, it is often suggested, have given cultural studies a unique access to forms of intellectual wholeness which, in turn, have provided it with a privileged insight into the social totality.

A more pragmatic objection, and one I have made already, is that if spatial metaphors are to be applied to the extramural sector, that sector is—when viewed as a whole and in the light of the history of its formation—more intelligibly viewed as the centre's outposts than as its margins. The issues I want to focus on here, however, concern the type of explanation that is embedded in such accounts. For they are rooted in the assumption that the history of cultural studies can be deciphered by retracing the steps of its most notable exponents. This is the kind of logic which, given that Hall, Williams, Hoggart and Thompson all worked in extramural departments, then imputes an institutional marginality to such departments in order that they might provide cultural studies with an appropriately radical originating context. Although not without value or interest, the most notable weakness of such accounts is that they are, so to speak, all agency and no structure—as if, in some way unique to it alone, cultural studies requires no archaeological excavations of the conditions which, even though they may have been entirely outside the frames of conscious intention of its notables, have nonetheless effectively influenced the contours of its development as a now extended set of intellectual and pedagogic practices.

This, certainly, was what I had in mind when, as Miller notes, I suggested the need for histories of cultural studies to concern themselves with 'the institutional conditions of cultural studies, and especially the changing social composition of tertiary students and teachers' (Bennett, 1992: 33). Carolyn Steedman, as we have seen, has suggested what such an account might look like in, from an historian's perspective, seeking the roots of cultural studies not in the trajectories of E.P. Thompson's intellectual biography but rather in the changing practices of history teaching in English secondary schools. This allows her to suggest that the concept of culture as a whole way of life, far from simply springing unaided from the furrowed brows of Williams and Thompson, was in fact an invention of English secondary schooling required to facilitate children's study of cultural materials in the history classroom as part of a Piagetian pedagogy of child development. Taking a leaf out of Steedman's book would suggest the need to see parallel roots for cultural studies in the uses to which the early texts of Hoggart and Williams were put—long before the days of the CCCS—in secondary school English teaching. In this context, the pedagogic function of the concept of culture as a whole way of life was to extend the reformatory reach of the moral machinery of English in allowing the culture outside the classroom to be brought into the classroom to serve as a vehicle for the political and moral education of a new demographic cohort of students.

Of course, a couple of points like this do not in any way comprise an adequate alternative history of cultural studies of the kind that I am suggesting. However, they do suggest a way in which such a history might be written, not as a move from margins to centre, from a de-institutionalised existence to its institutionalisation, but as an always-institutionalised set of practices whose functioning has, in part, to be assessed in terms of their role in organising a new set of relations between educational institutions and new generations of students who have either lacked, or been unreceptive to the value of, traditional forms of cultural capital.[3] This provides a perspective from which to question two of the assumptions which, if they shape Miller's discussion, do so because they now more or less saturate the field. The first is the assumption that the proper aim of cultural studies teaching is to nurture and cultivate the expression of student resistance. The second consists in the view that the institutionalisation of cultural studies is a danger we should be wary of rather than something to be welcomed and explicitly cultivated because of the limited but still worthwhile possibilities it offers.

RESISTING RESISTANCE

In the penultimate section of his article, Miller offers a detailed assessment of the types of essay and examination questions through which U203 students were assessed in the first year of the course's presentation. His major complaint is that these constituted the students in a largely passive relationship to the course, requiring little more than an ability to summarise and demonstrate a comprehension of the course's main arguments and of its study materials. In doing so, the course failed to encourage students to draw on their own experience or knowledge of popular culture. It neither required nor allowed students to 'wander somewhere beyond the landmarks and approved positions already clearly staked out in the readings' (Miller, 1994: 430). In this respect, he suggests, U203 fell prey to the institutional ideology of the Open University in its insistence that all student work should be 'subject to the same, relatively stable, standardised and objective system of evaluation, despite the fact that that work was produced all over the country by students working in very different circumstances' (1994: 431).

This characterisation of the first year's assessment policies of the course is a fair one. These were unduly cautious.[4] Whatever the reasons for this, Miller is right to suggest that, at least in the first year of its presentation, the course did not adequately encourage students to apply analytical or theoretical skills to new contexts. However, I think it is a mistake to attribute this shortcoming to the OU system. The earlier course *Mass Communications and Society*, had successfully trialled group-based projects carrying a collective grade, and many of the history courses produced in the Arts Faculty had been comparably innovative in their assessment strategies. Certainly, the Open University was, at that time, far more open to innovative and flexible forms of assessment than was true of the on-campus courses offered at the majority of British universities. It is also, in my view, a political mistake of the first order to view the bureaucratic standardisation of assessment in the Open University as anything but progressive. This is where the legacy of Williams' failure to appreciate the respects in which the Open University and the extramural department constituted wholly different contexts unfavourably affects the balance of political judgement in Miller's discussion. The work of Pierre Bourdieu and Jean-Claude Passeron (1979) has shown how, in the cultural sphere, forms of assessment which encourage the demonstration of forms of cultural *savoir faire* (including a cultural knowingness about popular culture) acquired outside the framework of an administered curriculum favour students from a bourgeois background.[5] Viewed in this light, the bureaucratisation of assessment Miller complains of has to be seen as an absolute necessity for an institution like the Open University if it is not to be culturally biased against students lacking traditional forms of cultural capital. U203's compliance with these principles was not so much a matter of a failure to resist such institutional constraints as—at least to speak for myself—one of active and principled support for the politics of pedagogy on which they rested.

The root difficulty here is that, for Miller, the bureaucratisation of the teacher–taught relation is a bad thing in and of itself and, when applied to cultural studies curricula, something of an oxymoron. Again, recourse to Williams is instructive here. Contending that it was out of the 'entirely rebellious and untidy' situation of the adult education class that cultural studies emerged, its interdisciplinariness forged in response to the need of adult students to relate knowledge to their whole life and experience, without respect or patience for disciplinary boundaries, Williams argues that the Open University, in grafting itself onto this situation, 'had this element in it of a technology inserted over and above the social process of education' (Williams, 1989: 157). The lingering nostalgia which allows the adult education class to be fashioned as both the residual trace of community life and the harbinger of relations of face-to-face mutuality and reciprocal exchange which will characterise the condition of a common culture is clear in such assessments. Their effect is to distract attention from the wholly new conditions of political possibility and calculation which the new technology makes possible and requires if its utilisation is to be at all effective. It is a position which places us in the same situation *vis-à-vis* educational technologies as we would be in relation to the politics of the visual image in conditions of mass reproduction had Benjamin not written his essay 'The work of art in the age of mechanical reproduction'.

Yet this might seem unfair. After all, Miller's primary criticism of U203 echoes that which Benjamin made of the revolutionary hack who makes use of available techniques of production to purvey a radical message without in any way contributing to a transformation of the prevailing relations of intellectual production (see Benjamin, 1973: 92). U203 thus comes to be interpreted as symptomatic of an historical juncture in which those engaged in cultural studies 'defined the politics of their pedagogical practice in terms of the material they transmitted rather than either the relations they established with their students or the educational environment they created for their students' (Miller, 1994: 431). As a corrective to this, and in specifying the pedagogic norm which informs his criticisms of the course, Miller endorses Henry Giroux's contention that a radical pedagogy must 'provide the conditions for students to speak so that their narratives can be affirmed and engaged along with the consistencies and contradictions that characterise such experiences' (Giroux, cit. in Miller,

1994: 433). This leads Miller to propose, as the litmus test for a cultural studies pedagogy, the degree to which it 'acknowledges and responds to student resistance' (Miller, 1994: 433).

Miller is, unfortunately, less than explicit about exactly what this might mean. Three possibilities present themselves. The first is that cultural studies teaching should seek to organise and promote resistance to the authority of the teacher. The second is that it should organise and promote resistance to the curriculum, encouraging students to draw on the counter-knowledge of their experience in order to pose alternatives to the formalised knowledges imparted by course contents. The third is that cultural studies teaching should enable and encourage the expression of student resistance to particular forms of cultural power. However, I do not think any of these constitutes a cogent norm from which to assess the pedagogy of a course produced in circumstances of the type which characterised U203 any more than they constitute valid ideals for the development of cultural studies teaching more generally.

The difficulty with the first interpretation is that it posits a pedagogical norm that is the direct opposite of that which provides Miller with his starting point. In face of the ideal of a mutually collaborative set of relations between teachers and taught in which the difference between these two categories is blurred, teachers, on this model, are to organise students in an antagonistic relationship to themselves. Miller seems unaware of the tension between these different standards of evaluation, and this may account for the 'heads U203 loses, tails it fails' flavour of his discussion. For it is clear that any concrete pedagogic practice can always be condemned for its failure to meet these two contradictory imperatives.

The difficulty with the second interpretation is that, in advocating that situations should be created in which students can speak so that their narratives can be affirmed, it supposes that all such narratives *should* be affirmed and that their being spoken will be a productive and useful activity for all concerned. There are good reasons for doubting this. Let me illustrate my point anecdotally. I well remember encountering a telling instance of student resistance when an obviously well-heeled woman student from the south of England, trembling with what was evidently real distress and indignation, told me how strongly she objected to the summer school module focused on Blackpool. She had, she said, no wish to see or even think about how the yobbo working classes of the north of England spent their holidays, let alone being obliged to do so and to actually have to go to Blackpool in order to meet her assessment requirements for the course. Such feelings have, of course, to be tactfully responded to and, hopefully, put to good use. But this is quite a different matter from planning a course in such a way as to encourage their expression. Yet if this is so, the view that the aim of cultural studies teaching should be to nurture the expression of more politically correct forms of resistance must be regarded as equally questionable.

The third interpretation suffers from similar difficulties in that, at least as applied to the Open University, it reflects a significant misunderstanding of the nature of the student body. Miller suggests at one point that U203 seemed to open up the prospect of 'a course on popular culture taught to "the populace" (broadly construed as those people excluded from pursuing higher education in a more traditional setting)' (1994: 424). This impression—which Miller qualifies only in a footnote—is highly misleading. It was perfectly clear by the time U203 was being planned that the demographic composition of the student population it would recruit would be highly variable. Certainly, the possibility that that population might be construed in populist terms was wholly unviable. It was clear by then that the Open University was recruiting only a very small proportion of its intake from the working classes. Equally, it was clear that it had substantial appeal to members of the professional classes, a good number of whom already had degrees. There were very few black students, as the University had made little headway with Britain's postwar migrant communities. The most noted success of the University in access terms consisted in its appeal to women, mostly from a middle-class background.

This was not, in other words, a student population that could be constituted or addressed in terms of a 'pedagogy of the oppressed'. This is not to deny that, for some, the issues the course engaged with would have touched directly on personal experience of cultural oppression or disadvantage in ways that, depending on the particular circumstances and issues concerned, would have acted either as an incentive or disincentive to engaging with the course materials. This was most obviously true of the women who studied the course insofar as the course addressed the role of popular culture in the organisation of gendered and sexed identities. For the most part, however, U203 students would have found themselves contradictorily positioned in relation to the different fields of culture and power the course addressed. Recruited, like the staff who taught them, mainly from the new *petit-bourgeoisie* and located mainly in the 30 to 50 age range, this was a student population many of whose members would have had good reason for considering themselves the targets rather than the potential subjects of resistance.

There is a fourth possibility, and one which Miller acknowledges at one point: namely, that the course should have recognised that the radical political content of the study materials would create learning difficulties for a student population with these demographic characteristics, and that the course-team should have developed more specific and more interactive strategies to take account of and respond to these difficulties. This is both a telling criticism and a helpful suggestion which, had we given it more serious consideration, might have resulted in more muted forms of political argument or in teaching strategies more clearly related to students' occupational needs.

However, in subscribing to Giroux's conception of the role of cultural studies in developing a 'border pedagogy', the general tendency of Miller's suggestions pulls in a different direction entirely, one which, at first glance, would resecure cultural studies back in the resistive margins from which it allegedly sprang. For Giroux, 'border pedagogy' is defined as a field of expressive practices, as itself 'a form of cultural production' in opposition to a view of pedagogy in which teaching is viewed as 'the transmission of a particular skill, body of knowledge, or set of values' (Giroux, 1992: 202). Its role, rather, is to assist in 'the production of knowledges, identities, and desires' (1992: 202). In performing this role in the context of the multiple cultural borderlands of the American school where subordinate cultures push against both the dominant culture and against one another, cultural studies teaching becomes a part of a broader politics of identity and community, and it does so, essentially, in functioning as a pedagogy of enunciation, a pedagogy and politics of voice and of difference. In analysing the forms of voicelessness produced by the repressions of subordinate groups and in encouraging a coming to voice of the repressed margins, this pedagogy of the borders 'serves to make visible those marginal cultures that have been traditionally suppressed in American schooling' (1992: 206). In this way, 'radical educators can bring the concepts of culture, voice, and difference together to create a borderland where multiple subjectivities and identities exist as part of a pedagogical practice that provides the potential to expand the politics of democratic community and solidarity' (1992: 206). Their role in this regard, in compensating for the failure of the political system to produce a democratic public sphere, is to constitute the public schooling system as a significant zone in 'the ongoing process of educating people to be active and critical citizens capable of fighting for and reconstructing democratic public life' (1992: 199).

One reaction to this might be to suggest that a pedagogy which can forgo the redistribution of skills and competencies so easily in favour of a commitment to the redistribution of identities is more deeply affected by the politics of American liberalism than it imagines itself to be. Another would be to say that the task of restructuring democratic public life is asking a lot of teachers and of the school.[6] Yet there is an important sense in which what Giroux proposes does not ask much more of teachers or of the school, or much that is different, from what public education systems have always asked of them. For what is most striking about Giroux's prescriptions is how governmental they are. The garnishings, it is true, are radical and libertarian. But the substance of the argument is wholly governmental in attributing to employees of the state (which, lest we forget it, is what most cultural studies teachers are) a role, performed within the pedagogical machinery of public schooling, in forming and shaping the attributes of a citizenry. A postmodern and radically democratic citizenry, it is true, but this does not alter the fact that Giroux's critical border pedagogue is accorded the same function to be performed in the same place as her/his pedagogic forebears. And that function, moreover, is to be performed in essentially the same way. For what else does the pedagogy and politics of voice he recommends depend on but the redeployment of confessional techniques within the moral machinery of the school? What else is this but the highly governmental organisation of voices in order that some voices might be supported, and others be corrected and revised, in the custom-built environment of the school with the teacher as a technician of the soul? And what else, finally, does this border pedagogy depend on but a coming together of the psy-complex and American multiculturalism with a dash of cultural studies thrown in for radical flavouring?

If my answer to these questions might be intuited as 'not much', this should not necessarily be interpreted as a hostile response. To the contrary, although I think he may expect too much from it, Giroux's arguments rest on a view of the schooling system as a governmental apparatus with a crucial role to play in forming the ethical and civic capacities of future citizens. It is therefore appropriate to argue and debate the role which cultural studies curricula might have to play in such processes. Indeed, a part of my point has been that, from the very beginning, cultural studies has been involved in precisely such governmental projects through the role that it played, from a very early stage, in British secondary schooling. Institutionalised from the very start, the institutionalisation represented by its trans-Atlantic passage—if we are to think clearly about it—has little to do with the cooption of its radical potential as a result of the careerism of the American academy and has everything to do with its take-up and use in a different educational system. What is at issue, that is to say, is its shift from one institutional context to another.

Still, it is far from clear, to return to Miller, to see why he should regard Giroux's theories as capable of providing a general model for cultural studies. For the way Giroux develops his own views is highly circumstantial: it is the secondary level of the American public schooling system he has in mind. Even supposing one supported his views regarding the pedagogical deployment of cultural studies in this context, this is no reason to grant them any relevance to the role of cultural studies in the university. This inevitably raises questions about the kinds of knowledges and trainings that are to be imparted to students; about the occupations these will equip them for; about the roles they will play as future intellectuals; and about how these roles will stand in relation to the role played by intellectuals trained in adjacent fields. These are vital questions and, if cultural studies is to have a worthwhile future, they are ones that need to be answered clear-sightedly, taking into account where cultural studies students are likely to be recruited from, what their career destinies are likely to be, and what roles they can intelligibly be expected to play as intellectuals in diverse fields of governmental and private employment. So long as institutionalisation is posed as a moment of danger which threatens cultural studies with the loss of its radical credentials; so long as it is a field in which intellectuals can cultivate and preen a chic radicalism through the grand gesture of turning their backs on the institutional contexts of cultural studies, as if it could have any existence independently of such contexts; so long as it is not realised that cultural studies has been wholly institutionalised and implicated in the field of the governmental from the word go—for just so long will it fail to appraise its situation and the modest but real possibilities which that situation presents correctly.

Endnotes

Introduction

1 In any case, the suit should surely now be an object for sartorial longing in Australia where its urbanising and modernising associations have been underscored in the transition from Keating's finely-cut Italian tailoring to John Howard's cavalry-twill racism.

2 For a recent example of this approach, see McGuigan (1996).

3 Although his terminology is not the same as mine, Nicholas Brown's study of the use of culture as a means of governing prosperity in postwar Australia points very much in the same direction. See Brown (1995).

Chapter 2

1 George Marcus discusses a related maneouvre through which specific knowledge claims are validated in and by the speech of subordinate groups. He thus refers to Paul Willis' *Learning to Labour* as a piece of 'ethnographic midwifery among the proletariat' (Marcus, 1986: 181) which authenticates Marxist criticisms of the capitalist division of labour by means of a ventriloquist ethnography in which those criticisms seem to be spoken—directly, without intellectual mediation—by the working classes themselves.

2 A degree of scepticism regarding this claim is called for, if only because of the mythological status it has now acquired. McKenzie Wark, for example, has Williams, Thompson and Hoggart creating 'the first cultural studies curriculum while teaching adult education courses at Cambridge' because 'they wanted to create ways of teaching the culture of everyday life to the people who lived it' (Wark, 1992: 13). In fact, of course, none of these taught extra-murally at Cambridge—Williams was at Oxford, Hoggart at Hull and Thompson at Leeds. I doubt also that any would claim to have organised cultural studies curricula in their extra-mural days.

3 Williams' retrospective account of his years with the Oxford Extra-Mural Delegacy is much clearer on this matter, especially in his discussion of the tension between the quite different educational objectives of 'adult education' and 'workers' education' and the postwar tendency of extra-mural

provision to move increasingly toward the former (see Williams, 1979: 78–83). In a later account, by contrast, Williams embraces the terms of Hall's account in attributing the early formation of cultural studies to postwar adult education. Even so, the stress of Williams' account is different in emphasising not politics, but the relations of democratic mutuality between teacher and taught within the extra-mural class, relations he views as holding out the promise of a common culture—a promise he sees as having been subsequently denied by the bureaucratisation of the teacher–taught relation involved in the development of the Open University (see Williams, 1989: 151–162).

4 The stress here on the language of 'skills' and 'trainings' is deliberate. One of the most disappointing aspects of the debates surrounding the calls of the Finn and Carmichael Reports for a greater stress on skills and competency trainings in tertiary education, and for a gradation of skills and competencies capable of connecting the TAFE and higher education sectors, has been the readiness of cultural studies intellectuals to fall into line behind traditional defences of the humanities as a form of education which exceeds the mundane calculus that the notions of skills, trainings and competences imply. In this way, intellectuals who, elsewhere, show a ready theoretical appreciation of Bourdieu's arguments regarding the unequal amounts of cultural capital associated with different trainings and knowledges, and of the role which the distribution of such capital plays in the symbolic legitimation and reproduction of relations of class power, display their practical commitment to cultic conceptions of knowledge on which the power and charisma of the traditional intellectual depend.

5 The issue, of course, is whether such a discourse of the truth should continue to be granted any leeway in the cultural sphere. This question is posed in a very pointed way by R.W. Birchfield in his review of *Keywords* (see Birchfield, 1976). As the managing editor for the OED, Birchfield was clearly stung by Williams' suggestion that the OED editors were out of touch with demotic usage, showing an establishment bias in the pattern of their inclusions and exclusions. In rebutting this allegation—and he does so in detail and convincingly—Birchfield proceeds to show how, judged by the standards of the professional lexicographer, much of *Keywords* is technically flawed. (He suggests the book should be classified in the Dewey system as Education 374 (Adult Education) rather than as a work of primary scholarship.) Birchfield's criticisms are lent special force in the objection he lodges to the argument that Williams might be especially sensitive to non-official speech because of the borders he has crossed biographically. Birchfield's reply is that, as the son of working-class parents in New Zealand, educated at Wanganui Technical College before going to Oxford, and as a non-conformist and lifelong Labour Party supporter, he might say the same for himself—but soundly concludes that to do so would be irrelevant as such factors have no bearing on the

lexicographical practices through which language uses are recorded and registered.

6 Inglis offers a similar assessment but, interestingly, one which sees the need to relate life and work together as a response to Williams' own tendency to push his life to the centre of his work by often forging his subject matter 'out of the intersections of career and history, of biography and eventuality' (Inglis, 1980: 170). Parrinder (1987) adopts a similar perspective but extends it in warning against sentimentalising Williams' biography via picturesque readings of his attempts to straddle the borders between Wales and Cambridge, working-class community and middle-class education, etc. Instead, Parrinder suggests, we should view this aspect of Williams' work as a formative intellectual strategy, one which asserts the demand that theory must be judged before the court of experience and gives form to the conviction that there is a deep unity to the culture even though its surface might seem fractured.

7 There is, in this sense, a connection between the difficulty critics have experienced in summarising Williams' accomplishments and the parallel difficulties associated with defining the concept of a common culture. For the latter, too, is not definable in terms of any definite set of attributes. The condition of a common culture, Eagleton argues, cannot be defined in that it refers to what is always a necessarily incomplete totalisation: 'the culture can never be brought finally to consciousness because it is never fully finished' (Eagleton, 1967: 51). Similarly, for Williams, a common culture was not a culture held in common but a common relation to culture understood as a process 'in which the people as a whole participate in the articulation of meanings and values, and in the consequent decisions between this meaning and that, this value and that' (Williams, 1967: 30). A common culture, as he summarises it at the end of the same essay, is a 'free, contributive and common *process* of participation in the creation of meanings and values' (1967: 33). There is a clear connection here between Williams' notion of a common culture and Habermas' concept of an ideal speech community. It is, then, perhaps no surprise that Habermas—as he has since indicated (see Habermas, 1992)—should have found Williams' work of major assistance in formulating his critique of the public sphere.

Chapter 4

1 I draw here on the perspectives of Nikolas Rose regarding the organisation of the self. See Rose (1990).

2 As is always the case, however, such crystal-clear beginnings turn out to be more complex on further inspection. Very similar notions, for example, had informed the mid-century debates concerning the relative merits of archaeological compared with aesthetic principles for the arrangement of museum displays. Those who advocated the former insisted on the need for works of art to be displayed in the context of the ordinary customs and manners of their time. See Newton (1880).

3 These two concepts, in effectively moving their objects from real historical time and thereby evacuating them of historical significance, evidently bear the impress of the terms in which antiquarianism was criticised by the new historical sciences, and especially archaeology, in the nineteenth century (see Levine, 1986). The connection was a fairly direct one in the case of Tylor in view of his personal connections with both John Lubbock and Henry Pitt Rivers.

4 Mauss expressed his unease with this aspect of the concept ('I do not like the word survivals for institutions still alive and proliferating'), although his preferred alternative in referring to the fruits of ethnography as a 'museum of facts' does not seem much of an improvement. See Mauss (1979: 62).

5 For telling discussions of the tendency, in Williams' work, for arguments to be developed to a point at which their resolution depends on an appeal to a set of processes and realities that are beyond the reach of discourse, see Simpson (1992) and Gallagher (1992).

6 For discussions of a selection of these issues, see, on indigenous media issues, Langton (1993), Michaels (1994) and Molnar (1995); on the relations between indigenous peoples and museums, McAlear (1996) and Simpson (1996); on the relations between tourists and indigenous cultural sites, Jacobs and Gale (1994); and on the management of the past, Attwood (1996).

7 The literature here is extensive. For a useful and representative collection, see Gunew and Rizvi (1994).

Chapter 5

1 For details of Cole's intellectual roots and affiliations, see Alexander (1983).

2 I am indebted to Michael White of Monash University for making available to me his unpublished papers on Jevons; these have proved invaluable to me in developing my argument. For details of Jevons' role in promoting the critique of classical political economy, see the introduction to Black and Konekamp (1972).

3 Since Bentham's hedonic calculus was concerned with achieving the greatest total sum of happiness rather than the greatest happiness of the greatest number, it was consistent with restrictive distributive policies provided that those who monopolised pleasure-yielding resources enjoyed them very greatly indeed. Jevons' theory provided a progressive corrective to this in suggesting that the marginal utility derived from an added item of consumption decreased with higher levels of consumption, thereby opening up the possibility that a greater amount of aggregate social benefit might result from broadening the social bases of consumption. See Bahmueller (1981: 99–100).

4 The concerns I am interested in here are those voiced by reforming opinion. Conservatives had their own special demons to wrestle with. For Antonio Panizzi, the Principal Librarian of the British Museum, the

prospect of opening libraries to the public conjured up unnameable horrors. When the 1850 Select Committee on Public Libraries asked him who used the French National Library, which, unlike the British Museum, allowed open access, Panizzi replied: 'Quite another sort of people: downright idlers, mostly, and persons influenced by political excitement, who go to read books which very few people read here; they read books on politics and on religion, and such topics; when I say, religion, I do not mean for religion, but against it.' (Report, 1850, minute 747)

5 These debates were paralleled by equally heated and protracted debates regarding whether the British Museum's natural history collections should be (as they eventually were) removed to separate premises at South Kensington. Opposition to this proposal was most usually based on the consideration that, precisely because they had proved so popular with the working classes, a central-London location ought to be retained for the natural history collections. The benefits of maintaining ease of access in this case would, it was argued, be greater than those that would accrue from retaining a central location for the national art collections. For details of these debates, see Rupke (1994: Ch. 1).

6 It is important to add, however, that this was only one aspect of the system. Sherman also shows how the power of cultural patronage embodied in the *envoi* system was used as leverage to reform the administration of France's provincial museums.

7 For Ruskin, the use of copies at any level in art education was unthinkable. It was, he said, tantamount to 'coining bad money and circulating it, doing mischief' (Report, 1857: para 2470).

8 I have discussed other aspects of this reply elsewhere. See Bennett (1992a).

9 A compromise solution was proposed by one Sydney Godolphin Osborn when he suggested the need for a 'moral beer-house' where the working-man might mix improving games with a pint, a ploughman's lunch and a pipe. See Hole (1853).

10 I have discussed the gendered aspects of nineteenth century discourses of culture more fully elsewhere. See Bennett (1992a).

Chapter 6

1 Aboriginal remains and artefacts had been interpreted, since the mid-century period, as evidencing the most primitive phases of human development in ways which played a crucial role in providing a negative counterpoint against which the theories of modernity of western sociology and anthropology were constructed (see Miller, 1995). For most of the nineteenth century, by contrast, the key debates concerning Egyptian remains centred on the need to identify the racial characteristics of the ancient Egyptians in ways that would disavow the possibility that western civilisation might have been based on the accomplishments of a black people racially connected to Negroes (see Schiebinger, 1993: 186–90).

2 See, for a discussion of the use of aesthetic principles in framing the display of ethnological materials, Coombes (1994: Ch. 3).
3 The doctrine of survivals was first systematically codified by Edward Tylor in his *Primitive Culture*, first published in 1871. For discussions of the concept and its role in the discursive formations of late nineteenth century anthropology, see Hodgen (1936) and Fabian (1983).
4 The 1860 Report of the Select Committee on the British Museum contains a rich vein of impassioned testimony against moving the natural history collections in view of their popularity with the working classes. It was feared that a location in London's western suburbs would make those collections considerably less accessible to people from the poorer and more densely populated eastern, southern and northern suburbs. The tenor of this evidence differs significantly from that brought before the 1857 National Gallery Site Commission, discussed in Chapter 5, which was advised by a number of expert witnesses that moving the national collections to Kensington Gore might be appropriate precisely because it would diminish their accessibility to the working classes and so prevent their appreciation being marred by the presence of rough and uncultivated persons.
5 Owen used the institutional power of his position at the British Museum to effectively dominate the relationships between British and Australian natural history. For details, see Rupke (1994: 71–85).
6 The Museum published special issues of both *The American Museum Journal* and *Natural History* dedicated to its education programs. See *The American Museum Journal*, vol. 9, no. 7, November 1911 and *Natural History*, vol. 23, no. 2, 1920 and vol. 27, no. 4, 1927.
7 In 1889, for example, a letter from the Under Secretary of the Department of Public Instruction to J. Sinclair, the Secretary of the Australian Museum, acknowledged the Museum's advice that 'with a view to encourage and assist the teaching of Natural History, the Trustees of the Australian Museum have arranged to make the collections available for teaching purposes on Monday afternoons, when the Museum is not open to the general public' and conveyed the Minister's thanks to the Trustees for 'the facilities which they have agreed to place at the disposal of the Public School Teachers in this matter'. See Australian Museum (1895–1904).
8 Anderson's advice did not go down well with R. Etheridge, the Curator of the Australian Museum. In an internal document, Etheridge went through each and every one of the respects in which Anderson sung the praises of the British Museum (Natural History) and, with a mixture of cold fury and an early manifestation of postcolonial sentiments, savaged the London institution as grossly inferior to its Sydney counterpart. See Etheridge (1912).
9 The summary of the collecting interests of provincial museums detailed in a report published by the British Association for the Advancement of

Science in 1887 makes it clear that these were the most common disciplinary areas. See British Association for the Advancement of Science (1887).

10 See Rudwick (1992) for details of the popular dissemination of these new representations of historical time.

11 Haraway's discussion, however, does not account for the whole of the American Museum of Natural History's public discourse. During the period in which Osborn and Akeley were constructing the African Hall and, in general, shaping an image of nature 'red in tooth and claw' in support of a particularly virulent form of social Darwinism, the programs of the Department of Public Education continued to emphasise nature's potential to serve as a soothing balm for the stresses of urban life. The point, however, has a more general applicability in that few museums can be discussed in convincing detail if they are treated as the site of a unitary discourse. They are more meaningfully approached archaeologically to the degree that, at any one time, museum practices resting on different principles are likely to collide with each other in contradictory ways as a consequence of the lingering influence of earlier classificatory frameworks and assumptions.

12 See Stocking (1987) for a discussion of the new forms of disciplinary synthesis that were forged between prehistoric archaeology and anthropology over this period.

13 This is an important aspect of the arguments of Rydell (1984) and Greenhalgh (1989) concerning the organisation and function of international exhibitions. See, however, Mitchell (1988) for a contrasting Foucaultian perspective on international exhibitions.

14 See, as well as Coombes (1994), Chapman (1981) and van Keuren (1984).

15 Pitt Rivers was explicit in comparing his display principles to those adopted in natural history museums. For a helpful discussion of this aspect of his exhibition philosophy, see Coombes (1994: 118–19).

Chapter 7

1 The report was prepared by Michael Meadows and Kitty van Vuuren as part of a joint project between the National Indigenous Media Association, 4AAA and the Australian Key Centre for Cultural and Media Policy.

Chapter 8

1 There was, however, an active engagement with other fields of policy, especially education policy. See Centre for Contemporary Cultural Studies (1981).

2 There is now a considerable literature touching on these questions. See, for a sample of the positions aired in the debate, Cunningham (1992), Miller (1993; 1996), Grace (1991), Knight (1989), Elmer (1996), Jones (1994), and the articles collected in the special cultural policy issues of *Meanjin* (vol. 51, no. 3, 1992) and *Media Information Australia* (no. 73, 1994). My concerns in this chapter are very much a response to the issues raised in this literature, although not by way of a detailed response to

particular criticisms that have been made of my own work by some of the authors mentioned. I have, however, learned much from these criticisms and have attempted, in the formulations offered here, to meet at least some of them.

3 But by no means the only one. See also Hawkins (1993) for a discussion of the discursive and institutional forms in which communities were produced in the context of the Australia Council's Community Arts Program. Harris (1995) provides a similar discussion of the Community Art Centre program of the Federal Art Project which comprised one of the centrepieces of the cultural policies of the New Deal.

Chapter 9

1 This is not to gainsay that there may have been particular circumstances which helped to auspice the development of such relations at the CCCS. The state of flux characterising the disciplines on which the Centre drew in its concern to provide some kind of coherence and a sense of a shared project for the emerging field of cultural studies may have assisted an unusually productive blurring of the distinctions between staff and students.

2 Williams' writings in this area are, I think, quite markedly influenced by his personal preference for speech over writing and his related 'vocalic idealism' or faith that there is something in the full presence of unmediated face-to-face interaction which always exceeds, is somehow beyond, the resources of written forms, a plenitude which writing cannot capture. See Simpson (1992).

3 I should add that considerations of this kind do not exhaust the issues that need to be taken into account in writing the history of cultural studies. The broader field of government policies bearing on the practices of educational institutions and the changing forms and relations of cultural production in the cultural industries have also to be taken into account.

4 My own recollection as to why this was so was that, as we were aware that students would be coming to the course from many different disciplinary backgrounds, and that many of them would find it difficult, we thought it important to keep the assessment tasks plain and simple so as not to unduly disadvantage those who had no prior acquaintance with the kinds of issues and arguments the course addressed.

5 This is not to suggest that bourgeois students have a greater or better knowledge of popular culture than the members of other classes. What is at issue here concerns different ways of displaying that knowledge and the fit between these and particular forms of assessment. Popular culture curricula which assess students from the point of view of their capacity to demonstrate a bourgeois-class *habitus* in evincing particular kinds of familiarity with specific regions of popular culture exist not just as a theoretical possibility.

6 For a history of the school which suggests the need to be more circumspect in what it might be expected to accomplish, see Hunter (1994).

References

Aarsleff, Hans (1982) *From Locke to Saussure (Essays on the Study of Language and Intellectual History)*, Minneapolis: University of Minnesota Press.

Adorno, Theodor (1967) 'Valéry Proust Museum' in *Prisms*, London: Neville Spearman.

——(1991) 'Culture and administration' in *The Culture Industry: Selected Essays on Mass Culture*, London: Routledge.

African National Congress (1996) *Draft National Cultural Policy* (obtained via ANC Website).

Ahearne, Jeremy (1995) *Michel de Certeau: Interpretation and its Other*, Cambridge: Polity Press.

Alexander, Edward (1983) *Museum Masters. Their Museums and Their Influence*, Nashville, Tennessee: The American Association for State and Local History.

Althusser, Louis (1969) *For Marx*, London: Allen Lane, The Penguin Press.

——(1973) 'The conditions of Marx's scientific discovery', *Theoretical Practice*, nos 7–8.

American Museum of Natural History 1896 and 1912, *Annual Reports*.

Anderson, Charles (1912) *Report on a Visit to Certain European Museums in 1911*, Sydney: Australian Museum, Miscellaneous Series VII.

Anon 1912 'In our Museum: Some comparisons', *Daily Telegraph*, 13 July.

Armstrong, Nancy (1987) 'The rise of domestic woman' in Nancy Armstrong and Leonard Tennenhouse (eds) *The Ideology of Conduct: Essays on Literature and the History of Sexuality*, London and New York: Methuen.

Arnold, Matthew (1971) *Culture and Anarchy: An Essay in Social and Political Criticism*, Indianopolis and New York: Bobbs-Merrill.

Attwood, Brian (ed.) (1995) *In the Age of Mabo*, Sydney: Allen & Unwin.

Australian Museum (1895–1904), *Series 12*, Department of Public Instruction Correspondence, Box 1.

Bagehot, Walter (1873) *Physics and Politics: Or Thoughts on the Application of the Principles of 'Natural Selection' and 'Inheritance' to Political Society*, London: Henry S. King and Co.

Bahmueller, Charles F. (1981) *The National Charity Company: Jeremy Bentham's Silent Revolution*, Berkeley: University of California Press.

Barber, Lynn (1980) *The Heyday of Natural History, 1820–1870*, New York: Doubleday & Co. Inc.

Barker-Benfield, C.J. (1992) *The Culture of Sensibility: Sex and Society in Eighteenth-Century Britain*, Chicago and London: University of Chicago Press.

Barry, Andrew, Osborne, Thomas and Rose, Nikolas (eds) (1996) *Foucault and Political Reason: Liberalism, Neo-Liberalism and Rationalities of Government*, London: UCL Press.

Bauman, Zygmunt (1992) *Intimations of Postmodernity*, London: Routledge.

Benjamin, Walter (1970) *Illuminations*, London: Jonathan Cape.

——(1973) *Understanding Brecht*, London: New Left Books.

Bennett, Tony (1980) 'Popular culture: A teaching object', *Screen Education*, no. 34.

——(1988) 'The exhibitionary complex', *New Formations*, no. 4, Spring.

——(1989) 'Holding spaces', *Southern Review*, vol. 22, no. 2, July.

——(1990a) 'Criticism and pedagogy: The role of the literary intellectual' in Tony Bennett, *Outside Literature*, London: Routledge.

——(1990b) *Outside Literature*, London: Routledge.

——(1992) 'Useful culture', *Cultural Studies*, vol. 6, no. 3.

——(1992a) 'Museums, government, culture', *Sites*, no. 25, pp. 9–23.

——(1992b) 'Coming out of English: From cultural studies to cultural policy studies' in Ruthven, Ken (ed.) *Beyond the Disciplines: the New Humanities*, Canberra: Australian Academy of the Humanities.

——(1992c) 'Putting policy into cultural studies' in Grossberg, Nelson and Treichler (eds) *Cultural Studies*, New York and London: Routledge.

——(1993) 'Being "in the true" of cultural studies', *Southern Review*, vol. 26, no. 2.

——(1995) *The Birth of the Museum: History, Theory, Politics*, London: Routledge.

——(1995a) 'The multiplication of culture's utility', *Critical Inquiry*, vol. 21, no. 4.

——(1996) 'Figuring audiences and readers' in James Hay, Lawrence Grossberg and Ellen Wartella (eds) *The Audience and its Landscape*, Boulder, Colorado: Westview Press.

Bennett, Tony and Woollacott, Janet (1987) *Bond and Beyond: The Political Career of a Popular Hero*, London and New York: Macmillan and Methuen Inc.

Bérubé, Michael (1996) 'Cultural criticism and the politics of selling out', *EBR* (n.v.).

Bickmore, Albert S. (n.d.), Autobiography with a Historical Sketch of the Founding and Early Development of the American Museum of Natural History, unpublished ms.

Birchfield, R.W. (1976) 'A case of mistaken identity: *Keywords*', *Encounter*, June.

Blundell, Valda, Shepherd, John and Taylor, Ian (eds) (1993) *Relocating Cultural Studies: Developments in Theory and Research*, London and New York: Routledge.

Borzello, Frances (1980) *The Relationship of Fine Art and the Poor in Late Nineteenth-Century England*, Ann Arbor, Michigan: University Microfilms International. (PhD Thesis, University College, University of London.)

Bourdieu, Pierre (1988) *Homo Academicus*, Cambridge: Polity Press.

——(1990) *In Other Words: Essays Towards a Reflexive Sociology*, Cambridge: Polity Press.

——(1993) *The Field of Cultural Production: Essays on Art and Literature*, Cambridge: Polity Press.

——(1996) *The State Nobility: Elite Schools in the Field of Power*, Cambridge: Polity Press.

Bourdieu, Pierre and Passeron, J.C. (1979) *The Inheritors: French Students and Their Relation to Culture*, Chicago and London: University of Chicago Press.

British Association for the Advancement of Science (1887) *Report of the Committee appointed for the purpose of preparing a Report upon the Provincial Museums of the United Kingdom.*

Brown, Nicholas (1995) *Governing Prosperity: Social Change and Social Analysis in Australia in the 1950s*, Cambridge: Cambridge University Press.

Brown, Peter (1988) *The Body and Society: Men, Women, and Sexual Renunciation in Early Christianity*, New York: Columbia University Press.

Burchell, Graham (1991) 'Civil society and "the system of natural liberty" ' in Graham Burchell, Colin Gordon and Peter Miller (eds) *The Foucault Effect: Studies in Governmentality*, London: Harvester/Wheatsheaf.

——(1991) 'Peculiar interests: Civil society and governing "the system of natural liberty" ' in Graham Burchell, Colin Gordon and Peter Miller (eds) *The Focault Effect: Studies in Governmentality*, London: Harvester/Wheatsheaf.

Burchell, Graham, Gordon, Colin and Miller, Peter (eds) (1991) *The Foucault Effect: Studies in Governmentality*, London: Harvester/Wheatsheaf.

Burke, Peter (1992) *The Fabrication of Louis XIV*, New Haven and London: Yale University Press.

Bushman, Richard L. (1992) *The Refinement of America: Persons, Houses, Cities*, New York: Alfred A. Knopf.

Candy, Philip and Laurent, John (eds) (1994) *Pioneering Culture: Mechanics' Institutes and Schools of Art in Australia*, Adelaide: Auslib Press.

Canghuilhem, Georges (1988) *Ideology and Rationality in the History of the Life Sciences*, Cambridge, Mass.: MIT Press.

Caygill, Marjorie (1981) *The Story of the British Museum*, London: British Museum.

Centre for Contemporary Cultural Studies (1981) *Unpopular Education:*

Schooling and Social Democracy in England since 1944, London: Hutchinson.

Chapman, William Ryan (1981) *Ethnology in the Museum: AHLF Pitt Rivers (1827–1900) and the Institutional Foundations of British Anthropology*, PhD Thesis, Oxford University.

Chard, John (1890) 'On circulating museum cabinets for schools and other educational purposes', in *Museums Association Proceedings*, London.

Chartier, Roger (1988) *Cultural History: Between Practices and Representations*, Cambridge: Polity Press.

Clifford, James (1988) *The Predicament of Culture: Twentieth-Century Ethnography, Literature, and Art*, Cambridge, Mass.: Harvard University Press.

——(1997) 'Museums as contact zones' in James Clifford, *Travel and Translation in the Late Twentieth Century*, New Haven: Harvard University Press.

Cole, Sir Henry (1884) *Fifty Years of Public Work of Sir Henry Cole, K.C.B., Accounted for in his Deeds, Speeches and Writings*, London: George Bell and Sons, 2 vols.

Collins, Hugh (1985) 'Political ideology in Australia', *Daedalus*, vol. 114, no. 1.

Collison Black, R.D. and Konekamp, Rosemond (eds) (1972) *Papers and Correspondence of William Stanley Jevons: Biography and Personal Journal*, London: Macmillan in association with the Royal Economic Society.

Colquhoun, Patrick (1796) *A Treatise on the Police of the Metropolis; containing detail of the various crimes and misdemeanours by which public and private property and security are, at present, injured and endangered: and suggesting remedies for their prevention*, London.

Coombes, Annie E. (1994) *Reinventing Africa: Museums, Material Culture and Popular Imagination*, New Haven and London: Yale University Press.

Crimp, Douglas (1993) *On the Museum's Ruins*, Cambridge, Mass.: MIT Press.

Cunningham, Stuart (1992) *Framing Culture: Culture and Policy in Australia*, Sydney: Allen & Unwin.

Dana, John Cotton (1920) *A Plan for a New Museum: The Kind of Museum it Will Profit a City to Maintain*, Woodstock, Vermont: The Elm Tree Press.

——(1927) *Should Museums be Useful?* Newark, New Jersey: The Museum.

Danziger, Kurt (1990) *Constructing the Subject: Historical Origins of Psychological Research*, Cambridge: Cambridge University Press.

Darnton, Robert (1996) *The Forbidden Best-Sellers of Pre-Revolutionary France*, London: HarperCollins Publishers.

Davidoff, Leonore and Hall, Catherine (1987) *Family Fortunes: Men and Women of the English Middle Class*, London: Routledge.

Dawkins, Boyd (1892) 'The museum question', *Museums Association Proceedings*, London.

Dean, Mitchell (1991) *The Constitution of Poverty: Toward a Genealogy of Liberal Governance*, London: Routledge.

de Certeau, Michel (1984), *The Practice of Everyday Life*, Berkeley: University of California Press.

——(1988) *The Writing of History*, New York: Columbia University Press.

de Certeau, Michel in collaboration with Dominique Julia and Jacques Revel (1986) 'The beauty of the dead: Nisard' in Michel de Certeau (1986) *Heterologies: Discourse on the Other*, Minneapolis: University of Wisconsin Press.

Department of Arts, Culture, Science and Technology (1996) *All Our Legacies, All Our Futures*, Pretoria: Government Printer.

Department of Arts, Sport, Environment, Tourism and Territories (DASETT) (1992) *The Role of the Commonwealth in Australia's Cultural Development*, Canberra: Australian Government Publishing Service.

Department of Communications and Arts (DOCA) (1994) *Creative Nation: Commonwealth Cultural Policy*, Canberra: Commonwealth of Australia.

Desmond, Adrian (1989) *The Politics of Evolution: Morphology, Medicine and Reform in Radical London*, Chicago and London: University of Chicago Press.

Desmond, Adrian and Moore, James (1992) *Darwin*, Harmondsworth: Penguin.

Douglas, A. (1978) *The Feminisation of American Culture*, New York: Alfred A. Knopf.

Dunn, Tony (1986) 'The evolution of cultural studies' in David Puntner (ed.) *Introduction to Contemporary Cultural Studies*, London: Longman.

Eagleton, Terry (1967) 'The idea of a common culture' in Terry Eagleton and Brian Wicker (eds) *From Culture to Revolution: The Slant Symposium*, London and Sydney: Sheed and Ward.

Edwards, Edward (1869) *Free Town Libraries: Their Formation, Management, and History in Britain, France, Germany, and America*, London: Trubner and Co.

Edwards, Elizabeth (1992) Introduction to Edwards (ed.) *Anthropology and Photography, 1860–1920*, New Haven and London: Yale University Press in association with the Royal Anthropological Institute, London.

Elmer, Greg (1996) 'US cultural policy and the (de)regulation of the self', *Continuum: The Australian Journal of Media and Culture*, vol. 9, no. 1.

Etheridge, R. Jr (1912) *Notes on a Report by C. Anderson, MA, DSc of a Visit to Certain European Museums in 1911*, Australian Museum: Sydney, Miscellaneous Series VII.

Fabian, Johannes (1983) *Time and the Other: How Anthropology Makes its Object*, New York: Columbia University Press.

Fergusson, James (1849) *Observations on the British Museum, National Gallery and National Records Office with Suggestions for Their Improvement*, London: John Weale.

Findlen, Paula (1994) *Possessing Nature: Museums, Collecting, and Scientific Culture in Early Modern Italy*, Berkeley, Los Angeles and London: University of California Press.

Finney, Colin (1993) *Paradise Revealed: Natural History in Nineteenth-Century Australia*, Museum of Victoria, Melbourne.

Fisher, Philip (1991) *Making and Effacing Art: Modern American Art in a Culture of Museums*, New York: Oxford University Press.

Flower, Sir William H. (1893) 'Modern museums', *Museums Association Proceedings*.

——(1898) *Essays on Museums and Other Subjects connected with Natural History*, London: Macmillan and Co.

Foucault, Michel (1978) 'Governmentality' in Graham Burchell, Colin Gordon and Peter Miller (eds) *The Foucault Effect: Studies in Governmentality*, London: Harvester/Wheatsheaf.

——(1979) *Discipline and Punish: The Birth of the Prison*, Harmondsworth: Penguin.

——(1980) 'Nietzsche, genealogy, history' in *Language, Counter-Memory, Practice*, Ithaca: Cornell University Press.

——(1980) *Power/Knowledge: Selected Interviews and Other Writings, 1972–1977*, New York: Pantheon Books.

——(1989) 'Technologies of the self' in Luther Martin, Huck Gutman and Patrick Hutton (eds) *Technologies of the Self: A Seminar with Michel Foucault*, London: Tavistock Publications.

Frow, John (1991) 'Michel de Certeau and the practice of representation', *Cultural Studies*, vol. 5, no. 1.

Frow, John and Morris, Meaghan (eds) (1993) *Australian Cultural Studies: A Reader*, Sydney: Allen & Unwin.

Gallagher, Catherine (1992) 'Raymond Williams and cultural studies', *Social Text*, (n.v.).

Garnham, Nicholas (1988) 'Raymond Williams, 1921–1988: A cultural analyst, a distinctive tradition', *Journal of Communication*, vol. 38, no. 4, autumn.

Garrison, Dee (1976) 'The tender technicians: The feminisation of public librarianship, 1876–1905' in Mary S. Hartman and Lois Banner (eds) *Clio's Consciousness Raised: New Perspectives on the History of Women*, New York: Octagon Books.

Gascoigne, John (1994) *Joseph Banks and the English Enlightenment: Useful Knowledge and Polite Culture*, Cambridge: Cambridge University Press.

Geertz, Clifford (1973) *The Interpretation of Cultures*, New York: Basic Books Inc.

Gilroy, Paul (1987) *There Ain't No Black in the Union Jack*, London: Hutchinson.

Ginzberg, Lori (1990) *Women and the Work of Benevolence. Morality, Politics and Class in the Nineteenth-Century United States*, New Haven and London: Yale University Press.

Ginzburg, Carlo (1980) 'Morelli, Freud and Sherlock Holmes: Clues and scientific method', *History Workshop*, no. 9.

Giroux, Henry A. (1992) 'Resisting difference: Cultural studies and the discourse of critical pedagogy' in Lawrence Grossberg, Cary Nelson and

Paula Treichler (eds) (1992) *Cultural Studies*, New York and London: Routledge.

Goode, George Brown (1895) *The Principles of Museum Administration*, York: Coultas and Volans.

Goodman, David (1990) 'Fear of circuses: Founding the National Museum of Victoria', *Continuum*, vol. 3, no. 1.

Gordon, Colin (1991) 'Governmental rationality: An introduction' in Graham Burchell, Colin Gordon and Peter Miller (eds) *The Foucault Effect: Studies in Governmentality*, London: Harvester/Wheatsheaf.

Gould, Stephen Jay (1987) *Time's Arrow, Time's Cycle: Myth and Metaphor in the Discovery of Geological Time*, Cambridge, Mass.: Harvard University Press.

Grace, Helen (1991) 'Eating the curate's egg: Cultural studies for the nineties', *West*, vol. 3, no. 1.

Gramsci, Antonio (1971) *Selections from the Prison Notebooks* (selected and translated by Quentin Hoare and Geoffrey Nowell-Smith), London: Lawrence and Wishart.

Gratacap, L.P. (n.d.), History of the American Museum of Natural History, unpublished ms.

Green, Michael (1993) 'Vox populi', *Cultural Studies*, vol. 7, no. 3, October.

Greenhalgh, Paul (1988) *Ephemeral Vistas: The Expositions Universelles, Great Exhibitions and Worlds' Fairs, 1851–1939*, Manchester: Manchester University Press.

Greenwood, Thomas (1888) *Museums and Art Galleries*, London: Simpkin, Marshall and Co.

Griffiths, Tom (1996) *Hunters and Collectors: The Antiquarian Imagination in Australia*, Melbourne: Cambridge University Press.

Grossberg, Lawrence, Nelson, Cary and Treichler, Paula (eds) (1992) *Cultural Studies*, New York and London: Routledge.

Gunew, Sneja and Rizvi, Fazal (eds) (1994) *Culture, Difference and the Arts*, Sydney: Allen & Unwin.

Habermas, Jurgen (1992) 'Further reflections on the public sphere' in Craig Calhoun (ed.) (1992) *Habermas and the Public Sphere*, Cambridge, Mass.: MIT Press.

Hall, Stuart (1977) 'Culture, the media and the "ideological effect" ' in James Curran, Michael Gurevitch and Janet Woollacott (eds) (1977) *Mass Communication and Society*, London: Edward Arnold.

Hall, Stuart (1980) 'Cultural studies and the Centre: Some problematics and problems' in Stuart Hall et al. (eds) *Culture, Media, Language*, London: Centre for Contemporary Cultural Studies/Hutchinson.

——(1980) 'The Williams interviews', *Screen Education*, no. 34, Spring.

——(1981) 'Cultural studies: Two paradigms' in Tony Bennett et al. (eds) *Culture, Ideology and Social Process*, London: Batsford. (First published in *Media, Culture and Society*, no. 2, 1980.)

——(1988) 'Only connect: the life of Raymond Williams', *New Statesman*, 5 Feb.

——(1989) 'The "First" New Left: Life and times' in Oxford University Discussion Group (eds) *Out of Apathy: Voices of the New Left 30 Years On*, London: Verso.

——(1990) 'The emergence of cultural studies and the crisis of the Humanities', *October*, no. 53.

——(1992) 'Cultural studies and its theoretical legacies', in Lawrence Grossberg, Cary Nelson and Paula Treichler (eds) *Cultural Studies*, New York and London: Routledge.

——(1993) 'Culture, community, nation', *Cultural Studies*, vol. 7, no. 3, October.

Hall, Stuart and Jefferson, Tony (eds) (1976) *Resistance through Rituals: Youth Subcultures in Post-War Britain*, London: Hutchinson.

Hall, Stuart, Critcher, Chas, Jefferson, Tony, Clarke, John and Roberts, Brian (1978) *Policing the Crisis: Mugging, the State, and Law and Order*, London: Macmillan.

Haraway, Donna (1992) 'Teddy bear patriarchy: Taxidermy in the Garden of Eden, New York City, 1908–1936' in *Primate Visions: Gender, Race and Nature in the World of Modern Science*, London: Verso.

Harris, David (1992) *From Class Struggle to the Politics of Pleasure: The Effects of Gramscianism on Cultural Studies*, London and New York: Routledge.

Harris, Jonathan (1995) *Federal Art and National Culture: The Politics of Identity in New Deal America*, Cambridge: Cambridge University Press.

Harrison, Brian (1971) *Drink and the Victorians: The Temperance Question in England, 1815–1872*, London: Faber and Faber.

Hartley, John (1991) 'Popular reality: A (hair) brush with cultural studies', *Continuum*, vol. 4, no. 2.

Hawkins, Gay (1993) *From Nimbin to Mardi Gras: Constructing Community Arts*, Sydney: Allen & Unwin.

Healy, Chris (1996) *From the Ruins of Colonialism: History as Social Memory*, Melbourne: Cambridge University Press.

Hebdige, Dick (1988) *Hiding in the Light: On Images and Things*, London and New York: Routledge.

Hedley, Charles (1913) *Report on a Visit to Certain American Museums in 1912*, Sydney: Australian Museum, Miscellaneous Series VIII.

Helsinger, Elizabeth (1994) 'Ruskin and the politics of viewing: Constructing national subjects', *Harvard University Art Museums Bulletin*, vol. 3, no. 1.

Hindess, Barry and Hirst, Paul (1975) *Pre-Capitalist Modes of Production*, London: Routledge and Kegan Paul.

Hinsely, Curtis M. Jr (1981) *Savages and Scientists: The Smithsonian Institution and the Development of American Anthropology, 1846–1910*, Washington, DC: Smithsonian Institution Press.

Hodgen, Margaret T. (1936) *The Doctrine of Survivals: A Chapter in the History of Scientific Method in the Study of Man*, London: Allenson and Co.

Hoggart, Richard (1959) 'An important book', *Essays in Criticism*, no. 9, pp. 171–179.

Hole, James (1853) *An Essay on the History and Management of Literary, Scientific and Mechanics' Institutions; and especially how far they may be developed and combined so as to promote the moral well-being and industry of the country*, London: Longman, Brown, Green, and Longmans.

Holloway, John (1953) *The Victorian Sage: Studies in Argument*, London: Macmillan.

Holub, Renate (1992) *Antonio Gramsci: Beyond Marxism and Postmodernism*, London and New York: Routledge.

Horsfall, T.C. (1892), 'The Manchester Art Museum', *Museums Association Proceedings*.

Hunter, Ian (1988) *Culture and Government: The Emergence of Literary Education*, London: Macmillan.

——(1992) 'Aesthetics and cultural studies', in Lawrence Grossberg, Cary Nelson and Paula Treichler (eds) *Cultural Studies*, New York and London: Routledge.

——(1993) 'Mind games and body techniques', *Southern Review*, vol. 26, no. 2.

——(1994) *Rethinking the School: Subjectivity, Bureaucracy and Criticism*, Sydney: Allen & Unwin.

Hutchinson, Jonathan (1893), 'On educational museums', *Museums Association Proceedings*.

——(1908) 'On museum education', *The Museums Journal*, vol. 8, no. 1.

Huxley, Thomas Henry (1882) 'On the method of Zadig: Retrospective prophecy as a function of science' in *Science and Culture and Other Essays*, London: Macmillan.

Inglis, Fred (1982) *Radical Earnestness: English Social Theory 1880–1980*, Oxford: Martin Robertson.

Jacobs, Jane and Gale, Fay (1994) *Tourism and the Protection of Aboriginal Cultural Sites*, Canberra: Australian Government Publishing Service.

Jameson, Frederic (1993) 'On cultural studies', *Social Text*, no. 34.

Jay, Martin (1973) *The Dialectical Imagination: A History of the Frankfurt School and the Institute of Social Research 1923–50*, London: Heinemann Educational Books.

Jenkins, Henry (1992) *Textual Poachers: Television Fans and Participatory Culture*, New York: Routledge, Chapman and Hall.

Jenkins, Henry and Tulloch, John (1995) *Science Fiction Audiences: Watching Dr Who and Star Trek*, London and New York: Routledge.

Jevons, W. Stanley (1883), *Methods of Social Reform*, New York: Augustus M. Kelley.

Johnson, Richard (1979) ' "Really useful knowledge": Radical education and working-class culture' in John Clarke and Richard Johnson (eds) *Working-Class Culture: Studies in History and Theory*, London: Hutchinson.

——(1986–87) 'What is cultural studies anyway?', *Social Text*, vol. 16.

Jones, Paul (1994) 'The myth of "Raymond Hoggart": On "founding fathers" and cultural policy', *Cultural Studies*, vol. 8, no. 3.

Karp, Ivan (1992) 'Museums and communities: The politics of public culture' in Ivan Karp, Christine Mullin Kreamer and Steven Lavine (eds) (1992) *Museums and Communities: The Politics of Public Culture*, Washington and London: Smithsonian Institution Press.

Karp, Ivan, Kreamer, Christine Mullen and Lavine, Steven (eds) (1992) *Museums and Communities: The Politics of Public Culture*, Washington and London: Smithsonian Institution Press.

Kasson, Joy K. (1990) *Marble Queens and Captives: Women in Nineteenth-Century American Sculpture*, New Haven: Yale University Press.

Kavanagh, Gaynor (1994) *Museums and the First World War: A Social History*, London and New York: Leicester University Press.

King, Anthony (1964) 'George Godwin and the Art Union of London 1837–1911', *Victorian Studies*, vol. 8, no. 2, December, pp. 101–130.

Knight, Stephen (1989) 'Searching for research or the selling of the Australian mind', *Meanjin*, vol. 48, no. 3.

Kohlstedt, S.G. (1983) 'Australian museums of natural history: Public practices and scientific initiatives in the 19th century', *Historical Records of Australian Science*, vol. 5.

Kohlstedt, Sally Gregory (1979) 'From learned society to public museum: The Boston Society of Natural History' in A. Oleson and J. Voss (eds) *The Organisation of Knowledge in Modern America*, Baltimore and London: Johns Hopkins University Press.

Koven, Seth (1994) 'The Whitechapel Picture Exhibitions and the politics of seeing' in Daniel J. Sherman and Irit Rogoff (eds) *Museum Culture: Histories, Discourses, Spectacles*, Minneapolis: University of Minnesota Press.

Kulik, Gary (1989) 'Designing the past: history-museum exhibitions from Peale to the present' in Warren Leon and Roy Rosenzweig (eds) (1989) *History Museums in the United States: A Critical Assessment*, Urbana and Chicago: University of Illinois Press.

Landes, Joan B. (1992) 'Rethinking Habermas's public sphere', *Political Theory Newsletter*, no. 4.

Langton, Marcia (1993) '*Well, I heard it on the radio and I saw it on the television* . . .', Sydney: Australian Film Commission.

Latour, Bruno (1987) *Science in Action: How to Follow Scientists and Engineers through Society*, Cambridge, Mass.: Harvard University Press.

Lentricchia, Frank (1983) *After the New Criticism*, London: Methuen.

Levine, Philippa (1986) *The Amateur and the Professional: Antiquarians, Historians and Archaeologists in Victorian England, 1838–1886*, Cambridge: Cambridge University Press.

Lewis, Geoffrey (1989) *For Instruction and Recreation—A Century History of the Museums Association*, London: Quiller Press.

Liss, Julia (1995) 'Patterns of strangeness: Franz Boas, modernism, and the origins of anthropology' in Elazar Barkan and Ronald Bush (eds) *Prehistories of the Future: The Primitivist Project and the Culture of Modernism*, Stanford: University of Stanford Press.

Livingstone, Archibald (1880) *Report upon Certain Museums for Technology, Science, and Art, also upon Scientific, Professional, and Technical Instruction and Systems of Evening Classes in Great Britain and on the Continent of Europe*, Sydney: Government Printer.

Marcus, George E. (1986) 'Contemporary problems of ethnography in the modern world system' in J. Clifford and G.E. Marcus (eds) (1986) *Writing Culture: The Poetics and Politics of Ethnography*, Berkeley: University of California Press.

Mauss, Marcel (1979) *Sociology and Psychology: Essays*, London: Routledge and Kegan Paul.

McAlear, Donna (1996) 'First peoples, museums and citizenship' in Tony Bennett, Robin Trotter and Donna McAlear, *Museums and Citizenship: A Resource Book*, special issue of *Memoirs of the Queensland Museum*, vol. 39, part 1.

McCarthy, Kathleen D. (1991) *Women's Culture: American Philanthropy and Art, 1830–1930*, Chicago and London: University of Chicago Press.

McGuigan, Jim (1992) *Cultural Populism*, London and New York: Routledge.

——(1996) *Culture and the Public Sphere*, London and New York: Routledge.

McNeil, Maureen (1992) 'Late show stars in the mainstream' *Times Higher*, 17 July.

Meredyth, Denise and Tyler, Deborah (eds) (1993) *Child and Citizen: Genealogies of Schooling and Subjectivity*, Brisbane: Institute for Cultural Policy Studies.

Michaels, Eric (1994) *Bad Aboriginal Art: Traditions, Media and Technological Horizons*, Sydney: Allen & Unwin.

Miers, Sir Henry A. and Markham, M.A. (1932) *A Report on the Museums and Art Galleries of British Africa*, Edinburgh: T. and A. Constable Ltd.

Miller, Peter and Rose, Nikolas (1992) 'Political power beyond the State: Problematics of government', *British Journal of Sociology*, vol. 43, no. 2.

Miller, Richard E. (1994) ' "A moment of profound danger": British cultural studies away from the Centre', *Cultural Studies*, vol. 8, no. 4.

Miller, Toby (1992) 'Film theory: An ethics of indeterminacy?', *New Researcher*, nos 1 and 2.

——(1993) *The Well-Tempered Self: Citizenship, Culture and the Postmodern Subject*, Baltimore: Johns Hopkins University Press.

——(1995) 'Exporting truth from Aboriginal Australia: "Portions of our past become present again, where only the melancholy light of origin shines" ', *Media Information Australia*, no. 76, pp. 1–17.

——(1996) 'Cultural citizenship and technologies of the subject, or where did you go, Paul DiMaggio?', *Culture and Policy*, vol. 7, no. 1.

Milner, Andrew (1993) *Cultural Materialism*, Melbourne: Melbourne University Press.

Minson, Jeffrey (1993) *Questions of Conduct: Sexual Harassment, Citizenship and Government*, London: Macmillan.

Mitchell, Timothy (1988) *Colonising Egypt*, Cambridge: Cambridge University Press.

Molnar, Helen (1995) 'Indigenous media development in Australia: A product of struggle and opposition', *Cultural Studies*, vol. 9, no. 1.

Moon, Brian (1993) *Reading and Gender: From Discourse and Subject to Regime and Practice*, PhD thesis, Curtin University.

Morris, Meaghan (1988) 'Banality in cultural studies', *Discourse*, vol. 10.

——(1990) 'Banality in cultural studies' in Patricia Mellencamp (ed.) *Logics of Television: Essays in Cultural Criticism*, Bloomington and Indianapolis: Indiana University Press.

——(1992) 'A gadfly bites back', *Meanjin*, vol. 51, no. 3.

Myers, Fred (1996) 'Representing culture: the production of discourse(s) for Aboriginal acrylic paintings' in George E. Marcus and Fred R. Myers (eds) (1996) *The Traffic in Culture: Refiguring Art and Anthropology*, Berkeley and Los Angeles: University of California Press.

Negrin, Llewellyn (1993) 'On the museum's ruins: A critical appraisal', *Theory, Culture and Society*, vol. 10, no. 1.

Newton, Charles (1880) *Essays on Art and Antiquity*, London: Macmillan.

O'Regan, Tom (1992) '(Mis)taking policy: Notes on the cultural policy debate', *Cultural Studies*, vol. 6, no. 3.

Osborn, Henry Fairfield and Sherwood, George H. (1913) *The Museum and Nature Study in the Public Schools*, New York: American Museum of Natural History, Miscellaneous Publications, no. 3.

Outram, Dorinda (1984) *Georges Cuvier: Vocation, Science and Authority in Post-Revolutionary France*, Manchester: Manchester University Press.

Paradis, James and Williams, George C. (1989), *Evolution and Ethics: T.H. Huxley's* Evolution and Ethics *with New essays on its Victorian and Sociobiological Context*, Princeton, New Jersey: Princeton University Press.

Parrinder, Patrick (1987) *The Failure of Theory: Essays on Criticism and Contemporary Fiction*, Brighton: Harvester Press.

Pateman, Carole 'The fraternal social contract' in Carole Pateman (1989) *The Disorder of Women*, Cambridge: Polity Press.

Paton, James (1898) 'A People's Palace', *Museums Association Proceedings*, London.

Pickering, Michael (1992) 'Cultural studies and the challenge to English', *Sites*, no. 24, Autumn.

Pitt Rivers, A.H.L.F. (1891) 'Typological museums, as exemplified by the Pitt Rivers Museum at Oxford, and his Provincial Museum at Farnham', *Journal of the Society of Arts*, no. 40.

Place, Francis (n.d.) *The Papers of Francis Place in the British Library, 1791–1854*, Sussex: Harvester Microfilms.

Pommier, Edouard (1989) *Le Problème du Musée à la Veille de la Révolution*, Montargis: Musée Girodet.

Poulot, Dominique (1994) 'Identity as self-discovery: The ecomuseum in France' in Daniel Sherman and Irit Rogoff (eds) *Museum Culture: Histories, Discourses, Spectacles*, Minneapolis: University of Minnesota Press.

Pratt, Mary Louise (1992) *Imperial Eyes: Travel Writing and Transculturation*, London: Routledge.

Preziosi, Donald (1989) *Rethinking Art History. Meditations on a Coy Science*, New Haven and London: Yale University Press.

Purbrick, Louise (1994) 'The South Kensington Museum: The building of the House of Cole' in Marcia Pointon (ed.) (1994) *Art Apart: Art Institutions and Ideology across England and North America*, Manchester and New York: Manchester University Press.

Rainger, Ronald (1991) *An Agenda for Antiquity: Henry Fairfield Osborn & Vertebrate Palaeontology at the American Museum of Natural History, 1890–1935*, Tuscaloosa and London: University of Alabama Press.

Ramsay, Grace Fisher (1938) *Educational Work in Museums of the United States: Development, Methods and Trends*, New York: The H.W. Wilson Co.

Report from the House of Representatives Standing Committee on Expenditure (1986) *Patronage, Power and the Muse: Inquiry into Commonwealth Assistance to the Arts*, Canberra: Australian Government Publishing Service.

Report from the Select Committee on Inquiry into Drunkenness 1834 (1971), Shannon: Irish University Press.

Report from the Select Committee on National Monuments and Works of Art, 16 June 1841 (1971), Shannon: Irish University Press.

Report from the Select Committee on Paris Exhibition, 11 July 1867 (1971), Shannon: Irish University Press.

Report from the Select Committee on Public Libraries, 1 August 1850 (1971), Shannon: Irish University Press.

Report from the Select Committee on the National Gallery, 25 July 1850 (1971), Shannon: Irish University Press.

Report of the National Gallery Site Commission, 1857 (1971), Shannon: Irish University Press.

Report on the System of Circulation of Art Objects from the South Kensington Museum for Exhibition, 1881 (1971), Shannon: Irish University Press.

Resch, Robert Paul (1992) *Althusser and the Renewal of Marxist Social Theory*, Berkeley and Los Angeles: University of California Press.

Richter, Melvin (1964) *The Politics of Conscience: T.H. Green and His Age*, London: Weidenfeld and Nicholson.

Robbins, Bruce (ed.) (1990) *Intellectuals: Aesthetics, Politics, Academics*, Minneapolis: University of Minnesota Press.

Rose, Nikolas (1990) *Governing the Soul: The Shaping of the Private Self*, London: Routledge.

——(1993) 'Government, authority and expertise in advanced liberalism', *Economy and Society*, vol. 22, no. 3.

Rosenzweig, Roy and Blackmar, Elizabeth (1992) *The Park and the People: A History of Central Park*, New York: Henry Holt and Co.

Ross, Andrew (1989) *No Respect: Intellectuals and Popular Culture*, New York: Routledge.

——(1990) 'Defenders of the faith and the new class' in Bruce Robbins (ed.) *Intellectuals: Aesthetics, Politics, Academics*, Minneapolis: University of Minnesota Press.

Rowse, Tim (1985) *Arguing the Arts: The Funding of the Arts in Australia*, Ringwood: Penguin.

Rudler, F.W. (1891), 'On the difficulties incidental to museum demonstrations', *Museums Association Proceedings*, London.

Rudwick, Martin J. (1992) *Scenes from Deep Time: Early Pictorial Representations of the Prehistoric World*, Chicago and London: University of Chicago Press.

Rupke, Nicolaas A. (1994) *Richard Owen: Victorian Naturalist*, New Haven and London: Yale University Press.

Ryan, Mary P. (1990) *Women in Public: Between Banners and Ballots, 1825–1880*, London and Baltimore: Johns Hopkins University Press.

Rydell, Robert W. (1984) *All the World's a Fair: Visions of Empire at American International Expositions, 1876–1916*, Chicago: University of Chicago Press.

Saisselin, R.G. (1970) 'The transformation of art into culture: From Pascal to Diderot', *Studies on Voltaire and the Eighteenth Century*, vol. LXX.

Schiebinger, Londa (1989) *The Mind Has No Sex? Women in the Origins of Modern Science*, Cambridge, Mass.: Harvard University Press.

——(1993) *Nature's Body: Sexual Politics and the Making of Modern Science*, London: Pandora.

Sherman, Daniel J. (1989) *Worthy Monuments: Art Museums and the Politics of Culture in Nineteenth-Century France*, Cambridge, Mass.: Harvard University Press.

——(1994) 'Quatremère/Benjamin/Marx: Art museums, aura, and commodity fetishism' in Daniel Sherman and Irit Rogoff (eds) (1994) *Museum Culture: Histories, Discourses, Spectacles*, Minneapolis: University of Minnesota Press.

Sherman, Daniel and Rogoff, Irit (eds) (1994) *Museum Culture: Histories, Discourses, Spectacles*, Minneapolis: University of Minnesota Press.

Simpson, David (1992) 'Raymond Williams: feeling for structures, voicing "history" ', *Social Text* (n.v.).

Simpson, Moira (1996) *Making Representations: Museums in the Post-Colonial Era*, London: Routledge.

Skinner, Ghislaine M. (1986) 'Sir Henry Wellcome's museum for the science of history', *Medical History*, no. 30.

Sparke, Penny (1995) *As Long as it's Pink: The Sexual Politics of Taste*, London: Pandora.

Steedman, Carolyn (1992) 'Culture, cultural studies and the historians' in

Lawrence Grossberg, Cary Nelson and Paula Treichler (eds) *Cultural Studies*, New York and London: Routledge.

Stocking, George W. Jr (1987) *Victorian Anthropology*, New York: Free Press.

——(1968) *Race, Culture and Evolution: Essays in the History of Anthropology*, New York: Free Press.

Streeter, Thomas (1996) *Selling the Air: A Critique of the Policy of Commercial Broadcasting in the United States*, Chicago and London: University of Chicago Press.

Taylor, Brandon (1994) 'From penitentiary to "temple of art": Early metaphors of improvement at the Millbank Tate' in Marcia Pointon (ed.) (1994) *Art Apart: Art Institutions and Ideology across England and North America*, Manchester and New York: Manchester University Press.

Thomas, Nicholas (1991) *Entangled Objects: Exchange, Material Culture, and Colonialism in the Pacific*, Cambridge, Mass.: Harvard University Press.

——(1994) 'Licensed curiosity: Cook's Pacific Voyages' in John Elsner and Roger Cardinal (eds) (1994) *The Culture of Collecting*, Melbourne: Melbourne University Press.

——(1994) *Colonialism's Culture: Anthropology, Travel and Government*, Cambridge: Polity Press.

Tomaselli, Keyan (1992) 'From resistance to policy research', *Text*, no. 1.

Turner, Graeme (1992a) ' "It works for me": British cultural studies, Australian cultural studies, Australian film' in Lawrence Grossberg, Cary Nelson and Paula Treichler *Cultural Studies*, New York and London: Routledge.

——(1992b) 'Of rocks and hard places: The colonised, the national and Australian cultural studies', *Cultural Studies*, vol. 6, no. 3.

Tylor, Edward B. (1874) *Primitive Culture: Researches into the Development of Mythology, Philosophy, Religion, Language, Art and Custom*, Boston: Estes and Lauriat.

van Keuren, David K. (1984) 'Museums and ideology: Augustus Pitt Rivers, anthropological museums, and social change in later Victorian Britain', *Victorian Studies*, vol. 28, no. 1.

van Riper, A. Bowdein (1993) *Men among the Mammoths: Victorian Science and the Discovery of Human Prehistory*, London and Chicago: University of Chicago Press.

Viswanathan, Gauri (1991) 'Raymond Williams and British Colonialism', *Yale Journal of Criticism*, vol. 4, no. 2.

Vogel, Ursula (1987) 'Humboldt and the Romantics: Neither *hasfrau* nor *citoyenne*—the idea of "self-reliant femininity" in German Romanticism' in Ellen Kennedy and Susan Mendus (eds) (1987) *Women in Western Political Philosophy: Kant to Nietzsche*, Brighton: Wheatsheaf.

Wark, McKenzie (1992) 'Cultural studies at the crossroads', *The Australian*, 23 December.

——(1994) 'Distorted view of black culture', *The Australian*, 12 January.

Weber, Eugene (1976) *Peasants into Frenchmen: The Modernisation of Rural France, 1870–1914*, Stanford: Stanford University Press.

Weiss, F.E. (1892) 'The organisation of a botanical museum', *Museums Association Proceedings*.

White, Michael V. (1992) 'Bridging the natural and the social: Science and character in Jevons' political economy', paper presented to the Economic Society of Australia, 21st Conference of Economists, University of Melbourne, July.

Williams, Raymond (1963) *Culture and Society, 1780–1950*, Harmondsworth: Penguin.

——(1965) *The Long Revolution*, Harmondsworth: Penguin.

——(1967) 'Culture and revolution: A comment' in Terry Eagleton and Brian Wicker (eds) *From Culture to Revolution: The Slant Symposium*, London and Sydney: Sheed and Ward.

——(1976) *Keywords: A Vocabulary of Culture and Society*, London: Fontana/Croom Helm.

——(1977) *Marxism and Literature*, Oxford: Oxford University Press.

——(1979) *Politics and Letters*, London: New Left Books.

——(1983) *Towards 2000*, London: Chatto and Windus.

——(1989) *The Politics of Modernism: Against the New Conformists*, London: Verso.

World Commission on Culture and Development (1995) *Our Creative Diversity*, Paris: UNESCO.

Young, Robert J.C. (1995) *Colonial Desire: Hybridity in Theory, Culture and Race*, London and New York: Routledge.

Index